Caroline M Fuller

Across the Campus

A Story of College Life

Caroline M Fuller

Across the Campus
A Story of College Life

ISBN/EAN: 9783744689915

Printed in Europe, USA, Canada, Australia, Japan

Cover: Foto ©Thomas Meinert / pixelio.de

More available books at **www.hansebooks.com**

Across the Campus

A Story of College Life

By

Caroline M. Fuller

New York

Charles Scribner's Sons

1899

Dedicated

IN ALL HUMILITY

TO

"THE FINEST CLASS ALIVE"

Contents

Across the Campus

CHAPTER I

THE WATCHERS OVER HARLAND

IT was a hot September afternoon, and in a pleasant third-story room of Mrs. Hemp's "Boarding-House for College Students," two girls were engaged in a lively discussion.

They had arranged both beds to suit one of them — no two room-mates ever entertained the same view with regard to the position of their beds — and had shifted the poor lame wash-stand but five times, although it had shed a castor at each one of these journeys, save the last, and would gladly have contributed another, had it not become reduced in circumstances. At present the intensity of their discussion was increased by the fact that Ruth had just upset a box of tacks, and Christine had stepped on them.

"That was a cowardly onslaught!" cried the victim, spinning around on one unhappy toe. "There is n't a thing about college that I like so far, although it does n't begin till to-morrow; and I had on my thin slippers too!"

"Sit down on my bed, and pick the tacks out of the soles, please, Chris," was the unsympathetic answer. "I must have them to put up these photographs with."

I

Christine followed the suggestion, but meanwhile relieved her feelings by reviling the dimensions of the room.

"We have a beautiful view," said Ruth, looking out at the far-away river, and the blue hills which lay dreamy and warm in the afternoon sunshine.

"Yes, we can keep a view, because it's out of doors," said Christine, stubbornly; "we may have to put the piano lamp out there too. Possibly we shall be tempted to move out ourselves. Just look at that tack on the floor; what a shadow it casts!"

"Silly girl," said Ruth, amiably, "where do you think I had better hang 'Madame Le Brun et sa Fille,' —between the two windows?"

"Do not venture to address me," was the stern retort; "this is the thirty-first that I have removed from the toe alone!"

Ruth moved about the room in obedient silence, unpacking the teacups from a "pocket-edition" bathtub, dusting books, and placing them according to size in a genial bookcase of sunny brown, along the middle ledge of which was printed in chalk, "Les hommes sont méchants, mais leurs livres sont bons."

"I don't see why we couldn't get on the campus this year, anyhow," said Christine, dismally. "My father's a Senator; and, besides, he has a white beard. I don't see how the Registrar dared tell a man with a white beard that there wasn't room for his daughter on the campus."

"Christine, you're too ridiculous," laughed Ruth; "you know that people have to apply months and sometimes years beforehand to get rooms on the campus. Now, do you happen to remember where you put the picture wire, and those hooks that we bought this morning? "

" Nothing in this world ever happens," said Christine, solemnly. "If I remembered at all, it would be the result of deliberate forethought."

Ruth searched patiently through the miscellaneous heap of things which adorned the floor, and finally found the wire in a shoe-bag.

"I put it there so that we could find it easily," explained Christine, coming to the rescue. " Now, Ruth, listen to what I say, for I'm obliged to be firm. You are not going to hang these pictures, and neither am I. How are they going to be hung? I shall don my new shoes, which are too tight about the waist, sally forth, and engage an African for the purpose."

" Engage a man for a little thing like this? Why, Chris, how perfectly absurd! You forget that I'm used to doing everything for myself."

" Down in the shop of Phipps, the storage man," said Christine, dropping her voice to a whisper, " is a dark accomplice, and him will I bring and lay at the feet of my lady dear."

"Oh, Chris! " protested Ruth, in horror, " please don't bring any miscellaneous kind of a creature up here without asking Mrs. Hemp if it's all right!"

" It is all right," said Christine, beginning to button her boots, "and in addition to its other charms, it has a naturally curly nose."

"Oh dear," said Ruth, disconsolately, "I wish your father had n't gone back to Burlington, or that your mother was here to settle you."

" My child, you speak as if I were a pot of obstreperous coffee, and my mother a well-meaning but absent egg; and such sentiments are very, very wrong. Now put on your hat and come."

But Ruth still hesitated. "What is that noise out in the hall?" she said, going to the door. "Oh, Chris, I believe Miss Carey's trunks have come at last, and she's gone down town. What shall we do about them?"

Christine listened, and heard an irregular heaving and bumping upon the stairs, accompanied by a terrific struggling, and the sound of paint which is being gently but firmly removed from the boards where it was wont to linger.

"Do?" she said coolly; "why, nothing. What should we do?"

But Ruth was already out in the hall, showing the men Miss Carey's room, and paying the express charges herself, — a proceeding to which Christine strongly objected.

"You see, it will cause that girl to have tender associations connected with us," she began, and then, catching sight of the negro who accompanied the expressman, she joyfully exclaimed, "By my life, 't is the accomplice himself, and come hither in the nick of time! Enter, African, and hang my pictures."

The negro boy grinned, and promptly obeyed; the pictures were soon hung, and the bureau shifted into a new position.

"I liked it very well as it was," explained Christine; "but you see it is well to get all such heavy work done while we have a man here."

The girls put the finishing touches to the room, and sat down to admire their work; while the African, who

4

had been meekly standing upon the radiator, begged leave to descend, and departed with his fifty cents.

"It does look pretty well, does n't it?" said Ruth, with a sigh of satisfaction; and so it did. The screen and the little tea-table were of white wood, burned in sepia-like designs; and several cheerful water-colors gave an atmosphere of life to the room. There were a few cream-colored bas-reliefs, a fine etching or two, and in one corner stood an exquisite bronze statuette of the Pompeian "Narcissus." The piano lamp gave promise of soft red shadows when evening should come; the little teakettle stood upon a doily embroidered in white and purple violets, while a few dainty teacups, hand painted with violets, were grouped around it. The Yale and Harvard flags were peacefully crossed above the bookcase; for Christine had a brother at Harvard now, and an older one had graduated in the class of '89. The Yale flag was in honor of Ruth's father, who had been a famous "Bones" man in his day, and who still disappeared periodically to attend certain dinners and reunions.

"Yes, it looks as well as it ever will," admitted Christine, " and now let's go down town and get an ice-cream soda."

The girls started out, and at the foot of the hill they met Miss Carey, accompanied by a friend.

"Allow me to present a stray classmate, surnamed Reade," she said with a flourish. "I can't vouch for her ancestry or private character, but she's treated me to an ice-cream soda, and I'm her friend for life. Hurrah!"

Miss Carey was a lively Kentucky girl, with Irish tendencies, and an irresistible twinkle in her eyes.

5

"It was awfully good of you to see about my trunks, Miss Burritt," she said, when Ruth had informed her of their arrival, "and I reckon that one of them contains something to reward you for this cheerful self-sacrifice. Drop into my room after supper to-night, and you'll find me the solid rock in an acid world. Come along, Miss Reade. Ladies, I bid you a fond good-afternoon."

"What an abominable girl!" said Christine cheerfully, as they pursued their way. "I wonder if they're all going to be like that."

"No, I don't believe so," said Ruth; "and besides, I rather like her, in spite of her funny ways. I think she's bright."

"She's gregarious," said Christine, gloomily. "They're all gregarious; but I don't intend to consort with them."

Christine had always done exactly what she liked, had everything that she wanted, and had come to college merely to escape something that she did not want, which was "society."

"Oh, Christie, I was looking forward so much to having you come out in Washington when you were eighteen!" said her pretty little mother with a sigh, when the plan was first proposed.

"But, mamma, I don't want to come out, and be turned loose to graze in society like any cow," was the discouraging reply. "If ever I am out, it will be because I was shot out, not because I came;" and Mrs. Arnold looked deeply grieved.

But the Senator and his boys held a solemn conclave in private, decided that Christine "had a head on her," and should go to college if she liked. So

Mrs. Arnold gave her consent, provided that Ruth, Christine's best friend, would go with her, and there was some difficulty about sparing Ruth, because her mother was delicate, and there were younger children; but finally Dr. Burritt yielded to supplication, and the two girls finished their college preparation together.

"The Alma Mater is n't at all imposing in appearance, is it?" said Christine, as they walked down Elm Street, under the shadow of the stately trees, which sent down sunny flickerings of light and seemed to be saying, "We, at least, are as imposing as one could wish."

"No, it is n't unusual in any way," said Ruth, simply, "but I think I am going to love it."

Every now and then the girls would meet an anxious mother, accompanied by a timid Freshman, who regarded them with shy eagerness as they passed.

"Gregarious!" said Christine, as she solemnly surveyed each new specimen, "hopelessly gregarious!"

Ruth did not answer, for, to tell the truth, she was not quite sure what "gregarious" meant, and always confused it with "amphibious."

When they reached Henley's drugstore, they found a number of girls eating ices around the cool marble counter, within reach of the wind which came from a revolving fan overhead.

"This is our first ice at college, Christie," said Ruth, with enthusiasm; "now, what had we better take? What have you that is good?" she asked, turning to the clerk.

A girl who was sitting near looked up pleasantly,

7

and said: "If you have just come to South Harland, you really ought to try a strawberry ice. Henley is famous for his strawberry ices, and everybody takes them."

Christine stepped forward with dignity. "You will give us two chocolate ice-cream sodas, if you please," she said distinctly, and the pretty Junior subsided with a look of surprise.

"I don't think you were quite polite to her," said Ruth, as they left the store; "she had on a sweet hat, and she looked like a nice girl."

"It is very hypocritical to pretend to like people when you don't," objected Christine.

"But you don't know anything about her," answered Ruth impatiently, and had the wisdom to add nothing more; for was she not proud to have it said at home that she could "get along with Christine better than any one else"?

It is to be observed that two people are very likely to get along well together, when one of them has her own way in everything! And while Christine was a gifted, tempestuous young person, whose character was often its own refutation, Ruth was one of those delightful people who have no talents themselves, but who find ample employment in repairing the mischief made by those who have.

"We must lay in a store of provisions in case we have callers," Ruth said, as they passed a grocery store; so they stopped and invested in a bottle of Crosse & Blackwell pickles, some Dundee strawberry jam, a tin of biscuits, and a bottle of Queen olives.

"Now I begin to feel settled," she added gleefully, as they turned towards home. "But we might just

8

as well have carried up the things ourselves. They were n't at all heavy."

"What! go along a public thoroughfare, clasping a load of groceries?" said Christine, with superiority. " I never did such a thing in my life."

When they reached the house the supper-bell was ringing, and they filed into the dining-room, accompanied by several other Freshmen who looked too frightened to speak, although they may have been merely suffering from reserve. It was a very silent meal, broken only by the chatter of several " old girls " who sat together, and by the time-worn remarks of Mrs. Hemp, who presided at one end of the table. Christine was put beside a bright-looking Sophomore, who might have been interesting, but received no encouragement. Kathleen Carey came in late, and was seated between two classmates whose silence effectually quenched her. Ruth, however, took an interest in all these new companions, and devoted herself to her little neighbor, who was a sweet child with large brown eyes, and a homesick look that went to one's heart.

After supper the girls collected on the back piazza to look at the mountains, which were still more beautiful in their evening glow; and Ruth's little neighbor said, "They are very, very lovely and comforting, are n't they ? I feel as if they would be my friends."

"They will help us to be good," answered Ruth, softly. " How nice it is that there are two of them ! I believe that even a mountain would be lonely sometimes, if it had no friend."

The hand of the small girl trembled a moment in

9.

hers, and Ruth said: "Come to the railing, and let's talk about them a little while. There, jump up here, and I'll put my arm around you so that you can't fall off. What do they remind you of—those great mountains? They seem to me like sentinels pacing the river bank, and although they have stopped for a minute now, I am sure that they will march on again to-night after we are all asleep."

"Oh, I don't believe that they would leave us," said the small girl, wistfully; "to me they are not like sentinels, but guardian angels. I think," she added, half to herself, "that they are watching over Harland!"

"Watchmen are they?" asked Kathleen Carey, who had come up behind her. "Well, look out that they don't spring a rattle on you some day. That's Rattlesnake Ledge up there on Mt. Gwynn, where Holmes sat when he wrote 'Elsie Venner.'"

"Oh, is that true?" asked some of the girls in surprise, and a friendly Sophomore said,—

"I doubt if Holmes wrote his book under the personal supervision of the rattlers, but that is really supposed to be the Rattlesnake Ledge of 'Elsie Venner.' The whole country around here is full of interesting associations. This house, for instance, used to be a school kept by Bancroft the historian, and afterwards, when it was a hotel, Jenny Lind stopped here for some time. We often think that her spirit comes back to tip over our water-pitchers."

"Oh, how interesting!" said the girls. "Do you know of any more associations?"

"J. G. Holland's story of 'Katrina' was located in old Hadley," continued Miss Robinson, "and there is a tree in our own campus that was planted by him

10

when he was here as a boy. It used to be called 'Jamie's tree,' but now everybody has forgotten which one it is."

"Why, I thought that the college was n't founded at that time," said one of the Freshmen, looking puzzled.

"And so it was n't, but Holland used to work for Judge Storey when the whole campus was nothing but Judge Storey's back yard. Then, when the college was started, this house was bought for a dormitory, and now presides like a white-haired grandmamma over its many descendants."

Kathleen Carey had dashed into the hall, and now returned with a copy of the "South Harland Gazette," which she waved triumphantly in the air.

"Friends and fellow-classmates, listen to this!" she proclaimed. "'Largest number of Freshmen on record! The town of South Harland opens its arms to an entering class of two hundred and sixty-four! Difficulty about finding accommodations for all, in the city limits! The following list of names has been obtained from the College Registrar, by Our Special Correspondent!' Now, girls, hold up your hands as your names are called." And a movement of interest went through the little group.

"'Adams, Beatrice Benedict, Richmond, Va.,' nice literary name, warranted straight from 'Much Ado about Nothing.' Any one claim it? Going, going, gone! 'Adams, Lydia Makepeace, West Harmony, Maine. Adams, Pomona Bufkins, Tombstone, Arizona. Allen, Amethyst Eliza, Holyoke, Mass.'"

A blushing Freshman raised her hand, and speedily put it down again, hoping that no one had noticed it.

"Welcome to our midst, Miss Allen," said Kathleen, with a bow; "make ready to welcome *me* to your midst later on. 'Appleyard, Araminta Daisy, Squaw Hunk, Wy. Arnold, Christine, Burlington, Ia.'"

"Christie, how can you be so stiff?" whispered Ruth, giving her room-mate a shake, and adding indignantly, "This is Miss Arnold, girls, although perhaps you knew it before."

"Ah!" said the Sophomore who had sat beside Christine at the table; "you must be the daughter of Senator Arnold, then, are n't you? Mrs. Hemp said one was to be here."

"I am Senator Arnold's *only* daughter," said Christine, with dignity, and Miss Gilbert was audacious enough to laugh.

"I'm sure I beg your pardon," she said, "for intimating that you might have a sister; and yet many nice people do have sisters, you know, and are still respected by their friends."

From that moment Christine condemned Maude Gilbert as a superfluous member of society.

"There has been a digression!" said Kathleen, peering over the top of the paper. "Parties will please return to business."

The next person who responded to the roll-call was Ruth Burritt, and then came Miss Carey herself, who said that, as circumstances prevented her from raising her hand, she would rely upon the testimony of all to prove that she was present.

"'Deland, Clare Edmonds, Hillside, N. Y.,'" was read; and the little brown-eyed girl said shyly, "I'm that one."

12

The last name that found an owner on the back piazza belonged to Philippa Fairbank, of Kalamazoo, Mich., a serious young person who looked (to quote one of the Seniors) as if she would go in for Heathen Missionary Work, and organize a new Needlework Guild.

"Now for a choice résumé," said Kathleen, irreverently. "'Elizabeth French Dane, Walla Walla, Wash.' What a plaster of nationalities! 'Edith Horton Standish, Boston, Mass.' Born in Beacon Street, died — no — came over in the 'Mayflower.' 'Katie Maria Dervish' — Hurrah! named for Grandma — "

"Clare Edmonds Deland," from Hillside, N. Y., stole away very quietly, and went upstairs to her room, where she hunted through her hand-satchel for another handkerchief, and sat down by the open window. She had taken her mother to the train that afternoon, — a slender, brown-eyed little mother, who did not look much older than Clare herself, — and the two had never been separated before. They had tried to tell funny stories and be cheerful when the time for parting came, but it was hard work, and each had cried when the other was out of sight.

Clare sat looking sorrowfully at her new trunk, which seemed in some mysterious way to be responsible for all the mischief. They had been such a happy little family at home, just mother and Ethel and Clare, and because there were so few of them, they had always felt like loving each other a great deal.

"Perhaps I'd better unpack my trunk," she thought tremulously, "and then maybe I won't think about what mamma and Ethel are doing this evening."

13

Mrs. Deland had taken out all the dresses that would crush easily, and hung them up in the closet; but she thought that it might amuse and divert Clare to unpack the rest of her trunk when she was alone.

She sat down on the floor now, and began to lay the carefully folded underclothes in a lower bureau drawer. She remembered so well the day when her mother had marked them, printing the letters very carefully in indelible ink, while Ethel stood by with a hot iron to press the name into each little garment as it was ready. Clare had not been allowed to assist in any of the preparations, not even to sew the tapes on the stockings, and it had all been great fun; but now, as each familiar thing came out of the trunk, it seemed to bring a fresh heart-ache with it. She felt quite comforted on finding the little red clock, which ticked sociably away, inside a flannel petticoat and did not seem to mind coming to college a bit. But when she took out other home-connected things, like her card-case, with the three birds on it, and the china dog that had stood on her table for so many years, they had a homesick and out-of-place look that made her feel more desolate than ever. The climax of woe was reached when she discovered a beautiful box of molasses candy, which Ethel had made as a surprise and tucked into the trunk at the last minute.

" Oh, how dear in them, how dear! " said Clare, and two sudden tears fell down upon the cover of the box, which was a second-hand Huyler box, tied up with blue ribbon; a third tear had lodged in the dimple of her chin, but she did not know it.

" I think I will take those girls some of my candy,"

she thought, "because mamma says that when you are very, very unhappy you must always try to do something nice for somebody else, and then you forget how unhappy you are."

She took the box, and tapped gently on Ruth's door, feeling sure that Ruth would accept the little gift as it was meant, and perhaps say something kind, to make her feel less lonely.

"Come in," called somebody; and Clare found Christine reading alone, with the red glow of the lamp on her face and hair.

"I beg your pardon," she faltered, "but I thought that you — and Miss Burritt, and you both, you know, might like some candy. My sister made it, and put it in my trunk for a surprise."

Christine leaned back in her chair, and looked at the small intruder with a decidedly bored expression.

"You are very kind," she said stiffly, "but we are fairly overwhelmed with candy at present. Miss Carey has just been in to get my room-mate, and has promised us a pound of Huyler's at least. You had much better eat yours yourself."

"I am sorry," said Clare, the tears springing to her eyes; and having said "good-night," she hastily slipped back to her own little room, thinking that "I am sorry" was not at all an appropriate thing to say.

"But I am so afraid of that tall girl with the flashing eyes," she thought. "I know that she will never like me, and I shall be afraid to go into their room again. Oh, mamma, mamma, I wish you were here!" and Clare threw herself down on the bed, to wrestle with that first great misery of homesickness, which we all find hard to bear even when we are more than seventeen years old.

Later in the evening came another surprise, for, pinned to the sleeve of her new pink wrapper, was a little note that had been written by somebody else who was lonely to-night, somebody who had sent her baby away from her because she thought that it was right.

My own darling Child, — When you find this, I am afraid that you will be wanting me very much, and not more, my dearest, than I shall be wanting you. But we can never be really separated, you know, while we think of each other. And if I believe you are happy, you know that I shall be very happy too.

Here there was a slight disturbance in the ink, and then came : —

Good-night, my own brave little Clare.

It was not easy for Clare to be brave after she had read this, and she lay awake for a long time, wondering about many things. A bar of moonlight crept in through the blinds, and she thought of the gleaming river, and of her friends the mountains, that were watching through the night. And then she fell asleep, with her hand on the dear note, and the tears on her lashes, like a child that is lost and far from home.

CHAPTER II

WHEN the rising-bell rang the next morning, Clare had been standing by her window for several minutes, looking out at the mountains. "They are like great beautiful birds, with wings of blue and gold," she thought, "and perhaps some day, if I am very good, I shall hear their song."

Before she was ready, Ruth Burritt knocked at the door to see if she would like to walk down to chapel with them, and Clare was very glad to accept the invitation. They started out after breakfast, chaperoned by Maude Gilbert, who with the greatest difficulty had persuaded them not to wear gloves.

"Every one will know you are Freshmen, if you do," she said, "and I am very much afraid that they will smile."

Christine had put gloves in her pocket before coming downstairs, but having no desire to be smiled at, she took pains to mention that very few people would think of wearing gloves to college on such a hot day.

As the girls walked down Elm Street, the chapel bell was ringing at regular intervals, and drew near like a welcoming hand stretched out to meet them.

"I 'm a little afraid," said Clare, keeping close to Ruth as they entered the side door.

2   17

"What on earth is there to be afraid of?" asked Christine, turning upon her with such scorn that the child shrank back in dismay. The broad stairway leading to the chapel was thronged with girls, and there was much hubbub of enthusiastic greeting and joyous laughter.

"I wonder if any one will ever love me as much as that girl in the pink waist loves that one in the brown skirt," thought Clare wistfully, as two beaming Sophomores toiled up the steps in front of her, holding each other's hands, and looking happily oblivious of surroundings.

"Oh, it *is* so good to see you again!" Clare heard one of them exclaim; and her companion responded with an impulsive hug that caused Christine to tread upon a member of the Faculty who was directly behind her.

"Such abominable sentimentality!" grumbled Chris, when she had duly apologized and inquired into the condition of the Faculty's toe.

At the head of the stairs was a large alcove, containing a bronze statue of St. George and the Dragon, which was at present adorned with several hats — one particularly jaunty sailor reposing upon the head of the saint himself. The sound of the organ stole out from the chapel, and wound about through the laughing, talking crowd.

"You can sit anywhere you like, this morning," said Maude Gilbert, as she hurried her party down the middle aisle, "but to-morrow we shall be divided according to classes."

"How much do I have to pay for my seat?" asked Ruth, in a stage whisper as they took their places.

"Nothing," answered Miss Gilbert, with a smothered explosion of laughter. "Here's the hymn-book, Miss Burritt, Number 294, in the 'Laudes Domini,' —you can see the number up there by the organ."

Clare sat between Ruth and a strange Freshman whose face attracted her attention at once. This girl was very fair, with regular features and black hair that contrasted strangely with her delicate coloring. But it was not the black hair that creeps and coils; it was the hair that fluffs and blows, and it had something in common with her eyes, which were of the deep dark blue that often withdraw into their own shadows, and leave one to wonder what the owner is thinking about.

Clare could not help looking at her, and said to herself: "She is the most beautiful girl that I ever saw."

Meanwhile Christine was saying to Ruth, "They're all crying, every one of 'em, and if they don't cry themselves they get some mother or aunt to do it for them, so it's all the same. I believe they'll irrigate the whole chapel."

"Chris, do be still," whispered Ruth, who did not wish to laugh. "I don't see but three Freshmen who are really crying, and the others are only looking homesick."

"There's one over there with green mitts on," persisted Christine, "and I shouldn't wonder if she's the Danish French woman — or the French Dane."

Her remarks were interrupted by the choir, who rose from their seats on the platform to give the signal for singing; the whole chapel followed, and soon the eight hundred young voices had joined in that glorious hymn beginning, "Lord, thy glory fills the heavens."

One can never forget that first morning in chapel! The music coming from every side, and the grand organ bearing the voices along on a solemn wave into the great closing chord.

Ruth choked, and the tears came to her eyes. Christine looked bored, but turned very white, as she always did, when determined not to show her feelings; and little Clare sang as she had never sung before. The Freshman who shared her book did not join in the hymn immediately, but soon, catching the enthusiasm of her companion, began to sing in a voice so full and sweet, so perfectly trained, that Clare stopped in amazement to listen. It was a beautiful voice, wide-spreading like a flower, and vibrating with all those exquisite overtones, or upper tones, that are so dear to a musician's heart. Other people stopped to listen too, and while the President was reading from the Bible, the girls who were sitting near the stranger studied her with naïve interest. She seemed entirely unconscious of herself, however, and when the next hymn began, sang a perfect second to Clare's soprano.

After the prayer was finished and the dear chant of "Our Father who art in Heaven," had been sung, the President made a welcoming speech to the entering class, and requested them to remain in chapel after the others had gone, to meet their Class Officer.

The music of the organ rushed forth again, while the Seniors and Juniors filed out, two by two, the Sophomores followed from the transepts, and the Freshmen were left by themselves, wondering what on earth a Class Officer was, — whether he would wear epaulets, and carry something to hit them with.

Presently a mild-looking man, who had been sitting in the Faculty Row, in the transept, hurried into the hall with an armful of recitation schedules, and having called the roll, he proceeded to distribute these among the new-comers, endeavoring to explain, meanwhile, the mysteries of "Elective" and "Required" studies, the undesirability of "conflicts," and the reason why the old Gymnasium was not the same as the new one.

"What *do* you make of this conglomeration?" asked Ruth, who was puzzling over her schedule. "Now, according to this, we have Latin, German, and History all at the same time, and that is what I should call overdoing it."

"Let's toss up and see which wins," suggested Kathleen Carey, who had taken Miss Gilbert's empty seat.

"Oh, Miss Burritt," said Clare, in an anxious voice, "I have Elocution at the same time that I have German, and they're both in the same room. How do you suppose they manage that?"

"It all comes of being gregarious," said Christine, in disgust; and the pretty girl, who had been studying her schedule in silence, looked up with a laugh. Now we all like to have our jokes appreciated, and the stranger had a pre-eminently ladylike appearance; so it was not long before she and Chris were consulting together as if they had always been friends.

"Suppose we write down the names of all the studies that every one has at the same time, and then draw lots as to which one we all go to," suggested the pretty girl, who was much amused by the whole situation.

Her plan was adopted, and the lot fell to German, which was represented as being in L. H. at nine o'clock.

"Now, what on earth is L. H.?" they said, and then some one happened to remember that Lincoln Hall was the name of the Science Building; so the little company sallied forth in quest of it, feeling very glad that there was not an old and a new Science Building to distract them. After having alarmed the Zoölogy Professor, and plunged in upon the Junior Physics, they succeeded in finding the German class, where it appeared that they were expected. The teacher gave them a list of books that they were to get for to-morrow, and after a lengthy dissertation on *Der, die, das* as found in emergencies, allowed them to depart.

The girls wandered about the campus until their hour was up, taking a mental photograph of the place, and wondering if they would be able to find any of the buildings after dark. They particularly liked the old Storey House, with its Pantheon-like pillars in front, and the group of genial pine-trees shading its back windows. Then they walked down the road that led between the cordial little Hadley, and its neighbor, the uncompromising Warren, and found the new Gym, which they invaded in a body, and had an impromptu dance. When they returned to College Hall the corridors were full of changing classes, but a friendly Sophomore piloted them to the Latin room, where Dr. Gillette, an active and alto-

22

together delightful man, dismissed them in a few minutes.

"I'm so sorry that you are not to be in our division," said Ruth to Miss Hathaway, the pretty girl, who, on account of coming later in the alphabet, had been relegated to the eleven-o'clock class.

"I wonder if it would be all right to go home now," said Clare. "We have n't any more studies this morning."

"Yes, you look tired!" said Ruth. "Chris and I are going down town now, to order the Livy and those German books, and I'll tell them to send up yours too, if you like."

"Oh, thank you so much," said Clare, gratefully; and presently she started for home, feeling as if she ought not to leave the college without asking permission of somebody, and half expecting that the Registrar would rush out to drag her back. Another Freshman, who also seemed uncertain of life in general, overtook her, and the two fell into a shy conversation.

"How do you like college?" asked Clare, who thought this must be a suitable thing to say.

"Oh, very much, don't you?" answered the other; and then conversation flagged.

"Do you like music?" again ventured Clare, who found it natural to speak of the subject nearest her heart.

"Oh, ever so much," said the Freshman, with enthusiasm. "I am studying the piano; are you?"

"Yes, — at least I was before I came away, but I can't help loving my violin a little the best. You see, it was my father's violin, and it knows me very well."

"How perfectly lovely!" was the appreciative response. "I do wish you would let me play your accompaniments sometimes. Are you going to take violin lessons here at college?"

"No, I'm to have piano now with Dr. Page, and next year my mother wants me to take up singing. Don't you think that the Analysis Class Concerts will be interesting? One of the girls told me that they often have string quartets, as well as the piano, and Dr. Page explains everything. That will be nice, I think; but oh, it is dreadful to be so far away from German Opera!"

"I haven't heard much German Opera," said the Freshman, respectfully. "Would you mind telling me your name?"

"Clare Deland. What's yours?"

"Rachel Winter. My room-mate and I are boarding at Dr. Gillette's, on the hill. He is ever so nice, and his wife is charming. You must surely come to see us."

"I surely will," said Clare, "for I live on the hill too. And now I wonder if we would be allowed to practise in the Music Building when there is a room vacant. Do you suppose so?"

"We might ask the President," said Miss Winter, seriously. "He would be sure to know."

There was a light step behind them, and a pretty Junior came up beside Clare with a look of apology which was both comical and charming.

"Forgive me," she said, "for overhearing a part of your conversation, but you really mustn't ask the President about practising in the Music Building. It's all right for you to practise there, and he doesn't

24

have anything to do with such things. If the Grind Committee should get hold of your little plan, they would give you no peace."

Clare and her companion looked at each other aghast. The Grind Committee! What new horror was this? The Junior began to laugh, and then, begging pardon for her rudeness, laughed again.

" Please don't look so frightened," she said. " You must have heard of the reception that the Sophomores give every year to the Freshmen, and you know they love to get all the grinds, or jokes, on the Freshmen that they can, to turn into souvenirs. You will have a very good time at the reception, if the girl who asks you takes pains in making out your card."

Clare was the first to recover herself, and said: " It was very, very kind in you to tell us about the practising. Of course we don't want to appear any sillier than necessary."

" I did as I would be done by," said the Junior, with a funny smile; "and now I want to ask you two ladies if you will come to the Hillard — that's the house near Lincoln Hall, you know — next Sunday afternoon, and play to us. We always have music after dinner, and it is very seldom that we can get a violin. We will play to you, too, if you will promise not to run away ! " and she looked so merry and cordial that the Freshmen immediately promised to come, resolving that they would practise every minute until the important afternoon arrived.

But as the time drew near, their courage oozed away, and when Saturday night came, Miss Winter confided to Clare that she wished they had n't said

25

they would go. "You play beautifully," she said apologetically, "but I get terribly rattled in my accompaniments, and with all those upper-class girls there I know I should simply ruin that 'Raff's Cavatina.'"

"We might write her a note," said Clare, who felt herself wavering in turn, "or perhaps we shall see her to-night at the Freshman Frolic. But what reason can we give for not coming?"

"I'm sure I don't know," said Miss Winter, dubiously. "Perhaps it would be better to compose a note to-morrow. You be thinking about what we'll say in it, and I'll come up to Mrs. Hemp's early, before church, so that we can combine ideas."

The Freshman Frolic was held in the new Gym, and was merely an informal dance, at which different girls took turns in being orchestra, and everybody was supposed to be very polite to the Freshmen. Let it not be recorded that there were certain mischievous spirits who went to the Frolic to mock and even to jeer at those who were there, or who repaired to Henley's and inflicted upon themselves a strawberry ice rather than assimilate the joys of this assembly.

Mrs. Hemp's girls were escorted to the Frolic by Maude Gilbert and Theresa Robinson; while Miss Snow, a spectacled Senior who was deaf in one ear, agreed to come later and do some introducing. Both Clare and Rachel Winter danced with their Junior, Miss Campbell, that evening, but studiously avoided the subject of the Sunday-afternoon performance, although she herself seemed inclined to dwell upon it. They had been much alarmed by the previous discovery that Miss Campbell was a member of the

Sigma, — the older of the two literary societies, — and was also a very prominent girl in her class. She introduced her two protégés to several delightful Seniors, who expressed the greatest pleasure at meeting them, and said they were really looking forward to the little Musicale of to-morrow! When the Frolic was nearly over, the Glee Club sang the well-known " Balm of Gilead," beginning with " Here 's to Ninety-two, she 's the best of all of you," and ending with " Here 's to Ninety-five, she 's the freshest class alive, Drink her down, drink her down, drink her down, down, down ! "

" 'The freshest class alive ! ' " muttered Kathleen Carey explosively, on the way home. " 'All them things that you say I are, you be.' Just wait till we get there."

" Well, Miss Arnold, whom did you meet that you liked to-night? " asked Maude Gilbert, as the girls sat down in Mrs. Hemp's great hall, to rest before going upstairs.

" Nobody," said Christine, conclusively. " They all stepped on my toes."

" You certainly looked fierce enough to frighten any but the bravest," said Ruth, with a laugh; and Kathleen Carey added, —

" It 's always the valiant what has the big feet."

" Well, I had an adventure," announced Ruth, proudly. " Somebody introduced me to a Miss Burritt, — a Ninety-three girl, I think, and she said that she had found me in the catalogue and was meaning to look me up, because we had the same name. Was n't that nice in her? And she asked me to go to the Sophomore reception."

27

"Perhaps you are relatives," said Theresa Robinson, looking at Ruth with much respect, for Louise Burritt was one of "the" nice Juniors in the college.

"We tried to find a relationship," said Ruth, "and we had just settled on one great-grandfather we had in common, when I unfortunately remembered that he was drowned in a tub of water at the age of two years; so we had to give him up."

"Oh dear, I had a great-aunt who fell down our back-cellar stairs into a barrel of soft soap," said Kathleen, mournfully. "Why does n't somebody ask *me* to the Sophomore reception?"

"I 'll take you with pleasure," said Maude Gilbert, who found Kathleen extremely entertaining.

"And I 'll take Miss Deland, if I may," said Theresa Robinson, laying her hand on Clare's. "I 've begun to think already about the girls that she would like to meet."

"Oh, how lovely in you!" said Clare, flushing with delight. And everybody laughed as the little company broke up for the night.

The next morning Rachel Winter came up to bring the note that she had composed, and also brought her room-mate, Salome Judd, a young lady who spoke so deliberately that one's idea of what she had last said would vanish before any more words came in sight.

"Now, what do you think of this?" said Rachel, producing her note. "Sally does n't approve, but I consider it the best thing I ever did." And she read an elaborate composition in which Clare figured prominently with a sprained ankle, and she herself
28

escaped with the minor ailment of a frightful toothache.

" I 'm — afraid — that — would n't — do, because " began Miss Judd; and Clare found time to read her own note, which ran, —

DEAR MISS CAMPBELL, — We want to come, but we 're too scared; so please excuse us.

Yours truly, CLARE DELAND.

" Oh, that is much too snippy," said Rachel, with decision. " She would never speak to us again if we sent that."

" Well, what shall we say then? " said Clare, who was beginning to feel discouraged.

" They 're — such — lies," continued Miss Judd, still referring to her room-mate's note.

Several more excuses were evolved and discarded, and it ended in not sending any note at all; the Freshmen simply did not go, when the time came, and Edith Campbell, who had invited a number of friends to hear them play, was unmercifully teased by those ungrateful ones.

" It is a good joke on me," she said, laughing, " but you can't expect me to be hospitable to any more Ninety-five girls."

" Hospitality I don't call it," said a Senior. " To ask the poor little souls to come and entertain us, without promising them even a sweet potato for their pains! I don't wonder they did n't respond."

" But I was going to ask them to our Dramatics if they 'd been obliging," explained Edith, " and I have a nice little cake and some tea for them upstairs."

" A cake and tea, did you say, Edith? " asked Miss

Burritt, slipping her hand through her friend's arm; "I'm so sorry those Freshmen did n't come! Girls, let's drop in on Edith before we disperse, — what do you say?"

"Agreed," answered the others; and a laughing company followed Edith up to her sanctum, where the tea-ball still reposed unused in the vacant cup.

"Did you know that you had a rival in the Freshman class, Edith?" asked one of the girls. "There is a certain Miss Hathaway, who is said to be more beautiful than you, and we are going to call upon her in a body this evening to satisfy our curiosity."

"Dear me, what fun! I'll take her to the reception," said Miss Campbell, who enjoyed the privilege of being the college beauty. "But I'm afraid I sha'n't be jealous of her even if her charms do surpass mine, for I think that we need — that is, girls won't you have some more cake?"

CHAPTER III

ARDIS HATHAWAY would have been annoyed, had she overheard this conversation, because her personal appearance was not a subject that interested her, except as a means to an end. She would have preferred to be singled out as a young person of inherent executive ability, or intellectual force, and was actually jealous of that beauty which distracted one's attention from her mental powers. Having lost her mother when a baby, she was left to the companionship of housekeepers, and a father who usually ignored her existence. But, his library being at her disposal, she imbibed much literature of an ethical, political, and epicurean nature, which turned her mind into strange channels. She saw through people easily, but did not let them know it, because they amused her too much. One of her favorite pastimes was to plan what a certain person would do under given conditions, and then provide the conditions in order to verify her deductions. She enjoyed stirring people up, and drawing out their most aggressive opinions; but she could make them like her when she chose, and her definition of originality was to say that such and such a person was " worth reading."

She and Christine Arnold found each other interesting, to their mutual surprise, and exchanged theories while investigating the fragrant wood-paths and hazy meadows around South Harland. One of their conversations remained in Christine's mind long after that first week of college was over. They had been walking through the quaint old street of Hadley, and, passing beneath the overreaching trees, were ushered into the presence of the mountains. For a while neither of them spoke, and then Christine said: "Is n't it hard that self-expression should be the ruling passion of mankind? When I see a thing like that I cannot be happy until I have written it down."

"It is true that we all have something to say," said Ardis, "and it is equally true that it is the main object of other people to prevent our saying it."

"Do people bore you to death?" asked Christine. "They bore me!"

"No," answered Ardis, "because I don't expect anything of them, in the first place. I simply go away. If you never expect anything of any one, you will never be disappointed."

Christine pondered over this in silence.

"I think, then, that I would rather be disappointed sometimes," she said, as they turned to go home. "When I cease to be disappointed in anybody or in anything, it will be because I have lowered my ideals."

The girls walked along for some time without speaking, and then Ardis said, "You should not have brought ideals to college with you; they take up too much room."

Christine laughed. "I fear that mine will do some trespassing in that case, for they are not even full-grown yet. In fact, I believe that they are just beginning to expand."

"Your idea of college, then, is that it resembles a huge corn-popper, into which we throw our undeveloped ideals, and when these have been shaken long enough over the fire of learning, they burst into nice fluffy kernels, which — to complete the simile — are eaten up as soon as we go out into the world?"

. "It would be better for an ideal to be eaten up than to be so tough and scorched that nobody would touch it."

"Yes," continued Ardis; "but if you try to swallow another person's ideal in addition to your own, you are very likely to choke yourself and die. Moral: Don't adopt other people's standard of right and wrong."

"It is curious," observed Christine, "that I happen to disagree with you in everything that you say; but I presume it makes our conversations more interesting."

"Certainly," said Ardis; "that is the cause of all interest, — disagreement. But we agree upon the main fact, that our conversations are interesting, do we not? And that Philippa Fairbank is n't. Perhaps that is why Philippa is emerging from the cemetery, at this precise moment, with Amethyst Allen in her wake, and they are both coming to meet us."

"Oh, Miss Arnold!" said Philippa, when she encountered the two girls, "the Sophomores had their class meeting to-day, after all; so there's no reason why we should n't have ours to-morrow. Is n't it all exciting?"

3   33

"Very," said Ardis and Christine, who were not excited in the least. "It's a beautiful day, — yes. Good-bye;" and they hastened on their way, to finish the afternoon on the back campus, where philosophy could be supplemented with apples.

On the following morning the Freshman class were electrified by finding this notice upon the college bulletin board: —

'95

CLASS MEETING!

TO-DAY

At 2 P. M. in Music Hall.

Everybody Come!!!

" Hurrah!" cried Kathleen Carey, tossing her red Livy into the air. "We've entered upon our political function!"

"Miss Carey, how could you?" exclaimed Amethyst Allen, in horror; "your book came right down on that Senior's head."

"Just hold her till I get it off, then, will you?" said Kathleen. " I've got to translate that remaining eye of Hannibal before chapel."

The Senior returned the book with a frigid glare, and passed on, privately concluding that Ninety-five was an unbearable class, fit only for extermination.

When 2 P. M. came, Music Hall was so crowded with enthusiastic Freshmen that they were obliged to overflow out of doors and windows, and several of them even elected to sit on the edge of the platform with their heads under the grand piano.

" Where is the Chairman? " inquired Philippa Fairbank, severely, as the meeting came to order. " Is the Chairman present? "

It seemed that no chairman was present, for the reason that none had been appointed.

"You be the Chairman," suggested a timid voice from the front row; and as several other voices supported this suggestion, Philippa solemnly " took the chair," which happened to be Dr. Page's music-stool.

" The first thing to do, fellow-classmates," she said with dignity, " is to elect a president, who will rule the class for the coming year."

" Please, Miss Chairwoman," ventured somebody in the back of the room, " we can't elect a president without having a Constitution."

" Is it the wish of this class that we have a Constitution? " inquired Miss Fairbank; and as there was a general murmur of assent, she finished pompously with, " It seems to be a vote, — it *is* a vote, and the motion stands as passed."

" There has n't been any motion," whispered Christine, who was perishing with laughter; " and, besides, she should n't call it a vote only because it seems to be one. There 's no judging by appearances ! "

" Has any one ' Roberts' Rules of Order '? " asked a sensible-looking girl, who carried a fresh notebook, bearing the name of Elizabeth French Dane.

" I 'll run around to Miss Roberts' and get it," said Amethyst Allen, who was an obliging little person; and several girls forcibly detained her, while somebody else explained that Miss Roberts, the young and pretty Chemistry assistant, was not identical with the author of " Roberts' Rules of Order."

Finally, the book in question was borrowed from a Senior in the Storey House, the meeting once more came to order, and the Constitution was drawn up in tolerably correct form; so that now it only remained to elect that unfortunate girl who was to " rule the class for the coming year."

" I nominate Miss Hastings as President," proclaimed a firm voice, and a frightened-looking Freshman rose to her feet, saying, " I decline the office," but was violently jerked down from behind by a friend, who whispered, " Be still, — you have n't got it yet ! "

The worst of it was, that no one knew anything about anybody else, and it did not seem reasonable to vote for an absolute stranger; but at last Miss Hastings, Miss Wyman, and Miss Standish were nominated as candidates, and requested to stand on the platform, that the class might inspect them. Miss Standish advanced with dignity from the back of the room, Miss Hastings was propelled forward by two anxious friends, and Miss Wyman emerged from under the piano. There was no doubt that Beacon Street produced the best impression, and Miss Edith Horton Standish was unanimously elected President of her class, amid congratulations and hearty cheers.

" Miss Standish will please take the chair," said Philippa Fairbank, stiffly; and Miss Standish proceeded to screw up the piano-stool, so that it would be high enough for her to sit on.

" The next thing to be decided upon to-day, I

36

think," said Miss Fairbank, "is the class color. Miss Standish will conduct the remainder of the meeting."

"If she has a chance!" murmured somebody, who was promptly suppressed.

"I believe it is the custom," said Miss Standish, with her cheeks slightly flushed, "for the entering class to take the color of the class that has just graduated; but this is, of course, not compulsory, — and the color of the college is white, you know."

"What was the color of Ninety-one?" asked some one; and a sepulchral voice from nobody knew where, answered "Nile green."

"Who's been up the Nile?" called out Kathleen Carey, in a very unseemly manner; "that's where the crocodiles come from!" A momentary disturbance was caused by this speech, and then came a long discussion about the suitability of various colors, — one faction being strongly in favor of a Scotch plaid.

"We have to choose a color that will be suitable for decorations," interposed the President firmly, wishing that the piano-stool would not wiggle so when she spoke.

"That is true," was one appreciative answer; "who ever saw a plaid flower, or even a plaid tree?"

Finally they decided to take green, — not the green that matches the crocodiles, but the green that Nature uses in all her decorations, the green of springtime and of summer, and the green of Ninety-five!

"Hurrah!" came in a chorus from under the piano; and the whole room joined in a triumphant cheer, as the assembly broke up in hilarious confusion, and rushed downstairs.

"I move that we adjourn," said Philippa Fairbank, feebly, as the last girl disappeared into the hall; but nobody heeded her except the plaster busts of musicians around the wall, and, being very comfortable, they did not second the motion.

Green bunting now became a prominent feature, both on and off the campus, for the class of Ninety-five had a color, and wanted other people to know it. Green hat trimmings walked into chapel, and green flags with a white '95 in the centre hung in every Freshman room.

"Union is strength," said Kathleen Carey, as she solemnly tacked a green petticoat around the edge of her table, "and no one shall dare to tread with his foot upon them that wear the green!" Ruth made a beautiful banner of silk, and hung it opposite the Yale-Harvard combination, where it caught the sunlight in its green folds, and looked "as if it were proud to begin life with a class like Ninety-five."

"You don't care enough for our flag, Christine," objected Ruth. "I think that you ought at least to get up a little class spirit before the Sophomore reception!"

Christine looked disgusted, and turned away in haughty silence, for she had not yet been asked to the Sophomore reception, and was distinctly annoyed by the fact.

"It's not that I want to go to their old dance," she said violently, "but one does n't like to achieve notoriety as being the only person who was not invited."

The truth was that Christine had gained the repu-

38

tation of being a snob among the girls who would have been her friends, and several of them had justly condemned her as being "too snippy to live," — a fact which did not shorten her existence, but did much to curtail her pleasures. The Sophomores always appoint a committee to see that every Freshman is personally invited to the reception, and it was one of the joys in Christine's life to know that Maude Gilbert was on this committee. Maude had been pursuing upper-class girls for a week, in behalf of her "left-over" list, and had purposely left Christine till the last, — intending, however, to give her a very nice partner when the time came.

One afternoon the two Freshmen were wrestling over their Latin translation, when there was a knock at the door, and Christine went to open it, feeling inclined to throw something at whoever was there.

"I beg your pardon," said a sweet voice, "but does Miss Arnold live here?" and Christine found herself ushering in a very pretty, light-haired little girl, who was a total stranger.

"We are very glad to see you," said Ruth, cordially; "won't you sit down?" and the face of the strange girl brightened, as she held out her hand.

"You are Miss Arnold, are you not?" she said, beaming with satisfaction. "I've come to ask you to the Sophomore reception."

Ruth looked confused, but turned to Christine, who was transfixing her with an irate glance.

"No; my room-mate is Miss Arnold," she explained. "But I am sure that she would love to go with you. Christine, wasn't it sweet in her to come and ask you?"

Christine turned crimson with rage, and said not a word. The little stranger looked troubled.

"I'm sure — I hope that I have n't come too late," she said timidly. "I wanted so much to have a Freshman for the reception, and one of the girls here said she thought you were still disengaged. My name is Marjorie Drew."

"I'm sure Christine will love to go with you, Miss Drew," said Ruth, ineffectually trying to reach her room-mate's toe and demolish it.

"It was very kind in you," said Christine, finally, "but I am afraid I shall have to decline your charitable invitation. I would prefer to go with a friend."

"Oh, if you have a friend here, of course it would be pleasanter to go with her," said Miss Drew, who was beginning to feel a little hurt; "and I hope you will pardon me for intruding, but I should have liked so much to take you myself. Perhaps your friend will give me a dance with you, if they are not all engaged."

Christine's honesty came to the front. "I have n't any friend here," she said slowly; "but what I meant was that I don't want to go with a stranger who asks me just because she was made to!"

Ruth looked terribly distressed, and Marjorie even more so. "I did not ask you because I was made to," she said, rising; "but in any case it appears that I've made a mistake, and I'm very sorry."

She turned to go, but suddenly crossed the room again and put her hand into Christine's.

"Won't you come with me, after all?" she asked impulsively. "I would n't have hurt your feelings for the world, dear child, because mine are always

40

getting hurt, too, you see, and I know just how it feels!"

"Oh, do not give yourself any uneasiness with regard to my feelings," said Christine, coldly. "I don't think that any stranger would be capable of hurting them;" and poor Marjorie felt too chilled to say another word.

"I suppose she has heard that I'm working my way through college," she thought, as the door closed behind her, and she went downstairs to tell Miss Gilbert the result of her interview.

Maude was justly enraged at Christine's conduct, and vowed that she should not go to the Sophomore reception at all.

"That would be a disgrace to your class," said Marjorie, with spirit, "and, besides, I almost understand how the girl feels about it. Perhaps I did not put my invitation rightly, — I don't know, — but it is very certain that she does n't want to go with me."

"She's an inexcusable, unbearable little snob," said Maude, fiercely, "and I shall give her a blowing up for insulting you so!"

"Don't be too hard on her, please," said Marjorie, gently. "She's only a mistaken child, that's all; and do you know, I rather liked her in spite of everything. I think she would be incapable of a mean or underhand action, and there's a certain greatness about her too. Yes, I liked her!"

Maude did speak to Christine, and represented to her that to be absent from the Sophomore reception would make her the subject of much unpleasant comment, especially if it were known that she had refused the invitation of a Junior like Marjorie Drew. Now, it is quite probable that Christine's absence would not have been noticed at all, but if it had been, the blame would naturally have fallen upon that member of the committee who had failed to do her duty; so Maude did not cease her indignant protests, until Christine had consented to accept the invitation of a Kansas Senior, a distinctly patronizing young lady, who sent up a dozen feeble carnations when the night of the dance came.

" I would not have advised you to throw *all* those flowers out of the window, Christine," expostulated Ruth, who was engaged in fastening a cluster of pink roses beneath her pretty throat. " You know the girls always expect you to wear at least a few of the flowers they send, even if they are hideous."

" They were the color of ducks' feet on a Japanese screen," said Christine, miserably, " and they would n't make me look beautiful."

" Well, you shall have some of mine, sweetheart," said Ruth, offering the only consolation in her power; " and I don't know as I would care what Miss Jenkins thinks anyway. She ought to have sent you decent flowers, if she expected you to wear them."

The reception was a great success, the new Gym being beautifully decorated with green boughs and red bunting, — the two class colors; while fastened to the farther end of the running track was a big '94 in red carnations, and on the opposite side hung an oak-leaf '95. The girls had stripped their rooms of sofa-pillows and divan covers to lay along the seats, and silk screens glimmered brightly in and out amongst the green. With the music by a good orchestra, the light dresses and flowers, and last, but not least, the two big bowls of frappé in one corner, it all seemed to Clare like a lovely, bewildering dream.

"I wish mamma could have seen it," she said to Theresa, as they stood on the running track looking down on the dancers.

"How beautiful Miss Arnold looks to-night!" answered Theresa, who was not thinking about her mother. "I had no idea that she was so pretty!"

People always found it hard to describe Christine, for the reason that she never looked twice the same. Her hair was gold in the sunshine and brown in the shadow, like two of her own moods; and her eyes were of the changing gray that often indicates an imaginative temperament. She was tall, and carried herself with so much dignity that people were inclined to be afraid of her before they knew her well; but she had an unmistakable air of distinction that disarmed all criticism of a petty nature. Strangers visiting the college later in the year often pointed her out to Miss Carlisle, — the most influential woman on the Faculty, — and asked respectfully if that young girl had not done something unusual. And Miss Carlisle, who saw and heard and knew everything about all the girls, though they seldom suspected it, would answer with the utmost conviction, "Not yet, but she will!"

To-night Christine was thinking about the hard lesson that she had learned, and wondering if she had not made a mistake in holding herself so aloof from the other girls; this impression may have been confirmed by the change which a pretty evening dress made in most of her companions.

"I suppose," she reflected, "that being at college, and not entering into the college spirit is like sitting

43

on the end of a wharf, and trying to judge of the temperature of the water by the other people that are in swimming!" The longer she thought about it, the less attractive the wharf side of the question became, and presently she found herself giving a very civil answer to a tired Senior who asked her "how she liked college."

Miss Jenkins regretted that she had not taken more pains in making out her partner's card, but Christine did not care. She was constructing a new code of ethics for her future use, and this new code did not include the old rule that "Thou shalt snub thy neighbor."

CHAPTER IV

A RENEWED ACQUAINTANCE

CHRISTINE lived up to her new principles so well that when Mountain Day came, she meekly fell in with the plans made by Ruth and Kathleen for an all-day drive and picnic, which would include two carriages, and endless cans of potted ham. Clare's friends, Rachel Winter and Salome Judd, were invited, together with Ardis Hathaway, and Kathleen's strawberry-ice acquaintance, Miss Reade. When the little party assembled on that brilliant October morning, Miss Winter and her room-mate were the last to arrive, — a delay which appeared to have been caused by Miss Judd's vacillating temperament.

"Sally never decides what she is going to do until every one else has done it!" explained Rachel, indignantly. "I went down town for something, and when I returned she was still sitting on the floor in profound meditation. And when I asked 'Why?' she merely said, 'I can't decide whether to button my boots first, and then put on my hat, or to put on my hat now, and button my boots afterwards.'"

Salome looked embarrassed; but just then a nodding equine head appeared at the top of the hill, and Kathleen rushed wildly around the little group, shaking hands with every one in it.

45

"Congratulate me, all of you!" she said, "for I engaged this beast, and yet the beast that is to come, — a very neat and well-shaped beast, too. Isn't it myself that should be set up with regard to the matter?"

Now it must be understood that every equipage in South Harland has to be engaged weeks beforehand for Mountain Day, and Kathleen was justly proud of the two carriages which drew up before the door. But the other members of the party passed mocking comments upon the appearance of these, and jeered unceasingly.

"This harness is too short-waisted," objected Christine, who was examining the forward horse, "and his tail! Why, Kathleen, where is it?"

"*I* haven't got it," shouted Kathleen, wrathfully. "Don't look at me in that suspicious manner!"

"The poor beast's met with an accident," said Ardis, thoughtfully, "and it has embittered his whole nature. In addition to that, his lower lip resembles a mattress, with the upper lip pulled down over it and tucked in!"

"This other horse has more spirit," announced Ruth, with satisfaction. "He chewed me when I patted him, so perhaps he'll go. Come, girls, let's put in the lunch-baskets, for we ought to be off."

"Catch that cheese, Honey," said Kathleen, tossing a brown paper parcel into Ruth's lap. "Now for an all-day jubilation!"

When the party started out, Christine went ahead in the first carriage, with Ardis, Kathleen, and Grace Reade; while Ruth followed, driving the sedate Sam, who dreamed of corn all the way. Christine rather prided herself upon her driving, and whipped up the lively Maggie Rafferty until she danced with rage.

"Christine, do be careful!" called Ruth from the remote rear, as they approached the top of a steep hill.

Now Christine had intended to be careful, but, objecting to Ruth's admonishing tone, she touched Miss Rafferty again with the whip, and Maggie flew down that hill like a whirlwind. To hold her was impossible, and to the credit of the girls in the carriage, they neither seized Christine's arm nor screamed. The horse made an abrupt turn at the bottom of the hill, the carriage went over with a smash, and Maggie tore off down the street, dragging the broken shafts behind her. There was a cry of terror from the other carriage; but Ruth was obliged to attend to her own horse, who "saw bears" with his ears, and pretended to be terribly frightened — not one word of which was true.

When they reached the scene of disaster, the girls were crawling out from the wreck, and regarding each other with white faces, — all but Christine, who lay very still with the blood flowing from a cut in her head. The unfortunate driver had been on the side of the carriage which turned over, and, as she afterwards objected, the whole of the party had sat on her at once. Ardis, who had a big bruise on her forehead, was holding Christine's head in her lap, and trying to stop the blood with her handkerchief. A toothless old woman emerged from a neighboring house, fell over a fragment of harness, and called out in a shrill voice, "Anybody want some Pond's Extract?"

Water was brought from a neighboring well by
Kathleen, who was gesticulating wildly, with the
crown of her hat jammed in, and the rest of it
balanced upon one ear. Christine was effectually
deluged by her friends, and presently sat up in a
rage, with the water trickling down her back.

"It's no more than could be expected," she said
indignantly, "of a horse with no tail!" And the
girls drew a long sigh of relief.

"I hope," she continued in a wrathful tone, "that
Maggie Rafferty will have a bad Easter, and die by
the sword."

"Oh, my darling, are you very much hurt?" asked
Ruth, making explorations up and down Christine's
back with a trembling hand.

"Stop tickling me," said the victim. "I hope that
this horse will be outlawed and derided of other
horses — that the loss of its tail will cause it to pine
away and die."

"She's out of her head," said Rachel Winter, in an
awed whisper.

"Nonsense," answered Ardis, sharply. "It's the
way she always talks. Come, Christine, if you are
able to walk, we will take you to the carriage."

Clare, who had been left in charge of old Sam,
towed him reluctantly to the wreck, and Christine was
helped in, not without some dizziness, which struck
terror to the hearts of her companions. When the
pathetic little procession reached home, Mrs. Hemp
put Christine to bed, lent Ardis the arnica, and sent
for a doctor. He was a good doctor, but his eyes
twinkled inexcusably when he heard the details of
the escapade.

"Guess I 'll just step into Rafferty's and inquire after the horse," he said, when he had assured the group of damsels in the hall that Christine would not die.

"A few days in bed, and perfect quiet, Mrs. Hemp," he had said; and Christine, who hated to stay in bed, pretended that the bookcase was the doctor, and threw a shoe at it.

"Is n't there anything that we can do?" asked a kind little voice at the door; and Christine grumbled from under the bed-clothes, "Tell her to go away and die."

"Thank you so very much, Miss Deland," said Ruth, gratefully, "but I think everything has been done. How is Miss Hathaway feeling?"

"The girls drove her down to Miss Taylor's in the carriage," said Clare, "and she seemed to be all right. Do you know — it 's so funny — there has been a procession of small boys coming to the house every few minutes with fragments of the lunch that was spilled out. The last one brought a corkscrew and a piece of harness."

Christine exploded with laughter, and pushed her head from under the clothes.

"Have they found my half-pound of Huyler that I had on the front seat?" she asked.

"No, they have n't brought that," said Clare, delighted to be of service. "I 'll go back and see if I can find it."

Christine had scorned and snubbed her from the beginning, but it was possible for her to forget things like these. The Huyler did not come to light; and Clare, having counted up her small shekels, replaced

4   49

the lost box by one exactly like it at Henley's, taking a singular pleasure in the little deception.

"She'll have to eat my candy now, whether she wants to or not!" she laughed to herself.

Christine's convalescence took a much shorter time than any one had expected, but she refused to go to recitation long after she was perfectly well able to do so.

"What! go down to college with my head tied up in a red silk handkerchief, and my nose in a sling?" she said with scorn. "Never!"

"Well, I can't keep on saying 'Ill' every day, when it's only your vanity that prevents you from coming," said the exasperated Ruth, who was weary of being questioned regarding the health of her roommate.

"Don't give any explanation at all, then," suggested Christine, cheerfully. "A few cuts more or less, don't make any difference."

They do, though, as she was destined to learn by experience. About a week after she returned to recitation, Fräulein Schaf "sprung" a written lesson upon them, and as Christine had not looked at her German for many days, she emerged from this trial very ingloriously indeed.

"I have my suspicions," she said to herself when she handed in that tottering paper; and her suspicions were not unfounded. On the following morning she discovered an ominous note on the bulletin board, and went up to chapel casting searching and irate glances at her friends, to see if any of them had observed that little note before she did.

"An invitation to the Warren dance, Miss Arnold?"

inquired a rampant Freshman, whom she encountered in the St. George alcove.

"Go away!" was the stern answer. "How dare you speak to me?" and the Freshman retreated in alarm.

"'Miss Arnold will please review her German with a competent tutor, and be examined in it again before the Christmas vacation.' How ingenuous!" muttered Christine, "and I am to go to her 'as soon as convenient,' 'and get the address of the tutor.' Hope it's no one I ever saw before. Well, I can take pains to have it some one I shall never see again."

She sat there until the last stragglers had hurried into chapel, and the hymn began; then she rested her head upon her hands and read that humiliating note over again. She remembered how well Henry had done at Harvard, how well Stephen was doing now, and regretted that she had been born.

Perhaps some other girls can remember sitting in the St. George alcove during chapel time, and wishing that there were some hole in the back campus big enough for them to creep into and hide themselves forever from mortal eyes. It is certain that this particular St. George and the Dragon have been the recipients of many woes connected with the bitter-sweet of college life.

While Christine was writhing in mortification, somebody came softly into the alcove, and she immediately adopted a look of unconcern.

"What's the matter, Christabel?" asked Ardis, laying her books upon the window-ledge. "There, — you've already resolved that nothing on earth would induce you to tell me!"

This was so near the truth that Christine laughed, and with a sudden impulse gave Ardis the note.

"You are very much annoyed over this, are n't you?" observed Ardis, when she had finished reading it. "And it's exceedingly foolish in you to care at all. When you are older you will learn not to mind little things."

"I am eighteen, and you are nineteen," said Christine, sarcastically, "and this is n't a little thing. It's a large, horrible disgrace, and when my father knows about it — "

"Don't tell him," interrupted Ardis. "Don't tell any one about it, — not even Ruth; for, in the first place, it is not so important as you think, and in the second, sympathy would be your destruction. If you let people sympathize with you, it will keep this annoyance continually before your mind."

"I observe that you have offered no sympathy," was the grim rejoinder.

"Christine, I'm an Epicurean. Do you know what an Epicurean is?"

"A person that eats too much, is n't it?"

"*No*, but a person that believes in getting all the pleasure out of life that life can give. I believe in having a good time."

"But that's just the trouble," objected Christine. "I've been having too good a time and not studying enough."

"My dear child, you don't grasp the foundation of this theory. When you do something that will get you into trouble, don't you see that you 're not planning for a good time at all? You 've allowed a lesser joy to crowd out the possibility of a greater, that 's

52

all. Your getting yourself conditioned in this stupid way was merely a lack of foresight, — a little mistake in the time and place of economy."

The girls began to come out of chapel, and Ardis took up her books preparatory to depart.

" Remember what I say," was her last injunction, " and don't be so down-hearted about this, for there's nothing to be ashamed of. You have only made a mistake, which, being wiser by experience, you will not make again. Farewell." And as Christine walked over to Lincoln Hall, she tried in vain to disentangle the right from the wrong in what Ardis had said; her philosophy had an impressive sound that made one think she must have lived long, and suffered much.

Fräulein Schaf was busy that morning, and when her pupil appeared she merely handed her a slip of paper with the name and address of a tutor written upon it.

" Oh, Fräulein," implored Christine, when she saw who it was, " cannot you send me to any other girl? I have particular reasons for not wishing to take lessons of this young lady."

The teacher looked up in surprise.

" This is the most clever tutor in the college," she said severely, " and she also needs the money; so I must insist that you begin with her immediately the *Unterrichten*. I have given her your name." And Christine knew that further argument was useless.

That afternoon she took her books, and stole down through back ways to a street behind the Opera House, where, up two flights of stairs, in a little room that resembled an attic, lived Marjorie Drew.

"I am so glad to see you, Miss Arnold," she said when Christine came in. "It is so delightful for me to have an interesting pupil, that I'm selfish enough to be glad you were ill and had to fall a little behind. We shall have fine times over this old German, I'm sure."

Now this was tact; but Christine looked at her coldly and answered: "It wasn't illness. It was Mountain Day, and besides I hate to study. Have you a dressmaker here? This appears to be a sewing-room."

Marjorie colored sensitively. "I'm sorry that you dislike seeing work around," she said, beginning to gather up the pieces of blue flannel that lay scattered about. "But Elizabeth and I were fortunate enough to get a very large order for gym suits this week, and have been toiling early and late to finish them."

"You mean that you make them yourself?" said Christine, aghast. "Why, in the name of all that is horrible, do you do that? And who is Elizabeth?"

"Elizabeth Dane is one of your classmates," answered Marjorie, "and we both work because otherwise we should not be able to remain at college. Now, if you are ready, Miss Arnold, we will begin on *Germelshausen*."

Christine was in deadly terror lest the "Danish Frenchwoman" should return and find her there, but Marjorie reassured her by saying, "Miss Dane and I regard this room as a confessional, and no one ever knows who my pupils are, or when they come."

On the following day Christine felt more inclined to converse than to work, — a tendency which Miss Drew promptly discouraged.

"I'm sorry that you take no interest in your lessons, Miss Arnold," she said. " I had not supposed that you were that type of girl."

Now we none of us like to be ignominiously condemned as a "type," and Christine's spirit was aroused.

"You have n't any pride, have you?" continued Marjorie, thoughtfully. " I wonder why you came to college."

"I — not have any pride? *I*," exclaimed Christine, indignantly. "What makes you — how dare you say that?"

" Why, most people who are really proud, like to excel in the world which they make for themselves," explained Marjorie. " Ambitious girls like to carry out successfully everything that they undertake."

" But I *am* ambitious," protested Christine. " I want to write more than anything else in the world!"

" You are willing to ride your horse, but not to feed him; is that it?" said Marjorie. " Well, a certain class of people always go to work in that way."

" I'm sorry you think I'm a class and a type," said Christine, suddenly; and it surprised her to find how very sorry she actually was. Marjorie was a gentle little thing who did not appear to have much strength of character. Why should she care what Marjorie thought? And yet she did care a great deal. The next few days her lessons were perfectly prepared, and she rather expected that Marjorie would praise her for this new departure; but, on the contrary, Marjorie seemed to take it as a matter of course that her pupil should do well, and confined her conversation to the mysteries of separable and inseparable prefixes.

" My dearest friend has been taken into Sigma," she said, one afternoon when the German lesson had been particularly successful. " We were all so proud of her, and there was such a delightful excitement when she received the note."

" Is she a good writer? " asked Christine with interest, for she could not help respecting these two literary societies which admitted no Freshmen and included only the most brilliant members of the three upper classes.

" Yes, she 's worked hard at her writing," answered Marjorie, significantly, " and she stands well in other things too. The societies do not admit any one who is not known to be at least a conscientious student."

" Do you envy her? " asked Christine, scornfully; and Marjorie laughed.

" Not much," she answered merrily; " you see, I got in before she did."

Christine looked somewhat crestfallen, but said abruptly, " You don't wear any pin."

" No, there is the best of reasons why I should n't wear a pin. But I 'm in Sigma all the same, although I see that you cannot associate members of Sigma with makers of gym suits."

Christine said nothing; but henceforth she understood that if she wished to have a place in this new world she must earn it, and that in college people are judged for themselves alone.

CHAPTER V

THE term fled away into dreary November, leaving its golden mornings and crimson forests far behind. Hare and Hound parties were given up; base winds flipped papers out of unsuspecting books, and bestowed them gayly in adjacent mud-puddles. Everything turned brown, and whirled about in brown shadows through brown days, and there were a few red sunsets that blew away as fast as they came.

" It is the falling of the year," said little Clare, as she stood looking out at the chill mountains. " Oh, I wish I could see my mother! "

" Clare, Clare, are n't you coming in to do German with me?" called Ruth from the hall; and Clare picked up her books, devoutly hoping that Christine would not be in one of her obstreperous moods. A few days before, Christine had become exasperated by what she called Clare's " lack of spirit," and had scornfully insinuated that Clare would not dare to call her soul her own.

" Well, it is n't my own," had been the unexpected retort.

" Indeed! " with sarcasm. " And whose is it, then, if I may ask? "

" God's! " answered Clare, with flashing eyes. " Now don't you say another word about it."

57

Since then Christine had decided that if Clare had no spirit, she at least possessed the courage of her convictions.

When she came in, Ruth had already begun on the German, and Christine was throwing olive-pits at her, from the other end of the room.

"Do you see that new picture of two youths on the table?" she asked, as Clare sat down. "The handsome one is my brother Stephen, and the other is Stephen's chum at Harvard — a very stupid man. Ruth's been engaged to him ever since she was three months old and he going on seven."

"Oh — are you really engaged?" asked Clare, looking at Ruth with that timid awe with which a very young girl regards another who "has had experience."   .

"No, certainly not," said Ruth, indignantly. "Christine, what do you mean by telling her such things?"

"Why don't you put your mind on your lesson?" objected Christine, landing an olive-pit in the middle of Ruth's dictionary. "That's no way to study. They're going to take us to the Yale-Harvard game next week."

"Won't it be fun?" said Ruth, with enthusiasm. "If only we can get a chaperon! and Miss Roberts has almost promised to go."

"Why don't you attend to the lesson?" asked Christine, seriously. "Clare, what do you think of my brother?"

"He looks — very nice," answered Clare, slowly, for she was not accustomed to young men, and did not quite know what she ought to say about him.

58

" He is very nice," said Christine. " My other brother, Henry, and this friend of Ruth's, can't hold a candle to him."

" Christine, you know that is n't — " began Ruth hastily, and suddenly subsided.

" He composes things for the organ," continued Christine, " and paints everything, including his clothes and the carpets. I shall make you play to him, when he comes up for the Twenty-second. You won't be half so much afraid of him as you are of me."

Clare looked annoyed. " I 'm not afraid of you," she began with dignity, and then added truthfully, " at least, not much."

Christine laughed. " Well, you can't expect me to learn my German while you two are chattering at this rate. I think I 'll go down to college and study; so farewell."

" Perhaps I ought not to have come in here," said Clare anxiously, when Christine left the room.

" What perfect nonsense ! " laughed Ruth. " You know it was Chris who did all the talking, and she often goes down to college in the afternoon anyway. Do look out *verderben* again. I 've forgotten what it means."

" ' To spoil, injure, destroy ' and a lot of other things," read Clare from the dictionary. " Why do you suppose Chris could n't have gone into my room to study? She looked tired this afternoon."

" She says there 's a fly in your room that sits on her ear and sings, and she does n't like to annihilate him, because he 's your fly."

" I should n't wonder if he 's the same one who sits

on my nose every morning, and makes personal remarks," said Clare. "I wish she had annihilated him!"

There was a knock at the door, and while Ruth was frantically endeavoring to collect the scattered olive-pits, in walked Louise Burritt, accompanied by a friend, whose presence threw Clare into wild confusion.

"Well, if here is n't my little runaway!" exclaimed Miss Campbell, advancing with cordial alacrity. "Look, Louise, this is the child whose cake and tea you consumed. Does n't that make you feel guilty, Miss Deland? But I did n't know you lived here. To tell the truth, I have n't set eyes on you since that Sunday when you did n't come."

She would not have been surprised at this if she had known that the main object of the two little miscreants had been to avoid her.

"We were so ashamed," began Clare; but Miss Burritt broke in with a laugh.

"Don't begin to be penitent so early in your college course, my child," she said; "Edith did n't lay it up against you, and we were all particularly pleased, because, you see, it was one on Edith. I vowed then and there that I would ask you to Dramatics, so I found out your address, and brought Edith here as a kind of surprise party. Was n't that nice in me? Now open your hands and shut your eyes!" and Clare gasped with delight as a significant bit of pasteboard fluttered into her lap.

"Here 's another for you, fair cousin," continued Miss Burritt, presenting Ruth with a similar ticket. "And now we must bid these ladies farewell, as we have a hundred things to do, and it is very obvious that they wish to study."

"Did you ever hear of anything so lovely?" cried the girls in one breath, as the door closed upon their guests; but as they spoke, it opened again to admit the head of Louise Burritt.

"Edith is to be the heroine, and I am the stiff clergyman who's in love with her. Won't that be exciting?" she said, and before the girls could answer, she was gone.

"I wish Chris could have been invited too," said Ruth, with a little anxious expression stealing over her face.

Christine was at that moment sitting by the window in the college reading-room, translating *Germelshausen*, while the big shaft of the organ creaked, creaked, in sympathy, and faint strains of music crept down from the Chapel above. Two girls came out of the Music Building and went towards the Hillard House; a young member of the Faculty shot past on his wheel, and dismounted at the Science Building. A bird hopped over the brown grass, and pecked at the fading lime which marked out the tennis courts, but not finding it toothsome, possibly because he had no teeth, flew away in a rage. Presently the college clock struck four, and the organ shaft relapsed into silence, with a long sigh of relief. The girl who had been practising came downstairs, her footsteps echoing noisily through the empty halls, and Christine realized that she was due at Marjorie's.

It was the last lesson before her examination, and all the anxiety that she had secretly endured was beginning to tell upon her strength. She was very pale that afternoon, and Marjorie looked up with quick sympathy when she came in.

"I'm afraid you've been working too hard," she said, as her pupil began the *Erzählung* of *Germelshausen*. She knew it all so perfectly, the poor child, and conjugated every impossible verb, declined every insufferable noun, without a mistake.

"It's what you approve of, isn't it?" asked Christine, indifferently. "I did not suppose you thought any one could work too hard."

"No, it *isn't* what I approve of," answered Marjorie, with spirit. "Overdoing is as bad as underdoing, and far more dangerous. One ought to realize that to know what to remember is not so important as to know what to forget!"

"Perhaps that's why I forget everything, then," said Christine, with a faint smile. "I want to be on the safe side."

"Your examination comes to-morrow, doesn't it?" asked Marjorie.

"Day after to-morrow at two o'clock. Do you think that I shall pass, this time?"

The dreariness of her tone brought tears to Marjorie's eyes.

"I'm afraid I've been wrong," she said, as if thinking aloud, "but how could I help it? What was I to do? There was no other way, and yet I'm afraid it was wrong."

"Nobody has been wrong excepting me," said Christine; "and since you have been right, and I have been wrong, I suppose it is quite natural that you should despise me."

"I don't despise you," was the quick reply. "No

one could do that. I believe that this failure will turn out to be your first step towards success."

" In that case would you advise me to fail again? "

"That's *young*," said Marjorie, impatiently. "Excuse me, but there's so much greatness in you it makes the youngness seem very much out of place."

"You have made me mad a number of times by your cold-blooded speeches," said Christine, calmly; "but you are a little thing, so I've refrained from slaying you as I would have slain another. Everything that annoys us is good for us, isn't it, Miss Drew?"

" If I 've done you any good by being disagreeable to you, I suppose it was worth while, even if it has made you dislike me," said Marjorie, sadly.

Christine said nothing, for she was beginning to realize the wide difference between Marjorie's life and her own. "I know why she doesn't wear a society pin," she thought; "it 's because she can't afford it." And if she had been in the habit of saying gentle things, she would have said something gentle now, but of late years she had taught herself that tenderness implies weakness, and must therefore be suppressed.

Meanwhile Marjorie was thinking: "Well, she does dislike me, and I shall never see her again. There is nothing on earth so trying as to have to be horrid to people you care for, just because it 's good for them! "

Christine had remained beyond her usual time, and as she rose to go, Elizabeth Dane rushed into the room.

"Oh, Marjorie, I'm so hungry," she said, throwing her books into a corner. "Miss Arnold will stay and have some tea with us, — won't you, Miss Arnold? I've been in the Laboratory all the afternoon, and blew myself up four times. Behold these tortoise-shell spots on my hands! HNO^3 plus Spontaneous Combustion. Come, Miss Arnold, you simply must stay and have some tea." And she assisted Christine into a chair with a gentle lack of ceremony that no one could have resented.

Marjorie made the tea, and Elizabeth produced some crackers from under a bookcase.

"Have you done your Livy for to-morrow, Miss Arnold?" she asked. "Because, if you haven't, I warn you that it's perfectly abominable. I did mine last evening with Freda Hastings. Do you know Freda Hastings?"

Christine did not know her.

"Well, she's the only Freshman in the Hadley, and she's distinctly scientific, — goes in for bugs and batteries, and all that sort of thing. She went to drive with us Mountain Day, and whenever we stopped to admire the beautiful view, she would say, 'Girls, do you suppose there are any snails here?' And then she would climb out and look in every hole. She has a lot of snails already, and the girls say you can hear them squeaking and oozing around her room after dark."

"Has she a room-mate?" inquired Christine.

"No, I don't think any girl would room with her. No one in the house has set foot in her dominions since the night when the cockroaches got out. She kept them in a ginger-box."

"And did n't they like ginger?" asked Marjorie, laughing.

"They doted on ginger. But one night they opened their own box and threw it on the floor, and then they stood up on a chair, and shrieked for help; but when people came running in, they were nowhere to be seen."

"That was what Miss Carlisle would call 'subtle,'" observed Marjorie.

"Do you like Miss Carlisle?" asked Christine, who had not yet become interested in the Faculty.

"Miss Carlisle is the backbone of the college, as well as the inspiration of the Rhetoric Department," was the enthusiastic response. "If you're fond of writing, Miss Arnold, you must cultivate Miss Carlisle; and if she cultivates *you*, you'll grow!"

"Speaking of growing," said Elizabeth, "these gym suits are still in a primitive state, and if you will pardon me, Miss Arnold, I think I will hasten their development."

Further conversation was interrupted by the noise of the sewing-machine, and as Marjorie also had taken up her work, Christine thought it was time to depart.

"You will come again," they both urged; and Christine answered, "Indeed I will," with a cordiality that would have surprised her dearest friends.

"After all," she thought bitterly, as she walked home through the twilight, "it is not so much Marjorie who despises me, as I who am beginning to despise myself!"

But Fräulein Schaf expressed so much satisfaction over the results of the examination that college immediately assumed a more cheerful aspect, and the first thing that Christine did was to write a long letter to her father, telling him all about it.

It was the night of the Hillard House Dramatics, and Ruth and Clare having set forth, arrayed in their second-best gowns, improved by their very best manners, Christine was sitting alone upstairs, when Kathleen burst into the room with a thundering knock.

"Christine! Chris! It's time to start for Dramatics! Come quick, or all the best places will be gone."

"I haven't been asked to Dramatics, Kathleen, and neither have you — you know you have n't!"

Kathleen bent down and whispered two significant words in her friend's ear.

"Fire-escape!" repeated Christine, puzzled; "do people ever go up there?"

"People will be up there already — everybody! The whole *town!*" cried Kathleen, in a crescendo howl. "Hurry up! Oh, do hurry!"

A little excited color crept into Christine's face, but she responded with dignity, "I could never humiliate myself by going in such a way."

"Everybody does it," persisted Kathleen, dancing impatiently around the room. "There is not a light in this college but what has expended its tallow at some time upon that fire-escape. Come, *come*, or I shall go alone, and eat up all the peanuts."

"Whose peanuts?" asked Christine, with provoking deliberation.

"*My* peanuts, of course, Honey. Whoever goes to a show without peanuts? I'll let you feed the

66

ostrich, if we meet one. Now come along, and take an extra wrap, for it may be chilly in the last act."

Christine hesitated; but her natural love of fun, and a certain spirit of mischief which was never far absent, asserted themselves. Her anxiety about the examination was over; she felt all the exhilaration that follows the removal of a strain. Why should n't she see those Dramatics from a fire-escape?

The girls ran quickly down the hill, and turned into the campus from the little street that runs beside the lake, dodged trees, fell over hammocks, and finally brought up behind the old Gym, where several people had already established themselves upon the fire-escape. A shadowy foot hung conveniently within reach, and Kathleen grasped it with fervor, saying, "Just what we want; quick now, pull yourself up behind me;" and the owner of the foot stifled her pitiful cries, that she might not disturb the climax of the first act. The girls managed to see into the Gymnasium very well, and the back rows of the audience were too much absorbed in the play to notice these unbidden spectators. But when the applause began, they were discovered by the ushers, who, instead of resenting the intrusion, handed out programmes, jested pleasantly, and came back to converse with them while the Banjo Club was playing.

Christine did not speak for some time, but when at last she made some comment on the play, a hand stole out from the folds of a hooded figure near her, and Elizabeth Dane whispered: "I did n't expect to see you again so soon, Miss Arnold. That's Freda Hastings, next you. She 's brought her favorite

67

snail with her, and it's my private belief that she's sitting on him!"

"Did you pull off my shoe?" inquired Miss Hastings, peering into the face of a girl whom she took for Christine, but who wasn't and responded snappishly: "No, what did I want of your old shoe? Please tell that girl up there to stop throwing peanut shells down here."

None of the little party could recognize each other, because it was dark outside, and as the hall was dimly lighted, except from the stage, it was easy for complications to arise.

"Who are you all, out there?" whispered a pretty Senior, coming to the window, in her dainty evening dress. "Ninety-five girls?"

There was a dead silence.

"Well, do be careful when you come down. The first time I went up there, a girl stepped on my dress, and we both fell off together. We weren't hurt, because we fell on top of another girl who was just coming up, but she went home the next day."

"Who is she? She's been up here too," exclaimed the girls under their breath, as the fire-escape trembled perilously with laughter.

"That was Miss Elbridge, the Senior President," whispered the Freshman nearest the window; and the fire-escape swelled beyond reason with righteous self-vindication.

The play was becoming pathetic now, and the audience in the back row was feeling for its handkerchief. Kathleen Carey was a sympathetic soul, and couldn't bear to see the poor young clergyman so heartlessly rejected by the cruel heroine; so in searching for her handkerchief she accidentally pulled out the peanut bag instead, and turned it upside down upon the heads of the audience in the "pit." There was a wild howl of indignation, a scuffle, and a composite sneeze, before the whole group on the fire-escape descended to the earth with one angry thud, while the ushers ran to shut the windows, stuffing their handkerchiefs in their mouths to keep from laughing aloud. The people in the back rows were suffering also, and the wave of contagious giggle rippled up to the very footlights, where it seized the hero and made him forget his lines.

"Say you love me — *quick*," whispered Edith, stepping on the clergyman's toe.

"Ow!" cried Louise. "Oh, I love you!" and the curtain was rung down to prevent further mishaps.

"Those dreadful Ninety-five girls!" raged the heroine, behind the scenes. "They've spoiled everything! Louise, how can you laugh so?" and she shook the hero till his wig flapped wildly about his ears, and his mustache lay upon the floor.

Louise composed herself, and, picking up the mustache, fastened it on, upside down.

"The class needs to be suppressed," she said, " and we'll teach them a lesson at the tennis tournament, if not before. I hear that Miss Senator Arnold is a fine tennis-player, but she may be too haughty to offer herself as a champion."

If they could have seen the haughty champion at that moment, their doubts would have been dispelled, for the fire-escape party had plunged into the hollow behind the Hadley House to avoid detection, and were discussing the dramatic beauty of the situation.

69

"It's quite proper that every play should have an Interlude," said Elsie Dane, who was taking Sophomore Lit, "and the Interlude was not lacking to 'Miss Hapgood's Adventures.' We made it!"

"I think myself that it much more resembled a Miracle," said Kathleen, rubbing her ankle. "Come, let's off to our respective hearths, before the flame burns low."

"Or the janitor is upon us," said Freda Hastings, who was vainly trying to piece together the fragments of her shattered snail.

When Ruth and Clare reached home, Christine was in bed, with a "Please don't disturb" sign out; and on Kathleen's door appeared a piece of brown paper with the inscription, "Retired early. Please walk softly through the halls!"

"I feel terribly guilty to have gone off without them, don't you?" said Ruth, advancing on tiptoe; and Clare looked very sorrowful, as she answered, "I think it would have done Christine good to go, and she could have had my ticket — only I was afraid to offer it, for fear she would be angry."

A prodigious snore from Kathleen's room made them both jump, and further conversation was postponed until morning.

CHAPTER VI

OTHER FESTIVITIES

"I WONDER how it happens that I have two Dramatics programmes," said Ruth the next day, when she was clearing up the room. "I must have brought away some other person's by mistake."

"It was very careless of you," said Christine, severely, "but very likely the other person did not want it, so I would n't grumble myself thereover, as the Germans say." She preferred to maintain a discreet silence with regard to her own participation in the affair, and promptly discouraged Kathleen's proposal that they should write up an account of it in a serial story called "The Fire Escapade," for the South Harland "Gazette."

The Yale-Harvard ball game at Springfield was the next excitement, and when all the crimson and blue flags had been laid away for the following year, it was time to think about the Christmas holidays.

A great many girls had gone home for Thanksgiving, and others had visited Eastern relatives, who gave them three helps of turkey all round, and told them how much they had grown. Ardis Hathaway went to Baltimore; Ruth and Christine preferred to remain at college, and Kathleen, who did not prefer it, remained in spite of that fact, and consoled herself by getting up a dance in the Gym. Clare went home, and when her mother and Ethel met her at the Forty-second Street Station, she felt that life was too beautiful for words.

The Forty-second Street Station is a lively, lovable place at vacation time, — so many big thumping trunks from New Haven, South Harland, and a dozen boarding-schools along the line; so many beaming fathers, joyful mothers, and excited girls, all talking at the same time, to say nothing of the stately brothers from Yale, who stand around looking supremely unconscious of their latest society pins. There is nothing, after all, like one's first vacation. But if college people think that it is pleasant to return, mothers say that one should know the Forty-second Street side of the story, when the long train pulls in! And then it is so very pleasant to have the Christmas vacation come, almost before one has recovered from the Thanksgiving dinner.

Ruth was showing Clare how to embroider a sofa-pillow for her mother, and she herself had made all kinds of delightful contrivances for the children at home.

"I only hope mamma will like to lie on this pillow as much as I hate to sew on it," said Clare, as she patiently pricked her little violin fingers.

Christine never did fancy work, and seldom bought any Christmas presents until the last minute, but this year she had already made one purchase, and she sent it away just before starting for Washington. The next morning Marjorie Drew, who was staying with an old aunt in Hadley, received a note, and a dainty box with a Tiffany stamp on the cover. They were both directed in the handwriting of her Freshman pupil, and the box contained a beautiful Sigma pin.

"I can't accept it from her," she thought, and then she tore open the note.

My dear little Teacher, — Please do not say that you cannot keep my Christmas message, only because it is I who send it to you. You have done so much more for me than you can realize, because you have given me a new self to go hand in hand with the old one. Perhaps, if you are ever inclined to be unhappy like other people, the little pin may remind you of this verse by Emily Dickinson :

> "If I can help one fainting robin
> Unto his nest again,
> I shall not live in vain."

Yours always sincerely,
· Christine Arnold.

And Marjorie put on the pin.

"Perhaps I shall be glad to remember some day," she said, touching it gently, "that she was once my robin."

It was the Twenty-second of February, and only those who have experienced it can know what a bore the "old Twenty-second" used to be. Everybody went to it, and only square dances were allowed; but as some of the brothers and cousins who were present had never danced before, there was no lack of variety to the figures.

"Pretty chumpy-looking set of men," observed Stephen Arnold, with much satisfaction; and Christine was furious because she could not truthfully contradict him.

The whole Freshman class was mortified, and distinctly bored by the proceedings; but it began to make plans, and continued to meditate upon them in its progressive heart.

"Isn't there anything wrong that you *can* do?" asked George Slater, of Wyckham, dismally.

"Certainly," replied Ardis, with a twinkle of amusement, "you can dance more than once with the same girl. That will be sure to call forth unpleasing comments from the Faculty."

"Oh, I say," said the Junior, looking as if he would like to put his hands in his pockets, "let's go up to the tower."

"It's pitch-dark, and I have on a brand-new gown."

"I'll light a cigarette, and then we can see."

"You want to go up there so that you can smoke, I perceive," said Ardis. "Well, I'm willing that you should, if it will make you look less miserable. We'd better go out through the German-room door, as there are four Professors in the hall."

The stairs up to the tower were winding and intricate, with ladder-like apertures, that made climbing after dark a precarious proceeding. But the two young people reached the top without accident, and stepped out into the keen night air. The roof was covered with tin, which rebounded alarmingly under their feet, as Mr. Slater stopped to throw his companion's evening wrap around her shoulders. The lights of the town twinkled softly below them, and the roofs of the campus houses showed in angular lines across the lawn.

They seemed to be very near the sky.

OTHER FESTIVITIES

"Omar Khayyám was a clever old chap, was n't
he?" mused Mr. Slater, looking at the stars. "Not
understanding the ways of things, he held his life up
to the light like red wine in a goblet, and watched
the sun sparkle through it."

Ardis congratulated herself that the sky had put
George into one of his most desirable moods; but
she was soon disillusioned, for he began telling her
about a banquet that he had recently attended,
"where flat speeches fell, and lay like dead flies on
the table, with their legs folded."

"That's the worst of George," a friend once observed. "He says things that make you 'wish you
were a better man and knew more hymns,' and then,
before you have shinned laboriously up to the pinnacle
where he's sitting, he has slid down the other side,
and is giving you the loud laugh from the ground."

Ardis wondered why she was willing to stand so
much from him, and decided that it was partly because of his epigrams, which pleased her, partly
because he had asked her to the Wyckham Prom,
and mostly, perhaps, because he was really very fond
of her. Then she nearly forgot him, in looking at
that broad curving sky, with its distant melodies of
light, and felt as if she too must sing.

"You really don't mind if I smoke?" asked
George.

"Yes, I do," said Ardis; "we must go back now,
or we shall be missed. Come!" and they started
down again, guided by an occasional match and a
large amount of clever calculation. But just as they
reached the great bell, it suddenly began to strike,
and the tower shook heavily with the vibrations.

"Ow!" cried Ardis, sitting down violently on the steps.

"Confound it!" exclaimed Mr. Slater, plunging wildly forward into nothing, "I've turned my ankle."

"Oh, dear!" called Ardis, as the deafening strokes went on. "What did you want to do that for?"

"So that I could sit here all night, I suppose. Are you up there?" The bell stopped.

"Yes, are you down here?"

"Oh, Lord!"

"Don't say that. Can't you really go any farther?"

"Not without a light. It's a beastly twist."

"If you'll sit perfectly still," said Ardis, gathering her skirts around her, "I'll go down and interview your chum, Mr. Lane. He'll come up and get you."

"Not if I know it! He's over here with the Junior President, and there'd be a woodcut of me in the 'Gazette' to-morrow. Haven't you got a pull on any of the functionaries?"

"The night watchman would help us. I got locked into one of the campus houses the other night, and he saw me getting out of a window, and promised not to tell. I'll go find him."

"Say," came in a hoarse whisper from the darkness, as she felt her way down the steps, "tell him there's money in it!"

Ardis crept cautiously down two other flights of stairs to the main floor, ran quickly through the empty corridors, and found the night watchman, reading by the light of his lantern, in the Latin room. He smiled appreciatively at the situation, and muffled the lantern under his coat.

"I'm kinder feared they'll get onto me when I pass the German-room door," he said. "Can't you slide up somehow, and shut it?"

"I'll try," said Ardis hurriedly, speeding back through the hall.

She had just succeeded in effecting her purpose without attracting attention, when Miss Woodbridge, the Mathematics Professor, came up.

"Yes, it *is* warm," she was saying to one of the Seniors; "perhaps, if I open this door it will cool the room off a little."

Ardis waited until Miss Woodbridge had departed, and then furtively closed the door again; but unfortunately the Professor happened to turn around and see her.

"Oh, Miss Hathaway, do leave that open," she said, coming back. "It's terribly warm here."

"Yes, Miss Woodbridge," said Ardis, desperately, "but don't you think it's dangerous to have such a strong draught on the girls after they've been dancing?" She could hear the steps of the night watchman coming up the stairs.

Miss Woodbridge was over forty years old, but she still looked like a girl, and possessed, as one of her pupils said, "a large, fat, delightful sense of humor."

"Very likely you are right," she replied with a peculiar expression; "it would certainly be unwise to run any risks in the way of taking cold."

Then she considerately disappeared, and Ardis thought, "I will never cut Math again as long as I live!" Mr. Slater was sent down to the station in a carriage, and the next day a large box of American

77

Beauties came for Ardis, accompanied by two significant words: " Don't tell ! "

" Please don't think I'd be such a fool," Ardis wrote in thanking him. " Remember that it was I who asked you over here ! "

Clare Deland had not invited a man to the Twenty-second, for the reason that she did not know one who could come; but she enjoyed the evening immensely in spite of this, and enjoyed her talk with Stephen Arnold most of all.

" Chris tells me that you're an inmate of the music world, Miss Deland," he said, when his sister introduced them, " and I hope that you will take me there before I go, for I've just retired from the Pierian Sodality, and feel like an escaped convict."

" You must play to me too," said Clare, laughing, " only our piano is such a wicked old thing ! I sometimes think it's because I'm not noble enough to bring out the best side of it."

" Do you endow your instruments with personality too ? I never imagined that I had the monopoly of that nice, artistic little notion; but my organ always seems like a living creature to me, and when I'm in a thundering mood, it won't have a word to say. Yet it's better than a piano, because a piano gets mad at the least little thing."

" I think that some pianos get cross-grained early, because they've never had any one to understand them," said Clare. " I'm sure that I should grow cynical if nobody ever played anything on me but ' White Wings.' "

" That *is* hard lines for the Hemp piano," said Stephen, sympathetically. " But you play the violin too, don't you? I think it is a good plan to get acquainted with different instruments, because it teaches one to speak a new language. I tried learning the flute once, but my chum smashed so much furniture, throwing it at me, that I had to leave off."

"After all, the organ is the grandest language," said Clare; "it always reminds me of great mountains, with snow peaks perhaps, although I never saw a snow peak."

"You are thinking of the Jungfrau, with a sunset on it," said Stephen; "when you see that, you will have your music set to words."

Clare was silent for a minute, and then she said: "I have always wanted to go to Switzerland. Sometimes I try to imagine how the music goes climbing up the mountains, through the tops of trees and the throats of birds, until the flowers gather it in, and it is only a spirit song."

"I heard something just like that once in a pine forest," said Stephen, earnestly; "it was the kind of a song that you —"

"Stephen," said Christine, suddenly appearing, "the lancers are over long ago and Clare's next partner is waiting for her! Do hurry up, or Miss Winter will think you are an extinct species."

"Oh, come now, this dance ought not to be finished yet," said Stephen, rising with deliberation; "but we'll have a little mutual concert on the hill, Miss Deland, after this unseemly riot is over."

Clare always liked to remember that conversation with Stephen, and the little musical evening that followed it. Mr. Packard, Ruth's friend, contributed a five-pound box of Huyler, and an equivalent quantity of funny Harvard stories. The loquacious Mrs. Hemp appeared with lemonade, and was forcibly suppressed while Stephen played the "Moonlight Sonata" and a few exquisite bits from "Parsifal." Then Clare brought her violin, and Stephen accompanied her in the "Midsummer Night's Dream," and part of the overture to "Lohengrin," which was received with great enthusiasm. The two men talked of the Bayreuth Festival, which they had attended the summer before, and told some of their thrilling experiences with the German language; but at this point Christine abruptly changed the subject.

On the whole, it is very easy to sit up late one night, and forget that such a gentleman as Horace ever existed; but when he appears the next morning, with a low bow and a neglected ode, it becomes necessary to treat him with a certain amount of consideration. But his brief absence has involved a useful bit of stimulus from the outside world; work is resumed with increased vigor, and when Easter vacation comes, the hardest part of the year is over. One comes back to beautiful Spring term, with its pushing bloom, its dances on the green, and its outdoor singings.

Christine and Ardis went in for the tennis tournament, and carried the green banner victoriously through four well-played sets; but when they came to Campbell and Burritt, the successful champions of two previous tournaments, they agreed that matters had become serious indeed. Would two Freshmen stand any chance of winning, against such players as Campbell and Burritt?

"Fight for your lives!" said Elsie Dane, excitedly;

" they 've made up their minds that we 'll be easy to beat, and you two girls are all that stand between oblivion and Ninety-five ! "

An eager crowd had gathered around the tennis court, impatient for the game to continue, and the two Freshmen were surrounded by a circle of enthusiastic classmates, who praised, exhorted, and implored by turns. Ardis and Christine looked at each other with sparkling eyes, and their courage rose as the game began; but Campbell and Burritt had all the confidence that comes from the recollection of many victories, and they beat the first set.

" We let them have that one intentionally, did n't we ? " said Ardis to her partner, " because we wanted to hold ourselves in reserve."

Christine did not answer, but turned her eyes toward the green flag that floated at one end of the net. She did not care for college celebrity, of course, nor to be identified too closely with the interests of her class; but there was something about that green flag —

" All ready, Ninety-five ! " called the umpire; and the girls sprang to their places, with the rackets balancing nervously in their hands, like birds. It was a very close game this time, but that back-handed play that Ardis had practised so successfully on Mrs. Hemp's limited tennis court, made itself felt, and the green flag emerged triumphant through a chorus of cheers, and a perfect deluge of lemonade.

" Ninety-five, Ninety-five, O Ninety-five ! " cried the Freshmen, joyously; and there was so much enthusiasm that several people who were seated on dry-goods boxes in the suburbs suddenly disappeared from view.

6 81

The kodaks were busy now, and during the final set their ominous clicks were almost the only sound that broke the silence.

"Thirty-fifteen, Ninety-three leads," called the umpire, "Thirty all."

"Forty-thirty, Ninety-five leads;" and every Freshman pinched the arm of her nearest neighbor in wild excitement.

"Deuce!" And all the pinched neighbors pinched back again.

There was a moment of terrible suspense, and then the umpire called, "Game! Ninety-five wins!" And the whole assembly broke into impartial applause for the two plucky Freshmen who had actually defeated the champions of Ninety-three! Christine and Ardis became the heroines of the hour, and no two people were more sincere in their congratulations than "Campbell and Burritt" themselves.

"I took you to the Sophomore reception," said Edith, mournfully, to Ardis, "and I won't do it again."

"Miss Arnold, I'm proud to know you," said Louise Burritt, throwing down her racket to shake hands with Christine. "Henceforth there shall be no better friends in the world than the classes of Ninety-three and Ninety-five."

"Cheer them! sing at them! do anything to show them how we feel," cried the President of Ninety-five, casting aside her official dignity; and at these words a large circle of hilarious Freshmen joined hands to dance around their two classmates, like the frisky apprentices in the "Meistersinger." The Glee Club collected informally, and sang "Here's to Ninety-five," which so pleased the Freshmen that they responded with three cheers for the Juniors, and Ardis led her class in singing "Here's to Ninety-three, she's the only class for me, drink her down, drink her down, drink her down, down, down."

"We are one in glory, if not in philosophy," said Ardis, slipping her hand through Christine's arm, "and for this reason I will treat you to an ice-cream soda."

The next morning when the Seniors came to Ethics, they observed that the busts of Greek philosophers around the walls were decorated in a most extraordinary fashion. Aristotle wore a green cravat, Plato had a large bow on his left ear, and Socrates looked very coy, in a green sun-bonnet with voluminous ruffles, and green strings tied tenderly under the beard. Some time elapsed before the lecture could proceed, and subsequent dark rumors were circulated, concerning the remarks that had been made that morning by the class of Ninety-two about the class of Ninety-five.

"It is fortunate for *many* reasons, that we are soon to leave the college," said the deaf Miss Snow, turning her "game" ear upon Kathleen Carey, whose room had been recently found to contain certain unexplained shreds of green bunting.

"It's myself that agrees with you in the matter," answered Kathleen, and, slipping around to the ear that was intact, she filled it with taunts of a highly disrespectful nature, including several to the effect that it was safer for the Seniors to leave college before anything more serious happened to them, because the girls of Ninety-five were tired of being Freshmen, and had decided to become Sophomores!

CHAPTER VII

HOW THEY BECAME SOPHOMORES

"WHO's alive, who's alive! Ninety-five, Ninety-fi-i-ve!" came in a jubilant chorus from under the Storey House windows, and a Junior upstairs observed with a sigh, —

"They've come back!"

"Yes," answered her room-mate, sympathetically, "and they're worse than they were before;" "they" being the Sophomore class, which had elected its new President that afternoon, and was now departing in a body to serenade her.

This President had been chosen for her pluck and perseverance, and was one of whom Ninety-five had reason to be proud. She was a girl who had expected, on coming to college, that a life which began and ended off the campus would necessarily exclude her from positions of official importance in her class, and this great honor had come to her as a complete surprise. She was sitting by her window that night, sewing braid on the dress of an opulent classmate, and trying to realize what it meant to be President, when suddenly there arose, from the front yard of her humble dwelling, sounds which "savored of sport."

"Three cheers for the President of Ninety-five, Elizabeth French Dane, Rah — Rah — Rah," suggested a voice; and everybody shared this sentiment so enthusiastically, for three deafening minutes, that old Mrs. Barstow, who kept the house, put her head out of a lower window and cried " Scat ! " Elizabeth also put her head out of the window, but did not compromise herself with language of such frigid brevity.

"Speech, speech!" came in repeated demands from below; and struggling to collect her self-possession, she said, —

"Girls, I shall never forget the trust that you placed in me this afternoon, and — and I will try to do the will of every girl in this class ! "

It was a rather pathetic little speech, but Ninety-five liked it, and having cheered her once more, went off singing, " Good-night, Elsie, good-night, Elsie, we 're going to leave you now."

"Dear me ! " said Marjorie Drew, pulling Elizabeth into the room; " that 's what comes of rooming with a celebrity. Henceforth I shall claim half of your serenades, as damages for having to stand the whole of them ! "

"I don't care, Marjorie," said Elizabeth, disentangling her feet from the braid, which had wound itself neatly around her, " I 'm *proud* of my class ! "

"And you have reason to be," was the answer, as they sat down again to their work; but Elizabeth found it almost impossible to concentrate her mind upon that skirt braid of the opulent classmate.

"Everything is going on at the college to-night," she said restlessly. " I 'm too full of something — I don't know what — to sit still. Will you solemnly promise not to *touch* that skirt if I go out and walk off my excitement ? "

85

Marjorie promised; and Elsie set forth, saying, —

"I think I will go up to the Hadley and see if Christine and Ruth have come. Freda said they were expected this afternoon, and the little wretches are already four days late."

"Give my love to Christine," called Marjorie, as the door closed; but Elizabeth did not hear. She rushed out into the clear September night, turned the corner by the Opera House, and ran swiftly across that open space where three roads converge, and the electric cars swoop down with ostentatious creakings into the town below. Before her, up through dark rustlings, stood the college, like a mysterious shadow of its daily self, with the ivy creeping into deeper shadows against it.

She went up the sloping brick walk, and sat down for a minute on the steps, resting her cheek upon the cold wall beside her as if it had been a living thing. A little ivy, that had been planted by girls who were gone, stirred and rustled above her hair, and she said, —

"Are you awake, you great College? And do you know how hard I have to work, only to stay with you? Or are you fast asleep in your shadows, and cannot understand?"

There was a stir in the tower like a long-drawn breath, and suddenly the bell began to strike the hour. It was nine o'clock, and there was nothing unusual in that fact, but Elizabeth felt that her question had been answered.

When she reached the Hadley, the windows of Number 2 were all ablaze with light, and trunks of various sizes were scattered about in the upper hall.

Sounds of unrestrained merriment from behind a certain door led Elizabeth to conclude that the Burlington girls had arrived.

" Give me that tack-hammer, Ardis," she heard Christine say. " Well, what did she do when you sang under her window? I don't doubt that she died."

" You belie my reputation," retorted Kathleen, indignantly, " when it is I who was taken on the Glee Club yesterday, and told that it is well to have a giant's voice, but not to use it like — "

" Come in," called Ruth; and Elizabeth walked into the room.

" Hurrah ! " cried Kathleen, extricating herself from a group of five girls on one bed; " speak of an angel and you hear him smite himself on a trunk in the hall. Behold the President of Ninety-five ! "

Christine deposited her hammer in the water-pitcher, advanced with outstretched hands, and welcomed Elizabeth with the firm grip of mutual understanding. Ruth came and kissed her, Kathleen insisted on shaking hands again, and the very best sofa-pillow was forcibly wrested from another damsel to decorate the presidential chair. There was much joyous conversation and distribution of " ploughed field," — a particularly intellectual kind of " fudge " which Freda Hastings had made as a welcoming gift for the new arrivals.

When the twenty-minutes bell rang, the little company reluctantly dispersed, not wishing to incur the displeasure of Miss Carlisle by being found on her premises too nigh unto ten o'clock, when lights are supposed to be out. They all went downstairs in a laughing group, and stopped for a minute under the window to call up a last "Good-night" before they separated to go their different ways.

The hill settlement was well scattered over the campus this year, for Clare was in the Marston, — one of the new dormitories; Kathleen was rooming in the Storey, next her friend Grace Reade; Salome Judd and Rachel were in the Hillard, and Miss Fairbank had a room in the Warren, with Amethyst Allen. There was a strange new exhilaration about this campus life that the girls all liked, although they were obliged to keep a few simple rules, and have canned salmon very often for supper. But canned salmon is infinitely superior to chipped beef, and if one does not have chipped beef for breakfast, it is easy to keep the rules.

As the largest part of Ninety-five had spent its first year off the campus, the two new dormitories, Lathrop and Marston, were now overflowing with lively Sophomores, who stirred each other up to deeds of a daring and expressive nature. During the first two weeks of college the Marston indulged in three dances, four spreads, two plays, a cobweb party, and a circus. But these revels were not destined to last throughout the year. Other matrons came to call on Miss Timmins, who was an artistic person with weak eyes, — and there were no more circuses; there was also a dearth of spreads and a cessation of dances, so the Marston collected its shattered dignity, together with its budding talent, and gave a concert.

But all these minor fêtes were soon eclipsed by the greater glory of the Sophomore reception, which was a truly grand affair, implying many decorations, and enough ice-water to last through half the evening. There were also to be "grinds" for the Freshmen, although the class of Ninety-six was the best behaved in the world, and had done nothing worse, so far, than to chase eleven Sophomores down the fire-escape when they tried to effect an entrance into the first class-meeting. It was a shrewd class, and indulged in very few of those little mistakes which are awaited with peculiar avidity by the newly made Sophomore. But in spite of all precautions it had furnished a certain amount of material for "grinds" by nominating members of the Faculty and of the upper classes as candidates for its own class offices, and by serenading its President as the Sophomores had done. This concert happened to be attended by the President of the college in person, and did not last so long as a great many concerts do; but the incident was dramatically illustrated by the Grind Committee, and laid aside for future reference, together with another document which was obtained in the following manner.

Every Saturday the whole Freshman class had a lecture in the old Gymnasium at eleven o'clock, and the Sophomores had one at twelve, so it was natural that one class should be coming out exactly as the other was going in; and the little stone walk which led to the Gymnasium was very narrow indeed. The Sophomores selected one morning after a rain, when the mud was infamously deep, and having ranged themselves along that walk in a compact battalion, waited for the Freshmen to emerge. The Freshmen did emerge, and as they departed with sideward skips and splashes through that villainous mud, they were pursued by taunts and compliments on their agility, which irritated them extremely. But the class as a whole was too dignified to show its feelings, and merely went home to change its shoes.

After the next lecture, which came a week later, one of the Sophomores discovered this paper reclining under a vacant chair, and promptly sequestered it.

"To the Class of '96 ! Take Warning !!!
" It is rumored that the Sophomores intend to make us walk in the mud again to-day. Keep close together, as we go out, and charge upon them in a body. Await signal at door. (Please read, and pass along.) "

A copy of this document, tastefully arranged with sealing-wax and red ribbon, was presented to each member of the Freshman class on the night of the Sophomore reception.

The hill contingent of Ninety-five had held several violent altercations with regard to the people whom they wished to invite, — Ruth and Kathleen having decided upon the same girl, from the day when she first entered chapel, and Christine insisting that she would not take any Freshman who did not wear green mitts. But after this agitating affair was over, and amity, together with all the borrowed sofa-pillows, had been restored, the class of Ninety-five evolved a festivity which made all other festivities appear trivial and superficial.

One morning the President gave a patriotic address on the subject of Columbus, and the benefit that America had derived from being discovered. It seemed that the following day was the anniversary of that great event; but as land had been sighted at two o'clock in the morning, it appeared that two o'clock in the morning would be the correct time for a celebration. Now, this was a joke; but some of the girls preferred to take it seriously, and plans for a suitable celebration were communicated to all the campus houses, so that abundant preparations could be made.

As the celebration of an historical event demands chronological accuracy, the stillness of that night was shattered, at the stroke of two, by the blast of a horn from a Hillard House window. This was the signal for a grand patriotic uprising, and lights immediately flashed in other windows. Smaller horns tooted in derision at outraged sleep, and firecrackers went off on the Marston House green. Impromptu processions of gray-wrappered patriots sailed through the dormitory parlors, with comb orchestras and tin pans; national airs rang out from every campus piano, and loyal voices joined in " Hail Columbia," " Rally round the Flag, Boys," and " Marching through Georgia," until the town of South Harland woke up. It is needless to say that the Faculty had been awake for some time, and that their attitude was one of surprise. Some of them said that it was " abominable," " insufferable," and others retired to their rooms to laugh; but all came to the rescue at last, and the disturbance was quelled.

In the morning it was rumored that the President had stood by his window and said, " Ah, well, well! it makes me think of when I was a boy; " but afterwards these rumors were sternly contradicted, and it was said that on second thoughts he had become very angry. There was an immensely large attendance at chapel that day, and people waited breathlessly after the exercises to see if the President would make a speech.

He did!

But all this has nothing to do with the Sending of Maria Grumbagg, which was a private affair, and much more select. It began with reading Kipling, and ended with the night of All Hallow E'en, when nobody pretends to be well-behaved.

Maria Grumbagg was a Senior who lived in the Storey House, and she had been heard to observe that the class of Ninety-five was an unmitigated nuisance. She had also dropped a boot into a plate of ploughed field that had been put outside the window under hers to cool, and Kathleen insisted that she did it on purpose; so it was agreed that she should have a "Sending." But young kittens, to begin with, were very scarce, and Christine, who loved cats, said that she would not have anything to do with the "Sending" if young kittens were used; so it was suggested that frogs were abundant on the back campus, and that mice could be caught in the President's barn. A butterfly-net and a "catch-'em-alive" trap were bought, and a few days later Maria Grumbagg found this notice on her door: —

"On the 29th day of this month, which is to say two days before that Fête known to us as All Hallow E'en, you, Maria Lucilla Grumbagg, member of the Senior Class in this College, shall be visited with a Sending!"

Maria thought that this was very funny, and took it down to paste in her memorabilia; but when the appointed time came she was absorbed in a Psychology paper, and had forgotten all about the Sending, which, however, did not forget her! It darted out of the waste-paper basket that evening when she came up from supper, and scampered away in three different directions, while she was feeling for a match.

"Help! Murder! Mice!!!" shrieked Maria, climbing into a chair; but nobody came to her aid, and she was obliged to find that match with the Sending scudding about the floor. Finally it disappeared into the hall, and Maria sat down at her desk to write, but was suddenly alarmed by a violent thump under her pen, followed by a wriggling sound. She shut up the desk, took her umbrella, and standing at a discreet distance, hooked open the drawer, expecting to see more mice; but no mice responded. Instead of mice there was a flash of smooth white shininess, of moist greenness, and a frog descended upon the umbrella, two inches away from her hand. She stepped to the window and opened the umbrella suddenly, so that the frog might descend once more, and then she went downstairs to Mrs. Halifax. Unfortunately Maria was no favorite with the matron, because she was always complaining of something, and Mrs. Halifax hastily dismissed the frog incident as "some little prank," which it undoubtedly was.

On the following day Maria found a notice to this effect upon her door: —

"To-night there shall be five mice and two frogs; to-morrow there shall be four frogs and two mice; on the day following there shall be nine frogs and no mice, and after that there shall be no more Sending!"

All of these frogs and mice did not come true, because Maria kept her door locked; but there are ways of introducing frogs, even through locked doors, and on the night of All Hallow E'en there were seven frogs in Maria's room. These numbered two less than had been promised; but Maria strove to be content, and maintained a respectful attitude toward the ploughed field of the Sophomores throughout the remainder of that year.

All Hallow E'en, the night on which Maria enjoyed her last Sending, is the most delightful night of the year at this particular college. There is an entertainment of some kind at every house, and the whole campus goes visiting in masks and dominoes. But they are not the kind of dominoes that one sees at Nice and Rome; these collegiate costumes combine a greater variety of form and color, resulting from the fact that they are not bought, but have to be evolved. When crossing the campus after dark, one encounters black witches with spooky caps and glittering white eyes, red devils in curly shoes, ghosts and policemen, flowers and pussy-cats, and characters from every book that ever was written. Some of the matrons provide apples and water for the witch assembly; and one very nice matron, whose memory the alumnæ will always cherish, used to provide gingersnaps as well.

The Sophomores had not neglected to make special arrangements for this evening, and their first plan was centred upon a play that was to be given in the Storey House parlors at eight o'clock. The plan had been originated by Grace Reade, who was a demure maiden with a spirit of mischief running through her like a current of electricity. She suggested things to do, and Kathleen did them; then they took the consequences together, divided them by two, and gave what was left to their friends.

When the fun began, these two conspirators arrayed themselves in twilight colors, and stealing down the back stairs, let in two tall figures in black, one in white, and a mysterious little mouse in gray. All the Storey House girls were in the parlor, and Kathleen led her friends softly through the vacant halls to her own room, where the necessary instructions were imparted.

"Ardis, you and Clare go into Chapter 4" — the rooms in the Storey House were always referred to as Chapters, — "Christine and Ruth into 7, and, Grace, you stay here. I'll go into Belle Bovey's room, where I can blow, and hear what goes on too. Now go softly, and blow *hard.*"

Some one had told Grace that if a few people blew into the gas-pipes for a certain length of time, the gas all over a house would go out, and the girls wished to test the truth of this experiment. They blew and blew unceasingly, but still the sounds of revelry rose with undiminished vigor from below.

"I'm absolutely out of breath," gasped Ruth from her room. "We can't keep this up forever."

"The linings of my cheeks have given way," answered Christine, calmly, "but I continue to blow."

Suddenly there was a cessation in the mirth downstairs, followed by an anxious murmur, which terminated in a general excitement. The gas-blowers then descended into the midst of a laughing, stumbling crowd, battling about in absolute darkness, and without waiting to hear the apologies of poor Mrs. Halifax, who would "send for a plumber immediately," departed to attend a dance which was being given at the Warren.

After that they repaired to the Marston, to collect materials for a new kind of ghost, which was to take the campus by storm. There were many ghosts abroad that night, — terrible creatures which shot up to an extraordinary height as one approached, and then collapsed again; but this new creation would entirely eclipse the old-fashioned telescopic phantom, for this was to be the ghost of an elephant! Kathleen was afraid that it might be taken for a live white elephant, but Christine assured her that any person of judgment would know it was the ghost of a dead gray elephant, who used to take prehistoric baths in the landscape gardening. Christine had dislocated her shoulder the summer before, and was therefore unwilling to take any part in the elephant, although she was badly needed for the left hind leg. But she atoned for her incapacity in this direction, by promising to be the noise that the elephant made when he chased people. Clare was too little to be an active member, so she was allowed to be the man who walks beside the elephant, and hooks him by the ear.

When the disjointed beast was ready to start, it advanced in an ambling shuffle up the Marston House road, and halted behind the Warren to await victims. Soon footsteps were heard approaching, and almost before the two dark figures had turned the corner, the elephant charged upon them, urged on by strange unearthly sounds, and guided by one flapping ear. There was a moment of utter consternation, in which the elephant man departed, taking the elephant's ear with him. Then one of the figures turned around and said sternly, "Young ladies!" It was the President and Dr. Page, who had been taking a little moonlight stroll around the campus.

When the elephant returned later in the evening to collect its abandoned epidermis, together with its one paper ear, it was time for the original elements to retire, and they slipped into their various homes, feeling that the evening had been a success.

"There is nothing like All Hallow E'en!" said Christine, as she and Ruth settled themselves for the night.

"Isn't that moonlight on the floor beautiful?" observed Ruth, who had a romantic turn of mind. "It only needs some water to be reflected in, to make it perfect."

Christine solemnly rose from her bed.

"I will supply that deficiency with modern science," she said, and filling a wash-bowl, she set it carefully beside the window on a chair. Then they lay and admired it, until the silver light tangled itself in a dream, and when the witches looked in through the window on their midnight rounds, they were both fast asleep!

CHAPTER VIII

A SONG AND A SORROW

WHEN Clare found that Ardis Hathaway was to be in the same house with her that winter, she was overjoyed, and said to herself, "Now perhaps I shall really get acquainted with her, and she will let me be her friend."

She envied Christine, who knew Ardis well enough to laugh and joke with her, and even to contradict what she said. And in the Marston Ardis reigned supreme. There was no one else who told such funny stories, no one who knew so well the right thing to do, or who could look so beautiful while doing it. But Clare was far too shy to make any advances toward the people whom she wished to know, and although she and Ardis met often in the rooms of other girls, Ardis regarded her as a merely inoffensive little thing who roomed in the same house with Christine Freshman year, and never thought of seeking her for a friend.

Meanwhile Clare's musical powers were becoming more and more in demand, for people had discovered that she could play the piano as well as the violin, and it was said that she knew the organ too, — a rumor which arose from the fact that Clare, like other musical girls, would always attack any instrument that she could find. The violin was still her dearest friend, but she seldom found any one who could play her accompaniments well, and a bad accompaniment has a peculiar badness of its own, which all other evil sounds have struggled in vain to acquire. So it was not long before Clare allowed the violin to take protracted naps under her bed, while she cultivated the acquaintance of the Marston House piano, which was a new, happy little piano that seemed to like her.

She began with playing hymns for the Sunday morning exercises; then she launched off into dance music for the various house entertainments, and very soon she fell into the habit of giving little concerts all by herself, which were attended by an informal but wholly respectful audience. Every Sunday, after dinner, she was expected to play, and if by chance she slipped off to her room before any one saw her, she was invariably followed and brought down again. When she took her place at the piano, the girls would all assemble in the parlor, the company and first comers appropriating the chairs, and the rest sitting meekly on the floor. Other people from outside would steal in, one by one, until the room was full; and although Clare did not hear them come, she knew when they were there, and it seemed as if new melodies sprang up beside the singing path she wandered on. No one ever spoke while she was playing, and that sweet hush of sympathy surrounded her like the atmosphere of a happy world, in which sunbeams took the place of fingers, and turned themselves to chords.

But of all the people who listened to Clare's music, there was no one who loved it better than Ardis, who was a musician herself, and it was to Ardis that Clare spoke oftenest when she played. Perhaps Ardis understood this, for she would leave whatever she was doing, and stand beside the piano until Clare had finished; and then she would say, "Now, Miss Deland, think a little while in music, and let me see if I can tell what you are thinking about."

Clare always enjoyed improvising, and one day Ardis said, "You were thinking about me, then, and that you cannot quite understand me."

Clare laughed, and answered, "Yes, you were right. But why won't you let me understand you?"

This was the beginning of their friendship, which, like many other college cross-currents, was a strange one.

Clare made Ardis sing to her, and learned the accompaniments to her songs, so that they could "do" them together, without notes, when asked; but Ardis was curiously unwilling to sing before people, although she and Clare used to practise for hours together in the Music Building, and tried all kinds of experiments with the unfortunate organ in the corner room: this was not entirely satisfactory, however, as it obliged the prima donna to pump and sing at the same time.

One evening she and Clare effected an entrance into College Hall, which was empty and dark and a glorious place to sing in, but the janitor pursued them so wrathfully with a lantern that they were forced to depart. The next time they asked his permission, and he said that they might sing there for half an hour, if they would use but one gas-jet; so they agreed to the conditions, and felt their way up the dark stairs in triumph. Clare patted the closed organ

with longing hands, but, knowing that she must not
touch, was forced to content herself with a piano.
Their one dim light could not stir the heavy shadows
in the Chapel, and the little concert was practically
given in the dark. But Clare did not mind playing
in the dark, and Ardis said afterwards, —

" I would always rather sing with only you and
those shadows to hear me ! "

She had an exaggerated terror of showing her
feelings, and knowing that music cannot be music
unless one gives it all that one has, preferred to
remain silent altogether, adopting the cheerful rôle of
bird who can sing and won't sing, but whom everybody loves too well to make sing. Music was really
the only thing that the two girls had in common,
although the younger one did not know this, and
sometimes, when Ardis was talking and laughing with
her friends, would wonder if she could be the same
Ardis who had sung into the shadows that night.
Clare knew that Ardis liked to stay with her when
she was tired of other people, because she would
sometimes come into the room, and sit moodily by
the window for an hour without saying a word; but
when she rose to go, she would tell Clare that she felt
a great deal better. One day she came in after dinner, and taking Clare up in her arms as if she had
been a child, sat down with her in a big rocking-
chair.

" Clare," she asked suddenly, "do you remember
anything about God? "

" Remember anything about — Ardis, what do
you mean? "

" Oh, you are different from the rest of us, and I

thought perhaps you might remember; but it does n't make any difference."

She seemed disappointed.

"Ardis, why will you always insist that I am so different from you?" asked Clare, in distress. "You shut me away from you, and when I ask why, you only say it is because I am different!"

Ardis put her friend down on the bed very softly, and went out of the room without answering the question.

"Now, what in the world can I do with her?" puzzled Clare. "She puts me outside of the pale of humanity as if I were a monkey, — an undesirable, ordinary monkey, that is incapable of understanding the simplest human emotion!"

Most of the girls considered Ardis utterly devoid of feeling, for the reason that her face never changed, and no one could ever tell what went on behind those mysterious eyes. But her feelings would reveal themselves in unexpected ways; and Clare, who studied her with the peculiar insight, varied of course by the singular obtuseness, that love can give, learned to understand her better than other people did.

On the first Monday after Thanksgiving, Ardis was taken into the Phi Delta Kappa Society, which was even more literary than Sigma; and although this was the realization of one of her most cherished ambitions, she maintained a happy serenity through it all that amazed her friends.

"Why, Ardis, are n't you pleased?" asked one of the many girls who stopped on her way to chapel to offer their congratulations; and Ardis, whose hope and dream of happiness had, for more than a year, been centred in those societies, answered quietly, —

"Of course I am delighted."

Clare looked at her curiously, and thought, "Why does n't she tell them how happy she is?" not understanding that the gentle art of dissimulation acts like a magpie, in concealing trivial articles along with those of greater importance.

Elizabeth Dane, also, had been chosen for Phi Delta Kappa, and being one of the first two Ninety-five girls to gain that distinction, was suitably and proportionately agitated.

"It takes only five black-balls to keep a person out," she whispered to Clare during the hymn. "How *do* you suppose I got in?"

When Ardis came out of chapel, Christine was waiting for her at the door of the German room, and looked most enthusiastic; but just as she was about to speak, a Phi Delta Kappa Senior came up to shake hands with the new member, and Ardis turned her back upon Christine in a way which was rude, to say the least. She had no reason for doing this, and at first Christine was too astonished to be angry, but, soon recalling that omission, departed with much dignity. While she was taking her books from the little front corridor downstairs, Ardis appeared, with cordiality upon her countenance.

"Maude Gilbert has lent me her Phi Delta Kappa pin," she said, "and I wanted you to admire it. You see, this whole business pleases me, because it's a good beginning; and good beginnings often precede good endings, — just as, when you spill soup on the front breadth of a dress, the whole *menu* is sure to follow in time."

" Ardis," said Christine, seizing her firmly by the wrist, " why did you eschew me in that extraordinary manner a few minutes ago? I came upstairs to be festive with you, and you were not festive."

" I was waiting to be festive in private," explained Ardis, quickly; " but do fix your critical eye upon my — I mean Maude's pin, and see if it is n't becoming."

Christine looked at the significant little white and gold thing with its dainty pearl, and said slowly, " It means a great deal, Ardis."

This was the first college experience that they had not shared in common, and, in spite of their warm friendship, both felt that the little pin had made a tiny barrier between them. They stood looking at each other in silence for a minute, and then Ardis said, " O Christabel ! " and throwing her arms around Christine's neck, she gave her an impulsive kiss, which surprised herself no less than it did her friend. But unhappily Christine did not like to be kissed, and thought that sympathy under the circumstances was objectionable; so she turned resentfully away, trying to reconcile these last two sides of Ardis with the ten or fifteen that she already knew. Ardis did not show that she was hurt, although her eyes darkened perceptibly; and Christine never knew quite how much love had been offered — and misunderstood, in that kiss.

The next week Ruth Burritt and Edith Standish were taken into Sigma, and Christine was sincerely pleased about Ruth, but experienced the feeling that many of us have when we see a number of other people getting what we want most of all! For a few days she was so cross that her friends found it difficult to live with her, and then Miss Carlisle took her in hand and restored her to good nature again.

Ardis had not been to the Hadley since that eventful morning of Phi Delta Kappa, and was devoting her spare time to Clare, who knew how to appreciate the value of such attentions.

One day there was a first-soprano vacancy in the Glee Club, and several of the girls, including Ardis and Kathleen, were very anxious that Clare should try for it.

" The Glee Club is more fun than anything else in college, Miss Deland," said one of its loyal members who had come over to argue the matter. "We get in at ever so many of the house dramatics, and are asked to all kinds of funny performances in the town besides."

" We don't always accept, though," said Kathleen pensively, closing one eye. " There was a time, before I came on the Club, when we used to sing for cake and coffee. But now we do not sing for anything less than oysters ! "

" I do wish you would try for it, Miss Deland," said Virginia Paul, a first soprano who knew what it meant to have another first soprano gone. " You don't need to be afraid of Ethel Lindsay at all, because she is nearly always civil to new-comers." `

Miss Lindsay, the Leader of the Club, was an autocratic young lady, who ruled her girls with a rod of iron, and occasionally engaged them in little mutual expostulations, which were vulgarly referred to, by ignorant persons, as rows.

"I'm afraid she would not think of taking me," said Clare; "you see I have n't a very big voice."

"We don't want big voices," explained Ardis. "The necessity is to find voices that will blend with each other, without showing any dividing lines, — like a picture, you know; and I think that your voice is just what Ethel will know she needs."

"Dear Ethel!" said Kathleen, with affection. "It is myself alone that knows what she 's called me at certain times, — and at other times too."

"Has she such a bad temper?" asked Clare anxiously, for she was not used to people of that description, and did not feel quite sure how she should get along with them.

"Miss Lindsay is a very bright girl," answered Ardis, "and understands that there is no one in the college who could take her place on the Club, so she carries things with a high hand."

"She has an exceptional amount of talent, too," said Miss Paul, "but she has also an exceptional way of telling us what to do, so that when she says, ' Sing *pianissimo* in this passage,' we all have an irresistible desire to shriek through it, just to assert our independence."

"And sometimes we do," added Kathleen, thoughtfully, "*I* do!"

"I should think," ventured Clare, "that a girl in that position might have a great deal of influence in the college, — that is, if she chose to exert it."

"She exerts herself in obtaining what she calls her rights," said Ardis, grimly; "and she is fond of telling us that she hopes we know who is the head of that Club."

"Dear me!" said Clare, in alarm, "I shall never dare to sing before her."

"One night after rehearsal," continued Ardis, "I took her by the sleeve, and said, 'Miss Lindsay, it is true that you have your rights, and we have ours; but one right that belongs equally to every person in this Club is that of hearing civil language, and I should suggest that we help each other to maintain it!'"

The girls drew a long breath, and somebody asked what Miss Lindsay had to say to that.

"Well, I could n't think of telling you all that she said," answered Ardis, with a smile; "but the fact remains that we 've been good friends ever since, and I 'm going to take Clare over to her this afternoon."

Clare did not want to go at all, but when the time came, she found the ordeal much easier than she had expected. Miss Lindsay was a handsome, high-spirited girl, with a wilful mouth, and a fine touch on the piano, which aroused Clare's admiration immediately. The usual examination in scales, intervals, and sight-reading was successfully passed, and then Clare was asked to try a song — which would practically decide the question of her admission to the Club. Ardis had told her what to do; so, instead of producing any music, she went to the piano and played her own accompaniment to a little song which she had written several years before coming to college. Miss Lindsay was delighted, and when Ardis explained that Clare had composed it herself, she turned to her Music Committee, saying quickly, "Don't you think — "

" That she 's exactly what we want?" broke in one of the girls, enthusiastically. " Yes, I do ! "

Miss Lindsay laughed and said, " It is entirely against our principles to take any one without the second trial, Miss Deland, but we have heard of you before, you see, and — well, I think you had better come to rehearsal on Monday night."

" Oh ! " cried Clare, with a delighted jump ; and when the other Club members had shaken hands with her, she went up to Miss Lindsay in her own little-girl fashion, and said, " I will try to be good ! "

The tempestuous Ethel must have found something encouraging in this beginning, for there was less friction in the Club from that time on, and there were people who said that the new soprano had acted as a peacemaker between the Leader and her girls.

Miss Lindsay lived in Waverley, a large town about half an hour by train from South Harland; and one day, not long before the Christmas vacation, she invited Clare and Ardis to come there for an organ concert which was to be given in one of the churches. They were to take dinner with her afterwards, and start for home early in the evening; so the matron gave her consent, and the two Sophomores worked hard that morning to get their studying done.

Ardis had a business meeting of Phi Delta Kappa at two o'clock, and Clare waited for her in the Reading Room, so that they should lose no time in reaching the station. It was a strange .unwintry afternoon, with a certain crossness about the elements that comes when a really cold and stormy day has made up its mind not to snow. Ardis held her sable muff against her face as they walked down

Main Street, and Clare flew along beside her like a happy brown bird. She was so glad that they were going to Waverley, and felt like talking every minute; but when they had established themselves in the train, Ardis would persist in looking out of the window. She continued to look out of the window, although there was nothing to be seen but shivering trees, and great wastes of stiffened grass, with ice-pools frozen blue and hard.

"Ardis," said Clare, at last, "what would you rather be, if you could be the one thing in the world that you most want to?"

Ardis rubbed a little steam off the window with her handkerchief, and answered, "I think I would rather be a dispenser of other people's time."

"What a useful kind of dispensary to set up! Had you thought of making it a charitable or a paying institution?"

"I should, of course, have certain hours set aside for charity patients," said Ardis; and then she looked out of the window again.

"Well," continued Clare impatiently, after a protracted pause, "why don't you ask me what *I* would like to be, most of all? It's only decently polite, after my asking you."

"I do not ask," said Ardis, lightly, "because I know. But I do not think you would succeed as a musical composer. You were meant to be a clinging vine."

"Ardis, what do you mean? You know that I am not a clinging vine."

"I know that you are — a clinging vine."

"You 're a donkey, Ardis."

" It is n't pretty to call barnyard names."

" It is still more hideous to make perfectly abominable speeches. You had better look out of the window again."

" Christine said," observed Ardis in a few minutes, as if speaking to herself, " that Clare had a quick temper! How strange it was that Christine could have thought such a thing ! "

Clare meditated upon this in resentful surprise, and finally came to the conclusion that she had not often had a quick temper at home, because there very little had been said or done to irritate her. Being delicate, she had always been tenderly cared for, and spared in every way. "So now," she thought, " I must get used to having people say things that I do not like, and to not saying things that *they* do not like in return. I don't believe it 'll work, though."

When the girls reached Waverley, Ethel met them at the station, and they drove up to the church in high spirits, Ardis talking gayly, and Clare in raptures over the organ programme which Ethel had brought down to show them.

" This is the finest organ for miles around," said Miss Lindsay, as they entered the church, " and Mr. Boyd says that Clare may play on it afterwards if she wants to. How do you like that, Clare?" and she laughed at the joyous look which her two visitors exchanged.

It was very beautiful sitting there, with the shadows growing deeper every minute, and the red glow from the stained-glass windows fading gradually into dusk. There was a great bowl of roses on the chancel rail, and for years afterwards Clare associated

the scent of them with the sound of an organ. Mr.
Boyd had chosen a Bach Toccata for the opening
number, and his first vigorous chord sprang through
the church like a light, pouring its golden shaft of
tone down the great aisles, and dying away in fantas-
tic flickerings of sound. Clare thought that she saw
him enthroned as in a warmer glow of melody, with
bright sparks whirling from under his fingers, and
music beams around his head.

"Ardis," she whispered softly, when the Toccata
was finished, "this is one of the things that we are
going to remember!"

When all the people had left the church, Ethel
took her two friends up to the gallery, and introduced
them to Mr. Boyd, who stopped hunting through a
pile of music, to give them a cordial welcome.

"So this is the little organist, is it?" he said, shaking hands with Clare. "Just run your fingers over
her a minute, and see if you ever felt an easier
action."

"Oh, I don't really play the organ," protested
Clare, in alarm; "I only love it, you know. And
then sometimes I dream that I'm playing on a big
one, and it's terrible to wake up!"

"Let's not have any waking up to-night, then,"
was the friendly answer. "Just run your feet over
her pedals, and see if you ever felt anything like
her in your life. She's considered the finest in
Massachusetts."

Clare touched one of the notes with the end of her
little finger, and the organ responded with a great
roar, which thundered down the deserted aisles,
turned around, and came back again.

"I think I'm afraid of her," she said, looking doubtfully at the organist. "Does she often make a noise like that?"

"That was her biggest pipe," answered Mr. Boyd, proudly. "His Christian name is the Fire Engine, and I never use him except when people stay too long after service."

"Do play that Nevin 'Love Song,' Clare," said Ardis, "and the little Grieg thing that I like."

Mr. Boyd showed her how to arrange the stops, and then she began to play, rather tremulously at first, but gaining confidence as the great thing stirred beneath her touch, then waked, and followed at her bidding.

"She has a wonderful knack at managing her," said Mr. Boyd, ambiguously. "To tell the truth, she generally dislikes strangers, and tries to get even with 'em in all kinds of ways. Oh, Miss Lindsay, my wife wants to know if you'll step into the vestry, and see her about that song for Christmas Eve. It won't take but a minute, and the young ladies will excuse us, I know."

The young ladies were quite willing to excuse them; and when they had disappeared, Clare turned around on the organ-bench, saying, "Now, Ardis, now, the 'Lost Chord' before any one comes back. We'll never have such another chance." And she began to play the beautiful introduction which she had arranged from a part of the overture to "Lohengrin."

Ardis had not intended to sing; but the great empty church and the great wonderful organ carried her into the music against her will. And as she sang, her voice did not seem to be a part of herself, but came from some outer sphere of melody where she had never been, and curled around her like smoke-wreaths, until she could not hear for the echoes. At first it was joyous, because of the pure joy of singing; then a burden had crept into it, from the trouble which Ardis was carrying in her heart, and at last it became one cry for understanding, to the God who had made her as she was, and placed her, all helpless, in a great unhelping world.

"Ardis, my dear one," said little Clare, with a sob, as the music came to an end, "what is the matter?"

"The acoustic properties of this church are very fine, are n't they?" observed Ardis, calmly. "I wish that our chapel were half as good."

"You really ought to go in for oratorio, Miss Hathaway," said Mr. Boyd, who had been listening from the door, "or, with proper training, you could take a position on the stage. There's a fortune in that voice, if you take care of it — emotion, dramatic expression, and all that — Oh, must you go? Well, I'm sorry, but come again soon, whenever you want to, and Miss Deland shall play on her as long as she likes. Oh, not at all, don't mention it — Glad you enjoyed it;" and presently the girls were borne off by Ethel to a pleasant home evening, with a beautiful home dinner, which included everything, from spicy pickles to cranberry sauce.

"I wonder if people who love music always love to eat," philosophized Clare, as she and Ardis exchanged another pathetically happy glance over the dinner. And Ethel replied, with a comical look, —

"Mr. Boyd says that, next to Bach, he loves apple-dumplings; so I think we are justified in associating

8   113

dinner with art. Come, Ardis, you know that you could contain another piece of turkey!" And the evening passed so pleasantly that when eight o'clock came the girls felt really sorry to go.

"It has been the very nicest of all days!" said Clare to her hostess; and after they were in the train she told Ardis that she could not understand why people found so much to criticise in Ethel Lindsay.

When they reached home, Ardis asked Clare to come into her room for a few minutes, and while they were sitting in the dark, she said, "Clare, if you thought that I had ever done anything mean or — or dishonorable, what would you say to me?"

"I should say that it was n't true," was the staunch reply, "because I don't believe that you could do anything mean or dishonorable."

"But if you *knew* that I was dishonorable — if I were put in jail for stealing, or something like that — what would you do?"

"I would go to you and put my arms around you," said Clare, simply. "What else could I do?"

Ardis got up and walked over to the window.

"My head aches, Clare," she said, throwing her hat on the bed. "Help me to get out these miserable shell pins;" and she shook down the long troublesome hair until it lay, like a darker shadow, upon the shadows of the floor. "Now go to bed, you little thing," she said very gently; "you know that you 're tired."

"I will not go until you tell me what is troubling you," said Clare; and then something told her that it would be of no use to stay. "Good-night, my loved one," she whispered, and slipped away to her own room.

A SONG AND A SORROW

There was much to be told in her prayers that night, much about the music that she had heard, about the flowers in the church, and about that whole beautiful day. There was Ardis, too; and when she looked up, she saw that Ardis was standing beside her. She had crept in without a sound, and would have looked like a little ghost in her white wrapper, if it had not been for the long, wonderful hair which folded her in like dark wings.

" Clare, you silly child," she said with the tears in her eyes, " do you really believe that your philosophy of friendship includes constancy unto death ?"

Clare pushed back that soft shadow from the face of her friend, smiled a little sadly, and answered: " Unto death ! "

CHAPTER IX

THE BASKET–BALL GAME

It was a dazzling, snow-dancing afternoon in March, and Kathleen Carey was promenading up and down the Storey House walk with a hot apple-pie under her arm.

"What have you got there, Kaddy?" called Grace Reade from an upper window. "I am really interested to know."

"You can't have it," said Kathleen, walking rapidly away in another direction; and Grace saw that she must resort to strategy if she wished to gain possession of that pie.

"Kathleen, come here, you — Kathleen, have you heard what Chris found out last night about the Freshman team?"

Kathleen turned slowly around, and began to retrace her steps with reluctance in every movement.

"Well, no, I had n't," she answered. "But take heed what you tell me, for I'm casting a fierce, suspicious eye upon you."

"Come up nearer to the house," said Grace, mysteriously; "I don't want any one to hear."

Kathleen glanced lovingly at the circular package in her arms, and not wishing to involve it in icicle-drippings from the roof, set it down very carefully on a huge snow-bank at the edge of the walk.

THE BASKET–BALL GAME

"There is no one in sight," she muttered, and proceeded to listen with eagerness, while Grace explained the details of a certain new dodge which the Freshmen were preparing for the basket-ball game. Both she and Grace were on the Sophomore team, and there had been many exciting discussions concerning the merits of either side, because this game — the great athletic test of the year — was to take place on the following day. Every participating Sophomore had a green cheese-cloth '95 sewed on the blouse of her gym suit, and a strip of the same color around one arm. The Freshmen wore the same decorations in violet, but with a '96, of course, instead of a '95, and many of them said that the '96 was confusing, because it prevented them from knowing when the gym suits were upside down. Belle Bovey was Captain of the Freshman team, and Christine Arnold of the Sophomore; she was winning a fine athletic reputation for the class that wore the green, and Miss Carlisle was glad to have her undertake the work, because it kept her happy and actively employed during certain outside hours which otherwise might have been given to unprofitable meditation.

There was to be a game that night, in which the "regulars" were to play the substitute team, and Chris would provide some remarkable anti-play for this new throw of the Freshmen that might prove destructive to the Sophomore laurels. Grace rolled her handkerchief into a ball, and tossed it down on Kathleen's hand, to illustrate the Freshman secret; and Kathleen, not liking practical illustrations, turned around with dignity to pick up her pie, — but no pie was to be seen.

"Grace, you double-faced," she began, and then suddenly espied a round hole on the snow-bank into which the warm pie had mysteriously disappeared, having previously buried itself in a mass of sympathetic slush. She cast irate glances at the window, from which issued sounds of mockery and mirth, dug out her pie, and went off to the swimming-tank to eat it. The swimming-tank was at this time a compact little cellar of stone, with a tiled floor; but, lacking the one element most essential to aquatic achievements, it was used as a rendezvous by members of the Athletic Association, and other people who liked to study in a low temperature.

Kathleen found the captain and the sub-captain of her team sitting on the brick wall of the tank, with their slippered feet dangling gayly into its arid depths.

"What have you got on your gym suits for?" she asked in alarm. "Have some pie?"

"Thanks," said Ardis. "We've been having a little private practice upstairs by ourselves, Christine personating the Sophomore team and I the Freshman. I beat her."

"It's a bad omen," said the captain, kicking off one slipper into the tank. "There, Ardis, you can go down and pick that up."

"I certainly won't," said Ardis, amiably. "Have some of Kathleen's pie."

"Leonora Kent has turned her ankle!" said Christine, gloomily. "What do you think of that?"

"Why," said Kathleen, beginning to cut up her pie with a visiting-card, "I think she had better invest in a cork leg."

"There is no one else who can get the ball into the basket as Leonora does," said Christine, seriously. "Kathleen, this is no joking matter! Whom shall I appoint in her place?"

"Myself," answered Kathleen, serenely. "I will volunteer my services."

"To tell the truth, we had already thought of you," said Christine, "and we will now consider it settled. You may take Leonora's place to-night."

"That's another pair of sleeves!" cried Kathleen, in terror. "I certainly won't take it or attempt to take it. I never got the ball in the basket more than once in my life, and that was because another girl ran into me from behind. Oh, miserable day! Oh, sad mishap! No, you don't find me making a fool of myself in public, after all the private affairs of the same kind with which we are familiar."

"Kathleen," said Ardis, helping herself to a piece of pie, "do you ever tell lies?"

"Not always," answered Kathleen. "But when such a descent is necessary, I can be the best liar that you ever knew. I can elevate the profession so that a thousand rejected competitors fall back in a wilted line and wither. I can —"

"You can practise until evening comes," said Ardis, jumping down from her high perch. "We superior officers have no more time to waste upon you. Here's your shoe, Chris;" and presently the two girls went off together, arm in arm, leaving Kathleen to demolish her pie alone.

"As Mr. Arthur Sherburne Hardy has wisely observed," she said, with a dramatic flourish of the arm, "'Digestion is a solitary business.'"

That night all Freshmen and Juniors were excluded from the Gymnasium, while the Sophomores attacked and valiantly defeated their substitute team. Kathleen did so well in her new position that there seemed to be much cause for encouragement on the Sophomore side.

The excitement grew intense as the time for the game approached, and on the following night the running track around the Gymnasium was packed to overflowing with enthusiastic girls, while the Faculty .occupied the stage. As one maiden disrespectfully observed, it was their first appearance. One side of the track was draped in violet, and the other in green, while many flags danced through the railings, and competitive knots of spectators sang their class songs in rival keys. There was much cheering when Miss Carlisle came in wearing the green of Ninety-five, and Christine, who saw her from behind the door in the dressing-room, flushed with pride and satisfaction.

The Freshmen ran into the hall first, and when Christine heard the tremendous applause which greeted them, her heart sank, for she felt that all this cheering might mean " thumbs down " for the Sophomores, and she was responsible for their success, or if worst came to worst, for their failure.

" We can do anything while we have you," said Elsie Dane, as if she had been reading her thoughts; and Christine's courage came back with a bound. She gathered her team around her, lifted the green flag which stood in the corner, and holding it above them with one fierce gesture of love and loyalty, said, —

THE BASKET-BALL GAME

" Girls, it is for this ! "

Her classmates understood her, and clenched their fists in silent determination.

When they ran into the hall, Christine did not hear the tumult of cheering which greeted them; she began to toss the ball around from one to another of her team, that they might be ready for hard work when the umpire gave the signal. A beautiful banner of white silk, with a golden " H " in the centre, hung impressively from one end of the running track, and the color that came off victorious would take its place beneath this flag, to remain until another year had come and another game been played.

The Sophomores were singing

> " Highly waves our emerald banner,
> Pride of Ninety-five;
> Who to win it further glory,
> Ardently would strive,"

to the tune of " Hold the Fort," and little Clare was beating time with a flagstaff.

" Play ! " called the umpire, and the game began.

> " Now, as herald of our honor,
> Springtime is at hand;
> And our glorious green shall cover
> The awakened land."

" Three to one, favor of Ninety-six," called the umpire; and the violet flags waved wildly, like flowers in a storm.

" Play ! " and Christine threw up both arms to catch that nimble ball which was almost within her reach; when suddenly the right arm dropped to her side like a shot thing, and the Gymnasium whirled around.

"Let me get through, let me pass, for Heaven's sake!" implored Ruth, pushing her way through the crowd in the gallery. "Let me pass or I will walk over you. Let me get by!" and even before she reached the stairs, the cheering broke out again on the Freshman side.

Christine had been taken to the dressing-room by two of the substitute team, and Ardis, as sub-captain, was fighting bravely in her place.

"It is the shoulder again!" said Ruth, as she saw Christine's face. "Girls, one of you help me take her home. Mildred, go for the doctor immediately. Florence," to a Marston Freshman who was standing by the door, "tell Faith Bentley to tell Clare Deland I want her at the Hadley immediately;" and the girls flew away on their various errands, while Ruth and one of the substitute team took Christine home.

Mrs. Sawyer, the matron of the Hadley, was away that evening, but Miss Carlisle had seen the Sophomore captain leave the Gymnasium, and hurried over to find out what was the matter. She helped Clare and Ruth get Christine into bed, and then went downstairs to wait until the doctor came. It seemed as if he would never come, and Christine was in an agony of nervousness about the game. Ruth kept one girl stationed at the Gymnasium, and another in the hall downstairs, to come and report every few minutes; but the reports were not favorable, and meanwhile the shoulder was growing worse. At last the front door slammed, and footsteps were heard coming up the stairs. Over in the Gymnasium Christine could hear them singing, —

> " Courage, classmates, we are called
> The finest class alive ;
> Now uphold your reputation,
> Fight for Ninety-five ! "

" Ruth," she said quietly, "take down our flag, — the flag of Ninety-five. Hold it where I can see it, and then I shall not scream when my shoulder is set."

Ruth obeyed her with quivering lips, and had just hung it over the foot of the bed, when the doctor came into the room. He was not the old doctor, but Dr. Comstock, a younger practitioner who had recently come to South Harland; and Mildred Wyman called Ruth out into the hall to tell her that they had been everywhere and could find no one else.

" I have heard that he is very fine," said Ruth, " and, at any rate, he will know how to put a shoulder in place. Don't go away yet, Mildred; we shall need you and Clare in a few minutes."

She returned to Christine, and heard the doctor saying: " Does this hurt you, and this? Ah, yes; I thought so. It ought to have been attended to before. Can you roll a bandage?" he asked, turning to Ruth. And when she proudly assented, he said: " Ask some of the young ladies to help you, and get to work immediately. Miss Carlisle, if you would kindly close the door."

The doctor was pouring something from a bottle on to a handkerchief, and presently he came over to the bed, saying, " If you will lie perfectly still, Miss Arnold, this will soon be over."

" I won't lie still," cried Christine. "Doctor, I am not afraid of being hurt, I never was afraid of pain in my life. I will promise not to utter a sound, only don't give me ether. I am not afraid of pain, I tell you — I can bear anything. I am not afraid; " and then something cold, with a sweet and suffocating odor, was laid upon her face. She felt Miss Carlisle's hand in hers, and tried to ask her if she would not take away that dreadful handkerchief, when suddenly the walls darkened, and she was sitting in Number 6, College Hall, waiting for recitation to begin.

She wondered why they should have a recitation in the dark, and when Miss Carlisle called upon her, she answered, "Unprepared." All the girls laughed at her; Miss Carlisle pointed a scornful finger at her, and she suddenly realized that she had come to recitation with her gym suit on. " How could they see in the dark ! " she thought, as she rose and walked out of the room.

She was in the basement of the Gymnasium, and the game was going on overhead, but when she tried to get upstairs the door was locked. She ran wildly back and forth, hearing the girls call to her from above, and yet she could not go to them. She found a chair and knew that if she could climb into it, she would float up through the ceiling into the hall; but whenever she approached it, the chair trembled and looked as if it would fall in pieces. At last she did climb into it, and went up through the floor into the Gymnasium; but it was empty and dark, and a thousand voices screamed at her from the shadows.

"I could not help it," she cried, "I tried to be here in time!"

"Christabel," said a sweet voice not far from her cheek, "Christabel, my darling!"

She roused a little, and tried to cling to the voice, but it whirled away out of sight, and she was once more left alone. Directly before her was a stormy wheel, and it blew so wildly through the air that she thought it must be a cyclone.

"We always expected one in Burlington," she said to herself. "But what is that in the middle of it? It looks like our flag, and it will be blown into tatters."

The cyclone drew nearer with a roaring cry, and stopped with a slight jar at the foot of the bed. Christine saw that the flag had not been injured; and turning to Miss Carlisle, who still held her hand, she asked, "How's the game?"

"Fine!" answered the doctor, with a boyish laugh; and then he motioned to three breathless figures in gym suits who were waiting outside the door. They came in on tiptoe, and laid at the foot of Christine's bed a white silken banner with a golden "H" in its centre, and beneath that banner was tied the flag of Ninety-five!

Two of the figures in gym suits were weeping quietly, but the third was overflowing with dramatic importance and said, "Doctor, can we talk?"

"Not to-night," he answered; "to-morrow. Miss Arnold must go to sleep now;" and he pointed to the door. But on the way out the dramatic figure said:

"It is not myself that would talk, but, oh, captain, you ought to be proud of Ardis, for she did the whole thing. She played magnificently, and kept telling us all the time to be worthy of you. Leonora would go into the game at the last, and of course her old ankle turned over again, so now she's sitting down in the Gym with her foot bandaged up, yelling 'Hurrah for Ninety-five!'"

The door was speedily closed, and when Miss Carlisle and the doctor had gone downstairs, Christine said, "Was Ardis here in the room before I came out from the chloroform?"

"She ran over for a minute when the game was nearly finished," answered Ruth, in surprise, "but the intermission was so short that she had to rush to get back. How could you possibly know that she had been here?"

"I thought she was," said Christine, drowsily; and long after Ruth had supposed her to be asleep, she turned quietly upon the pillows and observed, "The finest class alive!"

Early in the morning the flowers began to come in, — great bunches of violets and smilax from the Freshman class, roses and roses from the Sophomores. Number 2 Hadley looked like a garden, and Ruth made the sweetest of gardeners, as she moved around among the flower children, clipping stems, filling wash-bowls, and exclaiming with delight over each new face.

Kathleen came in and illustrated her graphic account of the game by acting it out on the floor.

"Minnie Appleyard went down on top of Rachel once," she said, "and Rachel thought she was done for, sure, — you know how fat Min is, — and began to forgive all the people who had stepped on her feet in ferry-boats; when suddenly she remembered the power of mind over matter. Min was the matter, you know; so, as soon as Rachel had denied the existence of Min, she rolled out from under her and caught the ball."

" There is everything in the power of mind over matter," said Christine, " if what is subservient to the will can be guided by it; but unfortunately shoulders are not subservient to the will, and never can be."

" Not when they 're ' un-jinted,' " said Kathleen. " But, cap'n, are n't you going to be out for the April Fool's Eve dance? We can't have it without you, in the least particular."

" I asked the doctor," said Christine, indignantly, " and he said it was doubtful."

The " April Fool's Eve " dance was to be a masked ball, given by the Sophomores of the Hardwick, a large boarding-house on Elm Street, for the members of their own class. " Just like Ninety-five," said the upper-class girls, when they heard of the arrangement; but Ninety-five only laughed, because it was loyal enough not to mind being told that it was like itself.

Ardis and Christine had been making two Quaker costumes, exactly alike, to be worn at the dance; and as the girls were of the same height, they were hoping that no one would be able to tell them apart. Ardis came in that afternoon, and put the finishing touches on Christine's costume, for the making of them had been a great secret, and not even Ruth was to know. But when the night of the festivity came, it was very evident that Christine could not be there, for she had scarcely left her room, and no one suspected that the doctor had given her full permission to go, if she would promise not to dance. She received much sympathy from the girls in the house, who came in to show her their costumes, and consult with her over their funny disguises.

When they were all gone, she triumphantly arrayed herself in the Quaker costume, and set forth, wondering if Ardis would not be surprised when she saw her double walk into the hall. The Hardwick girls had engaged the Gymnasium of the Waltham Preparatory School for their dance, and when Christine arrived, the place was already gay with lights and resonant with violins. She marched boldly in, and bowed gravely to all the Hadley girls whose costumes she had seen, laughing meanwhile at their curiosity and surprise. Strange figures came up to peer through the eye-holes of her mask, and Ruth asked her, in a high-pitched voice, if she would not dance; but Christine shook her head and darted away.

She was looking around the room for another costume like her own, when suddenly a tall figure in cap and gown seized her arm, saying, " Come into the hall a minute. I want to speak to you ; " and Christine followed in high glee, anticipating revelations of an amusing nature. The girl took her into the little passageway near the door, glanced nervously around, and then whispered : " They say that Miss Carlisle has found out who it was that black-balled Christine Arnold."

Her companion gave a violent start, and she said, " Yes, I knew how you would feel about it. Of course some of the girls were wild at the time, and it seems that Christine — " At that moment somebody came into the passageway from the cloak-room, and the cap-and-gown slipped away, saying, " I 'll see you later."

In a few minutes the Gymnasium door slammed, and Christine was speeding home through the darkness. She felt very cold, and ran swiftly, to start up her circulation, but when she reached the Hadley she was shivering. "Do I care so much as all that?" she said between her teeth; and then she sat down in her room, to see if she could understand this thing that had happened to her.

"I have been studying, I have been — I have been studying," she said with quick, short breaths. "What have I done that they should treat me so?"

She still felt very cold, and, having exchanged the Quaker costume for a warm wrapper, she filled her hot-water bag in the bathroom, and lay down on her bed. Then she pulled the blanket and steamer rugs up over her with the uninjured arm, and lay very still.

" Miss Carlisle gave me ' Excellent ' on both my essays," she thought. " Dr. Gillette said I did well. Fräulein Schaf said I did well. Professor Thorne said — yes, he said I did well. What have I done that they should treat me so?"

We all understand that it is foolish to care so much about belonging to a college society, for the college world is doubtless very small; but when wrapped in shadow, the great and the little worlds become as one, and that one is the lost world which was the greatest of all!

9   129

Christine knew that the stranger had mistaken her for Ardis, and the color rose to her face at the thought that Ardis must have known about it all along. When did it occur? Why had Ardis not worked harder for her in the society? If she, instead of Ardis, had been in the Phi Delta Kappa, she would have left no stone unturned to make her friend a member. "But I am very stupid, and not at all popular," she thought. "It is more probable that Ardis did work for me and failed, — failed because I was not worthy to be one of them."

She lay awake far into the night, and the next morning her eyes were wild, like those of a child that has been misunderstood. Vacation came soon, and in the confusion of packing, her sadness passed unnoticed; but she knew that Spring term was awaiting her, with all its burden of joy.

For other girls, this year had grown like a flower; for Christine, it had gone out like a candle.

CHAPTER X

HAMMOCKS AND APPLE-BLOSSOMS

THE classes of Ninety-three and Ninety-five had always been friends.

On the first day of April the Seniors went to Ethics, and found a notice on the door, stating that the recitation would be held in a certain room upstairs, so they took their books, and wearily ascended another flight. In a few minutes they came down again, to find Professor Harding waiting for them, and to remember that the class of Ninety-five never failed to celebrate an anniversary. But the affection between the Seniors and the Sophomores was renewed when Spring term came, and the Sophomores planned to build a platform behind the Wyndham, that the Seniors might dance upon it. They felt great responsibility with regard to this entertainment, and the responsibility was shared by personages no less important than the Seniors themselves. They went to look at the bulletin board while the Sophomores were holding their class meetings in the Mathematics room, and wandered casually past the door when a gathering was about to disperse. The Sophomores had resolved to give the finest entertainment that had ever heaped coals of fire upon Senior heads, and entirely scorned the idea of having an exhibition of trained dogs, as Kathleen suggested.

131

" Above all, it is to be a secret!" said Elsie Dane, impressively, at the end of the final meeting.

"I'm awfully afraid it will warp," said Kate Dervish, a Glee Club girl who lived in the Lathrop and prided herself upon disliking men.

"It's a way that secrets have, so you'd better be careful," laughed Rachel Winter, whom Kate did not like, because once in the Chemistry class Rachel had alluded to her as Maria.

" It will take a great deal of lumber," said Mildred Wyman, thoughtfully; " but the apple-blossoms will be out, and if there is a moon — "

The platform was completed on the day before the reception, and there was a moon. The weather had been perfect, and the orchard was all adrift with pink; but on that festive morning, when the weather should have made a special effort to be good, the apple-blossoms hung drenched and spiritless in a pouring rain. The back campus sparkled wickedly with puddles, and the path out to the Observatory was full of mud.

Sophomores in gossamers and overshoes came out to look at their platform, and went away with gloom upon their countenances. The Reception Committee spattered pitifully about on the clinging boards, and said that when the platform was waxed, it would do very well. If only the sun would come out for an hour, and dry it up! But the rain continued to descend, and before long that platform curled up like a leaf that rests upon the fire, taking to itself strange hollows and excrescences, which would have made dancing, even under the most favorable circumstances, a dangerous proceeding. There was a hurried collecting of sofa-pillows and other decorations in the undecorated Gym, and that night a dejected class of Sophomores entertained the very most considerate class of Seniors that ever made light of a disappointing evening, and had a good time.

Elsie Dane took Edith Campbell, who was President of Ninety-three. Ruth took Louise Burritt, and Christine invited Marjorie Drew.

"You observe that I am not unkind enough to decline your invitation!" she said with a laugh, when Christine went to ask her. Ardis and Clare took Senior friends in the Marston, and Kathleen invited Maria Grumbagg "as a penance," she explained.

The evening passed off very pleasantly, but the Sophomores were terribly humiliated over the failure of their plan; and when the Senior Dramatics were given at Commencement, they managed to smuggle a large box of roses behind the scenes, together with a card bearing the following explanation:

"Although our platform never felt the pressure of your feet,
And there were limitations as to what you had to eat,
To show that we appreciate your efforts to survive,
We send these greens with humble thanks, and love from Ninety-five."

The Seniors were both pleased and touched, and the flower incident had a pretty sequel in due time.

That last Spring term of Ninety-three taught the girls of Ninety-five what it meant to lose the friends that one cares for, and to leave the college that is one's little world. Ninety-five may have been ill-behaved, but it loved its friends as sincerely as a better class would have done, and mourned for them long after people thought it would stop. Perhaps it began to grow up, from this time, for when it came back to college in the Autumn, it was a class of children no longer, although the old spirit of mischief continued to bubble over till the end.

But this is anticipating, for the spirit of mischief was in full force all through that beautiful Spring term, when everything was calling the girls out of doors. German lessons were translated on the back campus, where bluebirds flashed through the branches above, and pecked surreptitiously at the red bindings of forgotten dictionaries. Sea-like murmurs crept through the grass, and wrapped the meanings of Euripides in a drowsy song. Logarithms flew away in a cloud of apple-blossoms, and specific gravities vied with the relative merits of chocolate and strawberry ice-cream. The arbutus was twining through the woodland, like a wandering green puzzle, with pink answers, and the girls spent whole afternoons in quest of the tiny blooms. Hands stained with dandelions put down unruly problems in Calculus, and Zoölogy became the most popular study, because it involved long insect-hunting expeditions, which kept the students out of doors. Decoration Day was always spent in the country, for the girls were so full of the "wild joy of living" that nothing could keep them in town when stern old work stepped aside for one moment, and said "Go!"

The hill settlement, with Ardis and Grace Reade, started out in a beautiful bumpy wagon, and aimed in a certain direction; for Ardis thought that it would be safer to aim in a certain direction, although the horse did not exactly go; and Christine said that as

Ardis was driving, she ought to decide this matter for herself.

"Only steer clear of public thoroughfares," she added. "We might excite some comment from the fact that four of us sit at the same time in the bottom of the cart."

The horse expressed a preference for the first side street, and being entirely bit-proof, Ardis thought that it might be as well to humor him. He went along until he reached the yard of his paternal livery-stable, and then turned into it without offering any explanation whatever.

"Child alive!" said Kathleen, as Ardis tried in vain to stop him, "what kind of a pernicious influence are you exercising on the beast? Just stop driving him a minute, and he'll be all right. That's what he needs."

Ruth took the reins, and with repeated words of endearment induced the horse to back out of the yard, just as he was meditating a violent entrance into his own stall. The cart retraced its journey, with a faithful repetition of the same jolts, and Ruth turned down Main Street, because she wished the animal to forget those tender yearnings which the sight of home had aroused in his heart. They were slowly approaching another side street, when the horse stopped short, snorted violently, and stood upon one leg.

"It's that tired feeling," said Kathleen, peering over the edge of the cart. "Oh, girls, look at the crowd coming up the street. What do you reckon is going to happen?"

"Drive on quickly," said Christine to Ruth; "we don't want to be caught in a procession."

"He won't stir an inch," said the driver, looking despairingly at her horse, which stood as if transfixed with terror, and absolutely ignored the fact that she had been whipping him for three minutes.

"Let's get out," suggested Ardis.

"We can't," came in a dismal chorus from behind, "unless you take out the tail-board, — we can't move!"

Ardis was preparing to descend and remove the tail-board, when an Arab steed, gayly adorned with gold trappings, advanced in thoroughbred zigzags up the street.

"It's circus day!" said Kathleen, in delight; and the girls realized that she had spoken the terrible truth. Their horse started violently, as two camels, attired in red and gold petticoats, ambled past.

"It is a comfort to know that none of the people in the crowd will look at us," said Clare ; and Christine added wickedly, "They won't look at us, but they will surely look at Ardis, because she has such a conspicuous position."

"Christine," said Ardis, turning swiftly round, "don't you ever dare write up this experience."

Christine generally carried a little notebook on these occasions, which often afforded material for "Bain papers" of a startling nature; and several of these papers had been read in class. She took a malicious satisfaction in producing her notebook now, when eight little ponies, each ridden by one abject monkey, were trotting past. She then became absorbed in a spirited description of the trick donkey, which was arrayed in divided skirts of striped bunting, like the clown who walked beside him.

HAMMOCKS AND APPLE-BLOSSOMS

It is doubtful if any of the party were prepared for elephants, but it is always the unexpected that happens. Two good-sized specimens of the unexpected came padding up the street, with swinging trunks and wind-tossed ears; and the horse, who had been patient through many surprises, said, " Here I draw the line." He bolted abruptly down Main Street, turned off at the ferry-road, and ran without stopping till he came to the river. The girls were interested to see if he would try to swim across, but the old ferryman did not give him an opportunity.

"Whoa, there," he shouted, seizing the reins. "Stiddy now. Say-y," turning to the girls with reproach in his eyes, "you've been drivin' him too hard!"

The horse meekly allowed himself to be embarked, the front wheels of the cart followed, and after a few minutes the back wheels complied; and the unwieldy boat began to move sideways across the stream.

"Guess we're goin' to hev rain," said the ferryman, when they reached the opposite shore. "I never knew it to fail to rain on circus day."

"I don't believe a word of it," said Grace; but when they had started on again, they discovered that a ferryman's prophecy is not to be ignored. The air grew very close, and the scent of the flowers became intense, as if the warmth had crushed the perfume out of them; the maples flashed silver all of a sudden, and a whirl of dust scudded up the road.

"It is of no use," said Ardis, as a big drop splashed upon her nose, " but, oh, if I don't get even with that horse!"

A large barn, with a door at each end, stood invitingly near, and the girls drove into it, hoping that the proprietor would prove as hospitable as other Connecticut Valley folk. He soon relieved their doubts by emerging from the cow-shed, with a bucket and a beaming smile.

"You're college girls, now, ain't you?" he said, "and if you be college girls this barn's yourn. That's all I've got to say. This barn's yourn."

The girls thanked him so warmly that he immediately offered to provide hard-boiled eggs for the whole party, and prepared for the wicked horse a sumptuous lunch, tastefully arranged in a nose-bag.

"Now, that's just what I've always felt that we needed," said Grace Reade, gazing mournfully at the animal. "If each of us had a nose-bag, embroidered with her own initials, the necessity for packing lunch-boxes would be avoided."

The other luncheon was set out on the hay, and two perky-tailed kittens were the first to take advantage of it.

"Felines, avaunt!" said Christine, sternly; and the felines avaunted in such deadly terror that she promptly relented, and coaxed them back with bits of potted ham. There were lettuce sandwiches, and fat cool olives, and ginger ale. There were stuffed eggs with the stuffing lost out; there was a beautiful mould of pressed chicken, and there was an apple-pie, containing a broken glass of raspberry jam.

"This is a truly pastoral scene," said Clare, looking at the gentle-eyed cow that was softly shaking her chain, and gazing with interest upon the company. Two iron-gray cart-horses stamped in their stalls, and snorted indignantly at the strange, thin horse who was eating out of their nose-bag. Outside the rain swept down in long gray slants; inside was the sound of rhythmic crunching.

" Did you notice how sweet the flowers were before the storm?" asked Clare. "It was as if they had been singing all the time, and we had only just heard them because of the silence."

"Speaking of silence," said Grace, "Christine has n't made a remark this term. What's the matter, Christine?"

" I speak when I have anything to say," was the exhaustive answer, and the subject was tactfully dropped. She wondered if the girls knew what the matter really was, and thought of the comforting letter she had received from Stephen that morning. She had confided her troubles to him in the vacation, and he had given her a great deal of sensible advice. This last letter said: " Don't think any more about that trumpery society. I would n't want to join a society where the parties could n't tell a bright girl when they saw her, anyhow. Think, first of all, what you came to college for, and, last of all, that you can leave it again as soon as you like."

This appealed to Christine's pride, as Stephen knew that it would, and she had gained courage ever since.

"Let's drink somebody's health," said Kathleen, waving her glass in the air. " Whose shall it be?"

"That glass happens to be mine if you wish to know," said Grace. "You upset yours a minute ago into the pie."

"Let's drink to dear old Ninety-three," said Ruth; and a sudden shadow fell upon the party.

"Why did you mention them?" said Grace, sadly. "It does n't seem as if anything could be the same when they are gone."

"I wonder if we shall be the same," said Clare. "People say that the step between Sophomore and Junior year is the longest."

"We'll jump over it, then, or walk around it," said Kathleen, making a '95 out of olive-pits, on an upturned pan. "I myself shall remain the same."

"Christine has changed a good deal in one respect," said Ardis. "In Freshman year she considered it compromising to be seen in public with a paper bag; but the other day I met her walking innocently up Elm Street carrying a silk screen and a pair of shoes!"

"Do you really feel just as you did last year, Kathleen?" asked Ruth, who did not like to have Christine teased.

"If anything has led you to draw inferences to the contrary," said Kathleen, with a wave of the arm, "then my looks belie my appearance! Now, ladies! I will declaim the Anglo-Saxon lesson for to-morrow, so that you will see him prostrate at her feet, and the straw shall run with gore — "

"Instead of spiders," broke in Clare.

"The subject of to-morrow's lesson," observed Ardis, "is the story of Orpheus and Eurydice. I fear that you have confused your plot with the tales that appear in the 'Saturday Serpent.'"

"When that time comes," said Kathleen, ambiguously, "let me know."

She scrambled to her feet, and began to recite in a strange unearthly language, the like of which is seldom heard, because it is not a living tongue, and yet has never received the respect that is due to the dead. Her dramatic gestures were irresistible. and when she had finished, her audience was rolling upon the hay in merriment.

"Say-y," said a gruff voice from the door, "I used to know a deef lunatic gentleman up to the Hosp'tal, who was Portugee on his mother's side, and he used to talk just like you."

The girls exploded with laughter, and Christine said: "What would Miss Carlisle say to that? I suppose she would refer the lunatic gentleman to Grimm's Law."

"It's letting up now," said Grace, who had been casually collecting the lunch-baskets. "Don't you think that we had better resume our pilgrimage?"

"To resume our pilgrimage means to go home, I suppose," said Ruth. "Well, it is certain that we have found this the Palace Beautiful;" and their host volunteered, —

"I ain't no objections to your stayin' longer, no objections at all, but I guess you think your mas — or your schoolm'ams I'd oughter say — will be frettin' after you, and it ain't like me to want to git you a scoldin'. I jest hope you'll come again soon, though, and what I want ye to remember is that this barn's yourn!"

The girls thanked him again, and presently they were driving home through air that spoke of wet lilacs, while a long rift of sunshine, washed yellow and bright, followed them down the road.

"After all," said Clare, "the real Palace Beautiful is the place that you leave behind when you go out on your pilgrimage, and return to at night when the journey is done!"

A few days later, Clare found a new winding stair in her Palace Beautiful, which led her up where she could see the sky. Ardis came into her room with a little note, and when the other people who had been waiting outside the door, rushed in to kiss her, Clare knew that something delightful had happened.

"Is it really true that I am in Phi Delta Kappa!" she cried. "Do you suppose that perhaps they did n't know how stupid I am?"

"They understood everything," said Ardis, who was watching her with happy eyes. "Now come over to chapel, little dearest, and let them show you how well they understood!"

She fastened the pretty pin in Clare's dress, and when Clare said, "Oh, I am afraid that something will happen to it!" she answered, laughing, —

"The pin is your own, so you can lose it if you like. I telegraphed to your mother Saturday night, after you got in, and she telegraphed back to have your pin ready for you to put on Monday morning."

"My best beloved, did you do that?" asked Clare; and then she added to herself, "My mother is a happy mother to-day!"

This happiness that had come to her helped to make other people happy too, for she moved in a soft atmosphere of joy that encompassed her like a warmth.

"It is not only being in the society," she thought, "but to know that they really wanted me, that perhaps they must have wanted me just a little, to take me in. It is beautiful! "

The girls said that Clare had not realized until now how many people were her friends; and in speaking of that day afterwards to her mother, she said: " It was as if I had awakened one morning, and found a bird singing in my room! "

The birds were singing on the campus now, and the Senior roses were blooming through little Clare's joy. There was one bed of deep red roses, that blossomed late, and they were called the Senior roses, because when they came, it meant that the Seniors were going away. There were the last few walks to be taken together, — walks that led where one could see the mountains, and walks that wandered down the road beside the lake; evenings when the singing of frogs came up through the dusk of trees, and mornings when the chapel exercises seemed all too short. Then came the memory of days when the Seniors were dressed all in white, Edith, Marjorie, and the rest, and an Ivy Song on the college steps crept in between them and the girls who must stay behind.

"What is the meaning of it all? " thought Clare, when Commencement was over. " Does it mean that some time we — *we* must do that too? "

She was changing her room in the Marston that day, moving into one which she wanted, because it had " a twilight and a star; " the old one had been full of electric flashings from a light in the street. She carried books down the corridor, trying not to look in at the dismantled rooms, where ghostly forms, concealed under sheets, lay stretched upon the beds. Outside the rain was falling very softly, as if it would put to sleep the memories of the year, — that year which had led Ninety-three to the borderland, and watched her out of sight with fearless eyes, knowing that what her Alma Mater had given her would guide her safely on.

Clare and Ardis were the last girls to leave the house, and that afternoon they walked down to the station together.

"You are going to write to me this summer, are n't you?" asked Clare; and Ardis answered seriously, "I never correspond with people, but I am always perfectly willing to receive letters from them."

They both laughed, and when they parted at Springfield, Ardis said, "It will take us nearly all summer, I think, to realize that the girls of Ninety-five are Juniors!"

CHAPTER XI

"WHAT IT MEANS TO BE FRIENDS"

IT was the year of the World's Fair in Chicago, and during the summer there were many unexpected college reunions on the " Midway Plaisance." Friends who had worked in Laboratory together now floated in gondolas, past the shining steps of palaces, or wandered hand in hand through rooms full of beautiful pictures. Undergraduates encountered famous Alumnæ in the Street of Cairo, and regretted that they dared not offer the hero of Ninety-two Dramatics a ride on the camel.

Ruth Burritt had expected to go to the Fair with Mrs. Arnold and Christine, but, on account of the great financial depression that year, her father had been unable to afford it. She took the disappointment very sweetly, but Dr. Burritt did not forget that there were friends whom Ruth might have seen if she had gone to the Fair, and whom she would not see now. " I won't tell her the worst until she has pulled up from this," he thought; "she does not need to know until the last minute."

So the summer went by, and one morning in September Ruth was called into her father's office, to find him walking up and down with that look on his face which came when he had been working for nights over a patient.

"Papa," she said, "you have had more bad news about money! I know you have. Oh, won't that old tariff question ever be settled?"

"Heaven only knows!" answered the doctor, with a sigh; "I don't think Cleveland does. Come here, Ruth, I want to talk to you. Yes, I've lost money lately, although a doctor's income is not supposed to be affected by tariff reform. You see, I have n't had as much practice as usual this summer, because every one's gone to the Fair; but it is certain that I shall have a great deal more than usual when they get back!"

"Papa, you know that you don't feel like joking," said Ruth, anxiously. "Tell me all about it, dear. Is it so bad that—"

"So bad that you can't go back to college this fall. Yes, my poor child."

He had not expected that Ruth would take it as she did. He had thought that she would suffer terribly, that they would both suffer, and that would be the end.

"Papa," she said with a white face, "I must go back to college!"

He looked at her in distress, thinking that she had not understood him, and said, "But, Ruth, poor little girl, poor little Ruth, I can't afford it."

"Sit down here, papa," pushing him towards the big office-chair. "Now," and she put both arms around his neck, "you must listen to what I say, because it won't be long. Papa, there is nothing in the world, next to my family, that means so much to me as my college. It is what Yale was to you. Papa! think what Yale is to you now, what it always will be.

And I will work! I will tutor, and earn my own board as other girls do, and the college will give me my tuition until we can afford to pay!"

"Ruth, do you think that I would allow you to accept charity from your college?"

"Papa, it is not charity, — it is not, indeed, because the college is our mother, you know. We love her, and she loves us, because we are her children. I understand just how the college feels, when she wants to take care of us."

"But do you mean to say that Harland can afford to give away so many scholarships? I understood that you were a poor college."

"And so we are, papa, terribly poor. But you don't know what a President we have, and you don't know what a college that President has made! It *is* a poor college, and that's why it gives away the little that it can. It seems to me that it is nearly always the poor people, or the poor colleges, that think they can afford to give."

"But would the Faculty give a scholarship to every one, Ruth? Would they give one to a girl who was not a good student? And how do they know who the good students are, if there is no marking-system?"

"We have no public marking-system," said Ruth, with spirit, " but everything that we do is on the college records, and I think — Oh, papa, I have learned my lessons, I have indeed, and I think they would not refuse me a scholarship."

Dr. Burritt rose from his chair and began to walk up and down the room.

"How can a girl know what kind of work she's

doing when she receives no regular report?" he said. "I've often wished that I could see a report of your standing, Ruth."

"My dear, ambitious old father," said Ruth, jumping up to walk beside him, "all that a girl needs to know with regard to her work, and all that the Faculty expects her to know, is that she is doing her very best!"

"And have you done that, Ruth?"

"Oh, papa, yes! Don't you remember, Freshman year, when we had to make a metrical translation of that ode, — how Dr. Gillette said mine was one of the best? Don't you remember, papa? I wrote you about it; and then Professor Everest, in Greek, said that I was quite competent to tutor. And Professor Thorne in Chemistry — "

"But, Ruth, even if the college would give you a scholarship, I can't afford to pay your board away from home. Here in the family you would not cost me more than three or four dollars a week; but there — "

"Oh, papa," said Ruth, clasping his arm, "I could live grandly, magnificently, on three dollars a week. Oh, if you would only let me go back and live on three dollars a week! There is such a girl, our brave little Class President, who has no money at all, and she pays her own board, all through sewing and tutoring and teaching, sometimes, in the High School. I could live with her, and we'd cook our own suppers and breakfasts, and I can sew on dress braid. Oh, papa, there was never any other college in the world like our college. Let me go back and live on three dollars a week!"

"WHAT IT MEANS TO BE FRIENDS"

Dr. Burritt stopped, and blew his nose violently three times. "Ruth, you're a trump," he said; "yes, you're a trump. Shake hands with your old father. By Jove, you remind me of some of our boys. They had to be brave fellows in those days, Ruth; used to work like troopers to get through college. Some of them kept a night school in the town. You make me think of them when you speak like that. I used to think that colleges were different nowadays; but no, Ruth, when a young girl can speak as you have spoken, it shows that the old stock is still alive."

"And you will let me go back, papa?"

"Go to thunder, Ruth,—you shall do as you like! You shall do as you like, little girl. There was one fellow that went off to the war. He sneaked out the last night, and sat on the old fence for ten solitary minutes, just out of sentiment, you know, and his college wasn't ashamed of him, either. No, by Jove! it wasn't.—He never came back."

That night Ruth and her father had ginger-ale and ice-cream down town, and when Mrs. Burritt asked what they had been doing, her husband said,—

"Oh, we've been having a little college reunion all by ourselves, haven't we, Ruth? The Class of Sixty-five and the Class of Ninety-five, eh, Ruth? Come into the parlor now, and let's sing 'Here's to Good Old Yale,' my dear."

When Christine heard that Ruth intended to leave the campus, she said that she would go too, and Ruth was obliged to reason with her all the way from Burlington to South Harland, before she could be persuaded to remain.

"I am sure that Elsie Dane will like to have me

149

with her," she argued, " and, O Chris, you know that you would n't like to cook your own breakfast! "

" You could cook it," said Christine, gloomily, " and I would eat it."

" It will be so pleasant for you in the Hadley, with all those nice girls; and I will come up and see you every day, and you can have all your suppers with us. But, my poor darling, who will ever make you wake up in the morning? I 'm afraid that you won't wake up at all."

" I can pretend that the rising-bell is tied to a great savage cow, who is coming right up into my room," said Christine, dismally, " and I can pretend that I 've been awake a long time."

They were both searching for a cheerful side of this situation which would keep them from each other, but consolation was not to be found.

On the following evening they were sitting in Number 2 Hadley, with all Ruth's belongings packed into a box, ready to be moved the next day. Elsie Dane was enthusiastic over the prospect of having a companion; for Marjorie was gone now, and she had been dreading the long weeks alone, with nobody to be glad when she came home, or to say " I am sorry " when her little feet were wet and tired.

" We can have the other room now," she said in delight. " I gave it up when Marjorie went away, because I could n't afford two; but it is horrid to cook and sleep in the same room. You have no idea! One dreams of beefsteak, and then wakes up to find it is n't true."

Christine's mouth quivered when she looked around those little rooms which she had first entered as a Freshman, two years ago. They seemed so much more desolate when connected with the thought that Ruth was to live in them. There was the little gas-stove, the second-hand desk, and the home-made bookcase with its curtains of chintz.

" All of our pretty things belonged to Marjorie," said Elizabeth, briskly, " and she had to take them away with her, because the inevitable aunt wanted them for her parlor. Of course she's been good to Marjorie, and ought to have the things, but it makes the room look rather bare."

Christine tried to remember if she had ever seen anything pretty about the room, and decided that she did not know what Elizabeth meant.

That afternoon she sent Ruth out to drive with Clare; Elizabeth was off tutoring somewhere, and she had the field to herself. First she engaged an express cart, stripped her room of everything which was portable, and had it carried down to the lodging-house of Mrs. Barstow. She hung the familiar pictures upon the walls, festooned red cheesecloth in a marvellous manner, so as to conceal holes and cracks in the plastering, and put divan covers on both beds. She placed the " Narcissus" upon a new little table in the corner, and stood off to look at him. She discovered that the sewing-machine was rented by the week from Mrs. Barstow, and arranged to make it a permanent feature of the establishment upstairs. When everything was finished, she went wearily forth again, bought a little set of china, ordered a supper to be sent in, and placed flowers on the table.

Elizabeth Dane was the first to return. Her shoes

were muddy, for she had walked over to a school in Hadley to make arrangements for teaching there two afternoons in the week, and they were not going to pay her so much as she had hoped. When she saw the "Narcissus" and the flowers and the other things, she began to weep, and said that Christine should take them all back again. But Christine pulled off the muddy boots, pushed a piece of cake into Elizabeth's mouth, and said that if she, Elsie, cared for her, Christine, she would retract those unkind words about taking them back.

Soon Clare and Ruth came in, for Clare was in the plot, and had received instructions not to return before six o'clock, and there was a merry, tearful, affectionate time, which may have been silly, but was certainly a credit to every one of them.

"Come, Elsie, you're neglecting your duty as hostess," said Christine, as Ruth embraced the "Narcissus," and vowed that he should be sent back the next day. "Supper is on the table, and the oysters are getting cold."

"Christine Arnold, do you mean to say that you have actually invested in oysters?" exclaimed Elizabeth, lifting the cover of a dish. "Ah! sweet-breads and French peas! If it is not good to be alive. And cream celery! Christine, I'm almost sure that I saw a can of ice-cream in the hall downstairs. Tell me if I did."

"They sent it over too early, then," laughed Christine, "but now for chapter one." And the party of four sat down to the dearest, merriest, most pathetic little supper that ever was given in Harland College.

After everything eatable had disappeared, the girls brought out a schedule, and discussed electives, for recitations did not begin until to-morrow, and no one had any studying to do. It was a delightful evening, although Ruth had to stop talking now and then, because her voice would tremble; and when it was all over, Clare and Christine walked home together through the warm September night.

"She never suspected anything,—the dear!" said Clare. "She thought that it was I who asked her to drive."

They did not feel like saying very much, and when Christine reached the door of Number 2 Hadley, she stopped and waited for a minute, before she opened it. It was dark and desolate and bare, the pretty room that had always been so full of light and flowers. But there was no Ruth here now, and nothing to make one feel at home.

"I am a pig!" said Christine, thoughtfully, "I was always a pig;" and she sat down, like "His Wife's Father" on a left-over dry-goods box, in the middle of the room.

The next morning chapel was crowded, and they sang, "If o'er unruffled seas towards heaven we calmly sail," a favorite hymn with all the girls, but Christine thought that it did not apply to any one she knew! The opening exercises were more serious than usual, for the members of Ninety-four felt their responsibility as Seniors, and Ninety-six had resolved to be better Sophomores than some other people whom they might have mentioned. Every one extended a helping hand to pretty Ninety-seven, which had already begun to cherish an unreasonable

153

admiration for the class of Ninety-five. In fact, the whole college was watching with uncertainty to see what Ninety-five would do next; and in a very few days it found out.

The Juniors proclaimed new principles of rigorous discipline, and began to "bring up" the Freshmen! They obtained permission from the President to prevent students from taking books into chapel, and every morning two Juniors stood outside the door to see that this rule was enforced. It was a good rule, because it insured exemplary behavior during the exercises, and the upper-class girls were delighted with it. Then came the Junior presidential election, which was a source of interest to many people, because it was uncertain which way it would turn. The two final candidates were Ardis Hathaway and Christine Arnold, and as the friends of one were the friends of both, no one seemed to know how she ought to vote.

"I think Christine would make the best President," said Mildred Wyman, who was in the Marston, "but I won't vote against Ardis Hathaway, so I'm out of it."

"There is no doubt about who wants it most," said Kate Dervish, with a laugh; and Philippa Fairbank added, "No, I really do not think that Miss Arnold would object to the position!"

It was true that this unexpected nomination had aroused a storm of class loyalty and ambition in Christine, which she did not try to conceal. It was such a violent reaction from the experience of her Sophomore year that at first she could not realize what it meant. "Is it possible that Ninety-five still

154

wants me?" she thought. "Does it think that I could be an honor to my class?"

She regained all her old vivacity and enthusiasm in a few days, although she kept saying to herself, "I shall not get it, I know I cannot get it. I must not let myself think that I shall get it."

The other candidate had said from the first that she did not care for the position; but Christine worked for her loyally, until Ardis herself asked her, with some impatience, to desist.

"I don't want it," she said; "it would bore me to death, and in fact I won't have it. You had much better take it when you can get it, Christabel, for such a thing is not always to be had for the asking!"

Christine was touched, and yet wondered that Ardis should give up such an opportunity without a struggle. It was another of her eccentricities, no doubt, for one could never tell what she would do. "But it is so unlike her not to want it," Christine thought, "she is fond of having power, and likes to exercise it. I wonder —"

She went down to see Ardis that afternoon, and said: "It has occurred to me that you may be withholding yourself from this position, because — well, because you want me to have it. Ardis, tell me, is that true?"

Ardis' face never changed, and she continued to look at Christine with those impenetrable eyes.

"I say that I don't want it, because I don't want it," she answered. "What would be the use of deception in such a matter? Life is too short, as well as too ridiculous, to make a fuss about little things; and in a hundred years from now, what difference will it make what girl we had for a President?"

"Everything makes a difference!" said Christine; but she was too much excited to discuss the philosophy of the situation, and went away satisfied that Ardis did not care about the election, after all.

"And if I should get it," she thought pitifully, "I think it would make me feel more worthy — no, not really worthy, but more worthy of papa and the boys."

When she had gone, Clare slipped into the room and put her arms around Ardis' neck.

The election was held in the old Gymnasium, and when the Juniors went upstairs, they were obliged to make their way through a little group of Seniors and Sophomores who were waiting in the lower hall, to hear what President would be chosen by the class of Ninety-five. Ardis and Christine were almost the last to arrive. They came over the campus, arm in arm, as they always did, and spoke to some of the girls in the hall before going upstairs.

"It seems to have made no difference in their friendship," said one of the Seniors; and a little Sophomore who had been considering the question for some time said, "Perhaps that's what it means to be friends!"

The voting was very close, and the girls outside waited in vain for the customary burst of applause. The first ballot had resulted in a small majority for Ardis, and the last two had ended with a tie.

"This will never do," said Elsie Dane, rapping impatiently on the table; "you know we must have a two-thirds vote, to elect the President, and at present we are no nearer to deciding the matter than we were when we came in."

There was a buzz of excitement in the back of the room, and Elizabeth thought that an element of rage was creeping into the discussion.

"I understood that Ardis had decided not to run for President," said Kathleen, indignantly, to a Marston House girl. "Did she tell you all to work for her?"

"Certainly not," answered Miss Bentley, with dignity; "but when we all said that we were working for her, she did not tell us to stop."

"She knew that we were working for her," said Mildred Wyman. "Of course she knew that the whole Marston would go for her, and the Lathrop too, being so near, and then she has friends in the Warren."

"Three houses won't carry an election, girl!" said Kathleen, forgetting to be polite, "and I myself have canvassed every other house on the campus, — Storey, Wyndham, Warren — hm-m, I forgot the Fairbank contingent in the Warren."

"The Fairbank contingent controls a number of votes, however," said Philippa, who had been listening to the conversation. "I suppose you will concede us the enviable privilege of voting for whom we like."

"Vote for your grandmother!" said Kathleen, in a blaze of wrath. "It is not the class of Ninety-five that would demean itself by accepting any vote from you with regard to any matter."

"Are all the votes in?" called Elizabeth, from the platform; and when some had answered "Yes," she said, "The polls are closed."

Ruth and Rachel Winter were distributing the

significant bits of white paper among the girls, and Kathleen insisted upon knowing what they had discovered on their rounds.

" As far as I can find out," said Ruth, " the girls who know both of them well, are voting for Christine, and the girls who live off the campus, or who don't know either of them, are voting for Ardis."

" The freak faction is going strong for Ardis," said Rachel, with emphasis. " They say that they do not want a ' society girl ' for their President; but I 'd like to know if Ardis is n't even more in the rush than Christine, and every one knows what a good student Christine is."

" They don't know what they do want," said Ruth, indignantly, " but I wish they 'd decide upon somebody before to-morrow morning. Look at those dear children sitting there together as if nothing was going on! I don't think that I ever admired any two creatures so much in my life."

Christine and Ardis were engaged in discussing "The Deemster," and had just begun to disagree about the character of " Danny," when the President arose from her chair and said, " Miss Arnold has sixty-five votes, Miss Hathaway fifty-one."

Christine turned very white, and Ardis tried to appear unconcerned, but a look flashed over her face which Christine had never seen before. She told Ruth afterwards : " It was as if the shadow of some horrible wriggling thing had passed over her face, and then left it just as it was before. For a minute I did not know her." But Christine knew herself, and before Elizabeth could call in another ballot, she had risen to her feet.

"WHAT IT MEANS TO BE FRIENDS"

"Miss President," she said, "I move that the vote be made unanimous in favor of Miss Hathaway."

Ardis sprang up beside her and said, "Christabel, you sha'n't do it!"

Elsie Dane looked ready to cry, but said, "This proceeding is entirely unconstitutional. Is any one ready to second Miss Arnold's motion?"

There was no response, and after a moment of silence she asked again, "Is any one ready to second the motion?"

Christine turned slowly around until her eyes met Ruth's, and Ruth did as she was told, because that look had trusted her.

"I second the motion," she said quietly; and for a minute the echo of a footstep over by Lincoln Hall could be distinctly heard throughout the room. Some one laughed in the road outside, Elizabeth Dane began to speak, — stopped to steady her voice, and then said, "Will all those who are in favor of this motion signify it by saying 'Aye'?"

Christine's friends were terribly disappointed, but they loved her enough to do as she wished; and while the two girls stood there arm in arm before their class, Ardis was elected President of Ninety-five. The meeting broke up then; but as Ruth said afterwards to a Senior friend, "We were most of us pretty well broken up before that."

Ardis was overwhelmed with congratulations from enthusiastic Seniors, admiring under-class girls, and members of her own class who had voted against her, not because they wanted her less, but because they wanted Christine more.

"How beautiful she will look at the Junior-Senior

reception!" said Christine, as Ruth and Kathleen escorted her home; and suddenly Ruth remembered that she had never before heard Christine allude in any way to the beauty of her friend. She had spoken of her fine mind, of her high principles, and of her unusual gifts, but never before of her beauty. Ruth wondered if there were not something significant in the fact that she mentioned it now.

"What I don't like about Ardis," said Kathleen, "is that she had people working for her in every direction, and then gave out that she wouldn't be hired to run for President."

"How dare you imply that Ardis would be dishonorable?" said Christine, fiercely. "She told me herself that she did not want — I don't believe that she asked people to work for her. It would be impossible. And even if she asked them not to, they wouldn't stop for what she said."

"For my part, dear," said Ruth, "I would like to shake you, if, unfortunately, you had not made me love you more than ever before."

"And I myself should enjoy throwing you over a wall," said Kathleen, amiably, "if it wasn't that so doing would make you on the other side of it from me!"

When Christine reached her room, she was much cheered by finding an anonymous plate of ploughed field, sticky, voluminous, comforting, upon her bed, and it was labelled, "For the finest girl in Ninety-five!"

That night Ardis could not sleep, and Clare was unable to comfort her.

"It is all wrong," she cried. "It is all, all wrong!

But I did try to give it up to her. You know that I tried, and when the time came, I was weak and could n't. No, I could n't, because I had not the courage to be defeated. Clare, if you knew me as I am, you would not come near me."

"You could not both be elected," said Clare, quietly, "and one of you had to withdraw."

"Yes; and I let the younger one do it. I let Christine, after— Oh, Clare, the shadows in me are deeper than I knew. Oh, I hate myself, for I am a coward, — a coward, a coward!"

And that night, and the days that followed, brought no joy to the President of Ninety-five.

CHAPTER XII

SUNDAY is bounded on the north by Saturday night, and on the south by Monday morning, so it is natural that one should remember these two boundaries in recalling the characteristics of a certain day.

Christine had spent a restless Saturday evening on the back campus, in spite of the fact that five different people had invited her to open meeting of Phi Delta Kappa, and there was to be a lecture by Professor Waring Sims on "The Rise of the Drama." But she happened to be in a wild, unliterary mood, and preferred to investigate the darkness of the campus, with its uncertain slopes and many winding paths. Her love of darkness was inexplicable to people who could not understand the joy of being out alone with the strange night-cries and the great sighing trees; but Christine had found the answer to many questions in the companionship of trees, and they had been her friends from the time when she was young enough to live in them, like a little dryad, and be tossed in their strong arms. She made new acquaintances in every place, and her calling-list was large; but the most cordial of all the tree-friends lived on the back campus at college. She liked to start out at night, when it was so dark that she had to guide herself by the rough gravel of the paths, and when the trees were nothing but mysterious sounds. This evening, as she passed the Marston, its great elm was swirling in wind and shadow; but one branch caught the light from the kitchen window, and looked as if it had been hung with tiny lanterns.

"I will come over to-morrow," she thought, "and ask Clare." But she could not have told what it was that she wanted to ask. She only knew that it was something about the Great Reason Why.

The next morning was perfect, for the month of October likes to make Sunday a day for knowing God out of doors, a time for seeking Him through the mysteries of air and light; and the girls who went for early walks came in with those very mysteries of light in their eyes.

When prayer-meeting at the Hadley was over, Christine started out "to ask Clare;" and first she passed the Warren, where they were singing, "Oh, love divine, that stooped to share;" then the Lathrop, where she heard, "Lord, Thy glory fills the heavens;" and it took her back to Freshman year, when all things were possible and disappointments had not come. At the Marston they were singing, "In the hour of trial, Jesus, plead for me;" and she slipped up to Clare's room, where the hymn stayed with her until Clare came.

"Christine, you dear morning bird," she cried, when she opened the door, "I was just about to hie me across the campus and ask you down to dinner, and, behold, here you are. Our conversational talent is going out to dine at the Wyndham, but if you won't find it too dull without her, we want you to come."

"If 'we' means you, I will come," said Christine, laughing; "I want to see you, Clare."

"Do you, really? Why, how nice, how absolutely dear in you! I was afraid you would think it a bore."

She began to put the room in order, and said with a laugh: "Ardis and Maude Gilbert are having breakfast in Maude's room, and they've borrowed all my dishes, to say nothing of my table linen and hardware. I only hope they'll bring them back, and I also hope that they'll wash them first."

"Do you like Maude Gilbert?" asked Christine, who enjoyed hearing Clare evade a question of this kind.

"No," was the quick answer; and then she added: "Perhaps I ought not to say that. No, I suppose that I ought not to have said it; but I can't help thinking that Maude's influence upon Ardis is not very good."

"Do you think that Ardis is particularly amenable to influence? It seems to me that the utmost one could do would be to take the bad part of her aside, and ask it, as a special favor, not to interfere with the good."

Clare laughed. "Well, perhaps you are right, but it worries me a little."

"Don't make other people so much a part of yourself, child. Try to remember that sympathy is quite fatal to happiness."

"Oh, but I am happy," said Clare, with a smile, "and one likes to be sympathetic, now that Christ has been born."

"You speak as if that happened yesterday, Clare."

"It happens every day, does n't it?"

"Not with everybody. I think that the real love of Christ, the knowledge of his personality, is born in a person, like a talent, and cannot be acquired."

"Then you think it is not necessary for two people to know each other in order to become friends?"

"Tangible friendships are different," said Christine.

"But friendship itself is not tangible. Our love for our friends is part of the same material with which we love God."

"And do you really *love* God? What do you mean by the word God, Clare?"

"What do *you* mean by it, Christine?"

"I don't know, but please don't think I'm an Atheist, or anything of that kind. I believe, of course, that there must have been an original plan, but somehow I've missed — the friendliness of it all."

"What do you consider the greatest thing in the universe? There must be some one thing that you respect most of all."

"Why, — force," answered Christine, after a pause. "Force is what moves the world."

"Well, and is n't there something besides force in our great working apparatus? Force is what makes a horse run away; and a greater quantity of the same quality would make the world run away."

"I suppose there must be some restraining power, some kind of unity," admitted Christine, "but force and unity cannot make a God."

"I don't know what else they could make. Unity, which means the one, combined with force, which means the activity of all. What greater God could one have?"

"But that does not include intelligence, or that quality of love which you attribute to the God you know."

"I do not think that unity and force have ever been combined, without the assistance of intelligence to begin with. That order of things by which every trivial part works in relation to one magnificent whole, and never forgets, never goes wrong — "

There was a knock at the door, and Maude Gilbert came in, bringing Clare's household belongings, which consisted of three plates and a saucer, one red napkin, and a kerosene stove.

"Thank you very much for the use of them," she said. "If you had known how good our breakfast was, you would n't have thrown us over for a prayer-meeting."

"It was n't that I would n't rather have had the breakfast," said Clare, honestly; "but, you see, I was needed at the prayer-meeting."

"You would have been willing to do the wrong thing, then, if there had been anybody to take your place in the right, was that it?" laughed Maude, as Clare relieved her of the dishes.

"No," answered Clare, with spirit; "it would not have been wrong for me to have breakfast with you this morning, if there had been any one else to play, but there was n't, you know; so I had to."

"After all," said Maude, "you 're a good little thing. Are n't you coming in to see Ardis this morning, Miss Arnold?"

"I came to see Clare," answered Christine, who thought it was none of Miss Gilbert's business.

When she had gone, Clare said: "It is the fate of

all arguments in college to be interrupted. Now, how far had we got when she came in? We were saying that — "

" That God might be the infinite intelligence as well as the infinite force, — but what I can't understand is the personal part of it all. I never could feel the personality of God."

" But you have," said Clare, triumphantly, "although you may not have known it. Christine, do you like trees ? "

" Better than I like people. But what made you think of that ? "

" Because, next to people, there is more of God in trees than in anything else."

There was another knock at the door, and Ardis came in, dressed for church.

" Good morning, Christabel," she said. " I am surprised that you should deliberately keep Clare from attending the sanctuary, when I know how firmly you believe in having other people go to church. But if you are not going, Clare, may I borrow your prayer-book ? "

" Why, of course. No, Christine, it's all right; I don't want to go. Oh, Ardis, you are lovely this morning! Wait only one minute, and let us see you."

Ardis laughed, for she knew that Clare loved her beauty as she loved the trees and flowers and sky, and remembered that she had once said, " It does not belong to you at all, but to God."

Her dress this morning was long and close-fitting, of black cloth trimmed with tan, and she wore a large black hat, with a soft crown and two or three curling feathers. Her face behind the veil was fair and sweet, and the two girls who looked at her knew that she was like music. "I am coming back from the Wyndham at three o'clock," she said, drawing on her gloves, "and Christine is going to walk out to the bridge with me, are n't you, Christabel? Good-bye, children. I 'm sure that I know what you were talking about;" and she softly closed the door behind her, leaving in the room that effect of vanished sunshine which some unworthy people are destined to produce.

"Sometimes when Ardis leaves me I cannot help rushing out to call her back," said Clare, "and when she asks, 'What do you want of me?' I can only say, 'Nothing;' and then she laughs."

A shadow had passed over Christine's face, but she asked, "Why did you say that we could find God in trees, Clare?"

"The thankfulness that we feel in having the trees to look at is to love God," was the answer. "I believe that we will never be able to live without God in great joy, because you see it is necessary to have some one to thank. The people who really do not feel God must be the people who find no beauty in this beautiful world."

"Where did you get your philosophy, Clare?"

"Out of doors, mostly; but it has all been found and thought before."

"I am not so sure of that; but I 'm glad that you are willing to tell me your reasons for things. I was afraid that you might be like a little star that could n't give the recipe for its own light."

"There is more to a star than its silence," said Clare, looking amused; "so you must n't say that I

am like one, only because I don't talk all the time.
But I've always thought that even if the spiritual
part of ourselves can live on faith alone, the material
side demands reason; and it is only when faith and
reason are combined that we learn to understand the
'friendliness of it all.'"

There came another knock, and Clare said, " Don't
be discouraged, Christine. Come in!"

The intruder was Leonora Kent, one of those quietly
persistent workers who are seldom known by their
fellow-students until the last, — when some one accidentally discovers that they have taken the highest
marks. She was part of the steady and sturdy
material on which the success of a brilliant class is
always founded, and one of the people who helped
prove from day to day that *Ana* (upward), their
class motto, had meant something to the girls of
Ninety-five.

"I came to see if you and Ardis could help us at
the little chapel to-night," she said. "If Ardis would
only sing something, and you would play, we could
have a delightful meeting."

"I can't promise for Ardis," said Clare, "but I
think she will do it; and I'll come anyhow, Leonora,
if I can be of the least use."

"You are a comfort," was the grateful answer. "It
is really discouraging sometimes, or would be, if
there were not always a few people like you in the
world."

"I don't believe you know about the chapel," said
Clare, turning to Christine. "Tell her, Nora."

" Why, there is n't much to tell," began Miss Kent,
" but you know that the French quarter up there by

the Hospital is — well, they don't go to church very often, and there is a little forsaken chapel there that we are allowed to use. So every Sunday afternoon we — I mean Beatrice Adams and Philippa Fairbank and a few others — hold little services there for the children who cannot come down into the town. At first it was hard work, for nobody came; but now we are getting more and more, and it is so dear to hear them sing."

"They also have musical meetings, parents included, every third Sunday night," added Clare. " I sha'n't allow Leonora to omit her own statistics."

" The right hand of this glorious college does not know what the left hand does," said Christine, with enthusiasm. "Leonora, I never suspected that we had a philanthropist on the ball team."

"Some of the Sophomores are helping us now," said Leonora, "and we are so glad, because they will be likely to keep it up after we're gone. Come and see us some time, Christine. It's a dismal enough place, or I should have invited you before."

" Did you think that misery and I could not agree?" asked Christine, with a smile. "There you are wrong. But I'll come up to-night, Nora, if I may. And if there is anything that you need, I do hope you will let me know."

"'Anything that we need,'" repeated Leonora; and then she flushed.

"They have scarcely any hymn-books," said Clare, pitifully, "and the plaster will keep falling down from the ceiling; and they have no pictures on the walls — not a one."

"Oh," said Christine, "Leonora, why have n't you

told every one in the college about this? Why have n't you asked us all to help you?"

"Because we did not want to beg. Our time was our own, to dispose of as we liked, and that we could give; but we made up our minds, from the first, that we would n't ask for money."

Christine's feelings were so perturbed by all this, that she hastily arose and went home, having previously explained that she was coming back to the Marston for dinner.

"I suppose that Leonora represents what is called the 'freak faction' in our class," she thought, with a burning spot on each cheek. "She is not in the rush. She is not even in a literary society, and yet she manages to exist."

When dinner was over at the Marston, Clare asked a few of the girls to come into her room, and have some fresh gingersnaps, which had come from home yesterday, in company with a new dress. They were all girls whom Christine liked, and while Clare made the tea, they discussed the first number of the "Prism," — their college magazine, which had just been started, under the auspices of Miss Carlisle.

"The 'Prism' has as good a staff of editors as could be expected, when one considers that it is 'conducted by the Senior Class,'" said Mildred Wyman, cracking a gingersnap. "But I wish that Miss Carlisle had n't made 'our Maude' editor-in-chief."

"Our Maude is a very bright girl, nevertheless," said Faith Bentley; "and no one could say that her editorial is not original."

"I am particularly proud of the alumnæ department" said Christine, passing the sugar. "It is like a genial little college cemetery, in which we shall all meet when we are things of the past."

" Are you taking Junior Lit? " asked Faith, turning to Christine.

" Now, Fay, you did that on purpose," said Florence Homer. " You want to lead up to the fact that Madame Rigault called me a ' silly little girl ' this morning before the whole class ! "

" Be quiet, Ninety-six ! "said Faith. " Nobody gets through college without receiving one or more insults from that dear woman, and the fact that you mind them proves that you 're still a Sophomore. When you 're older you 'll find that she does n't mean a word of it."

" I don't care, though," persisted Florence. " I think that if she would treat the girls like women, they would n't behave like children."

" That may be true," said Faith, thoughtfully. " But I like her just the same. There 's a tonic element about her, like frosty air that bites at the same time that it stimulates."

" Yes," assented Christine, " the keenness of her mind always suggests the sparkle of very cool champagne."

" Only it is n't safe to pull the cork unless you know your lesson," said Clare, demurely.

" Don't talk shop," said Mildred, who was an energetic young person. " Besides, it 's Sunday. Let 's organize a secret society."

" To keep somebody out? " asked Florence; and Mildred answered, " Of course."

" We will call it the Society for Defeated Candidates," said Christine, " and the advantage of organizing it to-day will be that we can all hold offices. There will be enough to go around."

Clare took Christine's hand suddenly and kissed it, and the girls said, " Miss Arnold shall be our President ! "

" I was defeated for President, Freshman year," objected Mildred, " and if I can't be at least a Vice-President, I won't play."

" I was defeated for Secretary in the Symposium " (the Scientific Society), said Faith. " Does n't that count? "

" Let me be Treasurer," joined in Florence, " because somebody said once that she thought I'd make a good one."

" What am I ? " asked Clare, meekly. " I was never defeated for anything because I was never proposed, so I can't be in the society."

" You shall be defeated now," said Christine with sympathy. " We will defeat you for Vice-President so that you can be appointed Assistant Treasurer. Friends, I move that Miss Deland be elected Vice-President of our society. Contrary-minded? "

" No," came in a unanimous chorus. " Now, Miss Deland, you are legally entitled to membership, and I hereby appoint you Assistant Treasurer of the Society for Defeated Candidates, S. F. D. C., emblem to be a bit of sackcloth and an ash."

" But how about the constitution? " inquired Faith. " Are n't we going to have one? "

" Yes, indeed," said Christine. " I 'll write it now. Just wait a minute."

She went to Clare's desk and presently emerged with the following document: —

ACROSS THE CAMPUS

Article I. No person proposed for the Society can be black-balled more than three times in the same week.

Article II. One person must be black-balled at every meeting, and a notice of the same sent to that person within two days.

Article III. The Society shall have picnics.

" Now," said Christine, rapping on the table, " we must black-ball somebody immediately. Who shall it be? "

" Let it not be through the infamous bean," said Faith.

" ' I thirst for blood,' " said Mildred.

" ' I long for gore,' " said Florence.

" Hear! hear! " cried the society. But as Ardis came in at that minute, to claim Christine for the afternoon walk, the Defeated Candidates adjourned without further ceremony.

Christine wondered if Ardis would say anything about the Junior election; for the subject had not been mentioned between them since that memorable afternoon, and she was beginning to feel a little sore. We all know that when we have made a tremendous sacrifice for some person, our affection for that person is sure to increase, and it increases inversely with the amount of gratitude that we receive in return.

" Christine," said Ardis, when they had been walking for some time in silence, " the most interesting thing about life is to see how other people take it."

" I don't agree with you," said Christine.

" Good," returned Ardis, with a laugh. " Now that we have begun, it will be easy to continue. I

A COLLEGE SUNDAY

have been trying to define to myself the different kinds of dislike that one person can feel. What do you think about it?"

"I think that one kind is more than sufficient for one person, and that it should be the kind which leads one to take refuge in total abstinence."

"No," said Ardis, "I don't think that the term 'dislike' can be applied to the feeling that we have for everybody."

"I should hope not!" interrupted her companion.

"The term 'dislike,' continued Ardis, "applies to the people whom we don't respect, and to those whom we find personally objectionable. The term 'hate' applies to antagonistic people, whom we are forced to respect, and to those whom we have loved but love no longer."

"Ardis," said Christine, gloomily, "why all these sinister classifications? You used to laugh at me Freshman year, because I found too many people 'personally objectionable,' and yet I sported but one kind of dislike."

"I laughed at you because you disliked them so absurdly and ineffectually. It made no difference to any one whether you disliked her or not; but now — well, it does make a difference, and I, for one, intend to exercise my privileges. It gives one a sense of power."

"But not any other kind of power," said Christine. "Power, Ardis, is the greater opportunity for doing good or ill, — not a rat-trap."

"You are looking at the merely objective side of power, and the instrument to which you refer is irrelevant."

175

"What I mean, Ardis, is that power seems to trap certain people in the meshes of themselves, just as it sets other people free. But the world is, after all, a disappointing place."

"The objective side of power implies watching continually to see what will happen. It does not necessitate much thought."

"But what happens, and especially what has happened, may be held responsible for much of our thought, if not of our being," said Christine. "One has to be objective to get anything done."

"Being entirely objective is like looking out of the window to watch the carriages go by."

"It isn't," said Christine, exasperated; "it's like picking out a carriage with a good spirited pair of horses, and driving it yourself."

Ardis thought that Christine was not in a receptive mood, and changed the subject; but each concluded that the other had deteriorated, and the rest of their walk was not a success.

When they reached home the bell was ringing for vespers, and they slipped into a back row of seats, regardless of the pretty usher, who wished to give them superior places in front.

The President of Harland is particularly impressive at vespers, and the townspeople who wish to hear him are not always sure of finding a seat in the crowded hall. Many of the Wyckham students come over to these services, returning to their college so early in the evening that the matrons of the Harland campus do not feel constrained to turn out the lights before they are gone. The music is never so fine as when united with the "funda-

mental" of the men's voices, and the whole service
is so beautiful that misunderstandings soon become
absorbed in its peaceful atmosphere, and vanish quite
away. The closing hymn that night was "Saviour,
again to thy dear name we raise," and when it was
finished, the two big little girls in the back of the hall
were at variance no longer.

Ardis sang at the little chapel on the hill that
evening, and Clare played her accompaniments on a
wheezy melodeon. The front seats were filled with
a rapturous audience of small children, who listened
while she sang, sighed spasmodically when she finished, then punched each other in the ribs and
giggled. Leonora called them to order, and the
meeting ended with a hymn beginning, —

> "There's a work for me, and a wur-r-k for you,
> Something for each of us now to do,"

which made Christine feel insignificant.

"Leonora," she said, as the girls drove out the last
of their little flock and locked the door, "I'll see
about the plastering and I'll see about the pictures
too. No, don't thank me; I don't deserve it."

"Christine," called Clare from the foot of the steps,
"won't you walk down with me?" And presently
they started off together, while Ardis and Leonora
brought up the rear with a troop of small boys, who
were quite open-mouthed in their admiration of the
strange lady.

It was a beautiful moonlight night, and before
long the two girls had left their companions far
behind.

"Clare," began Christine, drearily, "do you think

that we ought to be condemned for falling over obstacles that are placed in our path, — things that we could n't help at all?"

"I don't think that we shall be judged for falling over the obstacles, but for the way in which we take the bumps. Don't you remember, Confucius says 'Our greatest glory is not in never falling, but in rising every time we fall.'"

"Such a quotation is like a hot-water bag to the emotions," said Christine, solemnly.

"No; but, seriously speaking, don't you think that our badness results from the privilege of choice? And is n't this privilege, after all, our greatest glory? Does n't the very fact that God gave us the option of choosing between right and wrong show that He had some faith in us?"

"But He must have been able to look ahead and see that we would not be worthy of that. faith."

"Oh dear, I suppose so! But, Christine, He must have known, when He gave us reason, that we would make mistakes. He must have known that we would experiment in every direction, with our own little outfits of creative power. Nature is the only thing that never makes a mistake. And yet I would rather have my share of incomplete reason, which continually leads me astray, than be part of a great Instinct that works according to fixed laws."

"Then the answer to the 'Great Question Why' is, 'Make the most of the best that is in us,'" said Christine. "We don't think about that often enough, Clare, not half often enough. We want other people's mosts, you know, — the kind that gets recognition and praise. But we ought not to go back on

178

our own, I suppose. After all, it *is* our own. It would be lonely if we did n't care."

" Very, very lonely," said Clare. "It is like a child, you see."

"And to despise what is best in ourselves is almost like despising God. Clare," she added suddenly, " I like to hear you talk about this Friend of yours ! "

The next morning, while Christine was arranging her room, Clare came in with a note from Ardis, which she said demanded an immediate answer. Christine tore it open and read : —

The Phi Delta Kappa Society of Harland College extends a cordial invitation to Miss Arnold to become one of its members. An answer is desired.

ARDIS HATHAWAY, *Sec'y.*

And this was the end of that college Sunday.

CHAPTER XIII

NUMBER 2 HADLEY

RUTH and Christine were studying their Physics together in Number 2 Hadley, and Christine was saying, —

"I don't see how the centre of gravity can fall outside of the object to which it belongs, even if the object *does* happen to be in unstable equilibrium. How can any object tell which its own centre of gravity is, when there are a lot of them lying around? I should n't think it would be safe to let a thing like that get loose, anyhow."

"Christine, if you are not good, I won't help you any more!"

"Well, let 's take Logic for a while, then. I wish to go forth and slay an illicit major."

"Very well," said Ruth, opening her Jevons, "what are you going to give in class to-morrow as an example of undistributed middle?" .

"A sofa-pillow. Oh, Ruth, how did you know beforehand that I was in Phi Delta Kappa, when we are all pledged not to tell?"

"I knew it from Elsie's face when she came home that night. She tried to appear gloomy and depressed, but I arose in my wrath and said, 'Elizabeth Dane, do you mean to say that you can walk into my room looking like that, and tell me that my room-mate is not in Phi Delta Kappa?' She gave me one big hug, but did n't say a word, and then we both stood on our heads for ten minutes and went to bed. We did n't either of us come near you Sunday, because we did n't dare."

"Ruth, who do you suppose stopped to congratulate me to-day when I was coming out of Lincoln Hall? Professor Burton! Was n't that nice in him? And I have never been in any of his classes, either."

The young Zoölogy professor was one of whom the college was particularly proud, because he wrote articles for the "Weekly Lamellibranch," and had discovered enough new legs, arms, whiskers, and other decorations, on various insects, to have made an entirely new genus if the fragments could have been properly combined. He knew people at the Smithsonian, and was respectfully spoken of by all the scientific magazines; but the best part of him was that he was only twenty-six years old, and remembered everything funny that he had ever seen or heard. He and his father lived alone in a little three-gabled house, and always went to vespers and Glee Club concerts together. They were very good friends indeed, and might be seen walking down Elm Street, arm in arm, on any fine afternoon. Sometimes they gave chafing-dish parties, and it was said that no one could cook oysters better than old Dr. Burton. He ranked next to Professor Thorne's children in the affection of the college, and was asked to everything that went on. The old man always had a seat in the front row at Dramatics, and stamped and applauded vigorously. He was very fond of Ardis Hathaway, because she was pretty, and one night when she took part in a Marston House play, he brought her a little bunch of violets.

"Do you know," said Ruth, "I believe that the Faculty are more interested in us than we have any idea of! They have been so good to me, every one of them, since — all this came." There was a knock at the door, and one of the maids put her head into the room.

"Please, Miss Arnold, Datisi's having a fit in the coal-scuttle!"

Christine rushed downstairs, leaving Ruth to think that she had become suddenly daft; but presently she returned, carrying an infuriated ball of fur, which spit violently when released, and shot under the bed.

"It's my new room-mate," said Christine, quietly, "and it wasn't having a fit at all. It was only playing with the coal."

Ruth looked at her in absolute consternation.

"I was lonely; that is all," she explained. "I don't think it agrees with me — not having any one to talk to."

"Oh, Christine, you haven't been as lonely as that! Don't tell me that you have been so lonely as all that;" and Ruth looked ready to cry, but a faint growl from under the bed made her laugh instead; and then came the rattle, rattle of a spool against the washstand.

"My room-mate is sportive, you perceive," said Christine, with a wave of the hand. "I knew it to be sportive, from the fact that when we first met, it was fanning itself with a bone."

"Christine, where did you find that animal?"

"Up on Hospital Hill. I was taking one of my solitary strolls, when I perceived the leg of Datisi's mother disappearing under a barn. I gave instant chase, and, behold, as I drew near, two round and cobwebby balls dashed away in the maternal direction. But one of these happened to fall into a saucer of milk on the way, and while it tarried to sneeze, I grasped it firmly by the tail. Incidentally this led to my concealing the feline in my muff and bringing him home."

"But will Mrs. Sawyer let you keep him?"

"Certainly. She said that the mice had been having midnight spreads in the pantry, and the very presence of Datisi would put their lights out at ten o'clock. Is n't Datisi a nice name? It's short for Barbara, Celarent, Darii, Ferio *que prioris ;* otherwise Bramantip; page 145, Jevons' Logic. I thought that it would be easier to remember the formula, if it happened to be my room-mate's name."

"Bramantip seems to be of a warlike disposition," said Ruth, laughing, as the growls increased in a rapid crescendo, and the spool rolled out from under the bed.

"Oh, he growls when he's pleased. I think that must be it, because, the other day when I washed him with tar soap, he purred."

There came another knock, and Christine received a call from the editor of Phi Delta Kappa, who wanted a paper for the next meeting. She said that "anything would do," but Christine understood perfectly well that it would n't. She also thought that it would be bold and unseemly to have a paper read at her first meeting, and said so; but the editor was persistent and finally departed in triumph, with a little sketch which Miss Carlisle had marked " Excellent."

" I think I'll go home," said Ruth, gathering up her books. "The oppressive quiet of this room is ' getting monotonous,' as the Western man said when the mule fell through the roof for the ninth time."

On the night of Christine's first society meeting, Ardis called for her, and they went over to College Hall together. Miss Carlisle heard them come downstairs, and went out to give each a rose from the box that had been sent her that afternoon. When they entered the reading room, Christine thought she had never before found herself in such a cordial community. Every one crowded up to shake hands with her, and say how glad they all were to have her in Phi Delta Kappa, and Christine thought: " Perhaps those girls who black-balled me last year were all Seniors, who have gone away." The room had been made comfortable with sofa-pillows; and the warm flicker of an open wood-fire danced over the hair and bare shoulders of Miss Genevieve Royce, as she took her place in the President's chair. A great cluster of pink roses stood on the table beside her, and threw a shimmering picture of themselves across the polished wood.

The roll was called, and then came the mysterious "Business Meeting," which dealt extensively in black and white beans. Christine deposited a fat white bean in every box, and felt distinctly aggrieved when two of the girls failed to be admitted. But the successful candidate was Grace Reade, and she grew warm at the thought of this delightful secret, which nothing could induce her to tell.

Then came the reading of the Phi Delta Kappa paper, and Christine's article received a little round of applause all to itself, although, as one girl said, "the suitable time for applauding, is when the old paper is done." Clare stole up to Christine several times during the evening and gave her a few soft little pats, as if to make sure that she was there; then slipped away, thinking that Christine and Ardis would rather be by themselves.

"Do you know, Ardis," said Christine, after one of these timid excursions, "I think that Clare has a better mind than we give her credit for."

"Than *you* give her credit for, you mean. I have always known what she was. But she gets no credit for her philosophy because she is a musician. You get no credit for your really excellent sketches and your dramatic ability, because you can write. I get no credit for anything whatever, simply because I've got a bridge to my nose and a decent complexion. It's the same way with Clare's music. People here think that a girl has no right to more than one gift, and if she happens to have that, why, exit all her other qualities."

"But, Ardis, you must confess that she doesn't often show those other qualities."

"That is one of her attractions to me. She never goes racing through College Hall calling out, ' Here, I've got an opinion. Now listen and see if it isn't a good one!' In fact, she is like a little flower-garden, and does not allow her blooms to stray outside the fence."

"No, I don't think that she is like a cultivated garden. She reminds me more of a patch of wood-

185

land where wild flowers happen to grow, and sometimes you can find it, and sometimes you can't."

This conversation was carried on between a series
of papers on " Poets of the Eighteenth Century," and
then came the social part of the meeting, when everybody talked, or gathered around the fire to sing
college songs. Christine could scarcely realize that
she was a part of it all, and went home that night
with vague dreams of literary success, and of an important place on the editorial staff.

The new editors would go on duty in April, and
bring out the last two numbers of the " Prism," so
that the Seniors might be free for their Commencement work; and Christine could not help wondering
what members of her class would be chosen to fill
that enviable position. She had always loved writing
better than anything else, and her literary career at
college had contained many amusing experiences.
At one time she had been known among her friends
as " The Arch-Heretic," because of an entirely sincere
essay that she had written on " The Ludicrous." In
it she had asserted that pleasure carried beyond a certain point becomes pain, and that we suffer more from
too funny a joke than from a joke that is not funny
at all. Miss Carlisle had scribbled in pencil at the
bottom of the last page, " Why was this paper written?
Most of your statements are arch-heretical."

Another early effort dealt with the story of a metaphor with a spiral tail. It was a convoluted animal,
which talked, crowed, and purred by turns; and Christine explained that being only an " implied resem-
blance," the metaphor could not be expected to
manifest all the characteristics of any one animal.

When this paper was returned, its margins bristled with " Sic? " which was Miss Carlisle's way of saying, "Do you really mean it?" and her criticism read: "You can do better than this. Try more serious work." But several papers, and particularly the last one, had received such warm praise that Christine thought, " Perchance the arch-heresy has fallen from me!" Her articles in the " Prism " were often " noticed " by other college magazines, and the loyal admiration of the Harland students stimulated her continually to further effort. It is an inspiring place, after all, this college world, and one in which we must be strange creatures if we fail to do our best.

But Christine's love of writing had begun with her very early childhood, and she had always felt that something must have been asked of her here, although the self-distrust that was helping her to grow brought its accompanying discouragements every day. And yet there were times when she had started up in the night, crying, " What do you want of me?" For it seemed as if something must have been wanted, else why was she made like this?

But when morning came, it convinced her once more that she was only very sleepy and commonplace; and she also realized that the world was continually raising its standard. Everybody wrote better; but fewer people wrote well.

" I wish I knew what Miss Carlisle really thinks of me," she thought. " She has so seldom said anything nice about my work and yet she is my friend. I'm almost sure that she is my friend!"

But Christine did not know that three years ago, when she came to college, she had been registered in a certain keen brain as "a girl whose greatness is hedged in by lack of discipline." Of Ardis, Miss Carlisle had thought, "A face that has possibilities of right, but probabilities of wrong."

She had watched the growing friendship between these two girls with a vague disapproval, which she herself could not explain. It seemed unreasonable to condemn Ardis as unreliable, simply because she never showed her feelings; and yet she often wished that Christine would see less of her. But this wish was not realized; for Christine had recently been elected to the Council — a committee chosen from the four classes to represent the undergraduates at Faculty meetings — and worked with Ardis continually to further the interests, and regulate the social events of the "student-body."

The sudden resignation of one of the three Junior members had resulted in Christine's election, and although nothing was said, the Juniors suspected that this resignation had been caused by some trouble with their President.

"Lucile Murray rooms next door to me, in Chapter 7," said Kathleen Carey, "and the other day she threw a book out of the window. She said it was an accident, but I rather surmised that she hoped Ardis might be passing by."

When the Councillor herself was interviewed on the subject, she remained quite non-committal, and refused to give any explanation of what had occurred.

"Did they think for a minute," she thought afterwards, with scornful eyes, "that I was going to say anything against the President of Ninety-five?"

The Junior Councillors were now absorbed in a

plan to abolish "the old Twenty-second," and have
in its place a genuine Prom, which the upper-class
girls could enjoy. The Prom would not come until
the spring, so Washington's Birthday must be cele-
brated by a festive rally in the Gym, with marching
and loud sounds. Everybody rejoiced when the arguments brought forward by the Juniors were finally
accepted; and Christine's mother, who faithfully
perused the Harland notices in the New York
"Tribune," wrote to say that she was coming up on
the Twenty-second to offer her congratulations in
person; while Stephen, who had heard of the arrangement, wrote that he would be there too.

As this was Mrs. Arnold's first visit to the college,
her daughter's friends were very anxious to see what
she would be like, and Christine invited a number of
them to meet her mother, at an informal spread in
the afternoon; but when the hour and the company
arrived, the guest of honor had not yet appeared.

"I've sent three telegrams, and met three trains,"
explained the mortified hostess, "but she hasn't
turned up, so perhaps we'd better eat the things."

Datisi had been dressed for company in a yellow
cravat, which went around his neck and lasted until it
reached his tail. He tried to back out of it several
times, and then pulled it around in front of him so
that he fell over it whenever he tried to walk. This
irritated him extremely, and when Christine took her
guests into Freda Hastings' room to lay off their
wraps, Datisi took the lobster and went downstairs.
When the girls assembled for the feast, their hostess
gazed at the table in horror, then began to look under
all the different pieces of furniture in the room.

"Christine, what *is* the matter?" they asked, as after an apparently futile search she sat down dejectedly on the floor.

"I've lost my mother, and I've lost my lobster, and my room-mate's gone."

"Never mind, we're here," said Freda, consolingly, "and the lunch is getting cold."

So they all fell to work upon the neglected viands; and just as they were consuming the last of them, Mrs. Arnold appeared in the door of Number 2 Hadley, with a great bunch of roses in each hand, and a box of violets crushed comfortably under one arm.

"I thought that you might want to decorate in honor of my arrival," she said, "so I've provided the ways and means."

"Oh, mamma," said Christine, in dismay, "we were afraid that you were not coming. I've been giving you a spread!"

So this was Christine's mother, — this dainty little person in silks and furs, with her arms full of flowers, and mischief in her eyes. She did not seem to be at all surprised to find the room full of girls, but beamed upon them all, and tossed her roses upon the bed.

"So you've been giving me a spread, have you, when I wasn't here?" she asked, as Christine helped her out of the fur-trimmed jacket. "Oh, Christie, Christie, how characteristic!" and sitting down among the roses, she laughed until she could scarcely see. The girls looked at each other in bewilderment, which gradually changed to consternation.

"There's nothing left but a plate of sandwiches," said one.

"Eaten it all up, have you?" asked Mrs. Arnold,

with a comical look. "Well, Christie, I like that! I think that Stephen and I will go down town to-night and give *you* a spread! — only you need n't trouble to come to it."

"But, mamma, how did you happen to be so late? We had given you up long ago."

"It was entirely the fault of the Russian minister. He came over on the train with us last night, and what did papa do but invite him to lunch with us to-day at the Fifth Avenue? I had to stay and be polite to him, or we would all have been involved in a European war. So that's why I was late. And now, please, introduce me to your friends, or they won't have the slightest idea who I am!"

But it is seldom necessary to introduce one's friends to a college mother, because she knows so much about them already.

"So this is Miss Carey? I've heard of how well she did Mr. Boffin in the Storey House Dramatics. And Miss Reade, too, — known also as 'Kathleen's Accomplice.' Ah, you good child, you have brought me a sandwich! And this is little Clare? Why, what a darling you are!" and much to Clare's astonishment, Mrs. Arnold pulled her down very gently and kissed her. "But where is my dear Ruth?" she asked, when she had met all the girls; "I was almost sure that she would be here to meet me."

"She's working," explained Christine; and Mrs. Arnold said, "Oh, the brave little soul!"

A shadow had come over her face, and Christine hastened to add: "Ardis could n't come, either. She has a man on her hands. But she's coming up to sing to you after supper to-night."

"And bring her accompanist," added Clare, shyly.

"Clare's Assistant Leader of the Glee Club now," explained Christine, proudly, "and plays all their accompaniments."

"Oh, how I shall enjoy it!" said Mrs. Arnold, delightedly. "And Stephen will like it too."

"But Stephen hasn't come, mamma."

"He's down at the hotel now, seeing about rooms. Christie, why don't you hang your pictures straight?"

"She *is* like Chris, after all," whispered Faith Bentley to Kathleen.

"I should have said — your picture," continued Mrs. Arnold, surveying the vacant walls. "What has she done with the rest of them?" she asked, — "smashed them or packed them away under the bed?"

"She's given them, or at least lent them all to Ruth," explained Freda Hastings. "I think she enjoys them more, having them down there."

Mrs. Arnold looked delighted, and began, "The dear — well, Ruth deserves to have them more than Christine, anyhow, for she is a better girl."

"Had you lost anything?" inquired an unexpected voice in the doorway. "I found them both in my room when I came home."

Miss Carlisle stood there, holding Datisi in one hand, the lobster in the other, and Datisi was sparring at the lobster with wicked paws. Christine's apologies were rendered somewhat futile by the mirth of the company; but Miss Carlisle was, as usual, quite equal to the occasion. "The kitten offered me a lunch, which I was noble enough to decline, because I knew that it was not his to give," she said; "but people who return stolen property often receive a reward, and those sandwiches look very good."

"Miss Carlisle, this is my mother," said Christine, laughing; and Miss Carlisle colored a little, as if she had been one of the girls.

"It is useless for me to try and make a dignified impression now," she said with dancing eyes. "But I'll stay long enough to explain to Mrs. Arnold that she missed a good deal in not coming to our rally this morning. We had a debate on the subject of whether the higher education of man unfits him for domestic life."

"And how did it come out?" asked Mrs. Arnold.

"Oh, we finally decided that a man can take better care of young children if he has studied Calculus, and can make more artistic puddings if he knows his Schopenhauer and Kant. No, Christine, I can't stay one other minute now. But Mrs. Arnold is coming to supper with us to-night, aren't you, Mrs. Arnold? We should all like to have you."

"Oh, Miss Carlisle, don't go yet!" pleaded the girls; but she answered with a funny smile, "One hundred and fifty-three Bain papers before to-morrow morning!" and departed merrily with the nearest sandwich.

The attention of the company was now directed to Datisi, who, having been formally introduced, spit at them all impartially and retired under the bed. Mildred Wyman, who liked cordiality in cats, confided to Grace that she considered his fur an unbecoming color, and Grace answered that she had no doubt it was put on only to conceal where his skin was pieced.

"And his eyes look like the inside of a blue grape," she added disrespectfully.

"Oh, Christine," said Faith, "there's your brother now, coming out of the old Gym. He's evidently been searching for the Hadley."

Christine ran downstairs to meet him, and Mrs. Arnold, who was never surprised at anything that her daughter did, presided gracefully at the leave-taking of the guests.

Ardis and Clare appeared promptly at the Hadley that evening with a big roll of music, and Ardis, who happened to be in one of her irresistible moods, yielded with quiet readiness to Mrs. Arnold's continual demands for "more." Miss Carlisle, who had already listened longer than her work allowed, went back resolutely to her Bain papers; and then Ardis sang the love song from "Samson et Delila," and the worker in the next room laid her cheek down upon the papers, and forgot them.

"What makes her so willing to sing to-night?" asked Freda Hastings, curiously, of Clare. "Is it the presence of Stephen?"

"No, it's Mrs. Arnold," replied Clare, with a little quiver of the lips. "Ardis has no mother, you know."

Christine had received permission to spend the night with Mrs. Arnold; and when they were in their room at the hotel, she said, "Now, mamma, tell me honestly, what do you think of Ardis?"

"She is very fascinating, and I can easily see why she should be popular; but I don't think that her influence upon any one would be particularly good."

"'Any one' means me, I suppose. Well, I hope

you don't think that I am weak-minded enough to be influenced by a classmate! "

Mrs. Arnold laughed. " My blessed infant, every girl in this college is a little planet, with an atmosphere of her own; and if you walk into other people's worlds, you must expect to breathe the air that is there. We never cease to be influenced by other people, — by the people that are near us, and most of all by the people that we love. Why, even a pickle is influenced by the close proximity of a red pepper."

" I don't see the force of your comparison," said Christine, with dignity. " You might as well say that a man who steps on an orange peel is influenced by the sidewalk."

. " He is, occasionally," said Mrs. Arnold, laughing. " Influence often comes from the quarter where it is least expected, and gains more force from finding us unprepared. But you love her very dearly, don't you? So, of course, I will try to love her too."

She sat looking at Christine rather wistfully, then put both arms on the table before her, and laid her head down upon them, like a little girl.

" Mamma, you might be a Freshman studying Horace in the Reading Room."

" I am studying something more interesting, my dear."

She lay awake until late that night, and smiled now and then, with the tears in her eyes.

" Perhaps I am wrong," she thought, " but when she is with her friends, there is certainly a different look on the child's face. She is more gentle than she used to be. I am so glad that she has learned to care for some one, — since she could not care for me."

Christine did not know her mother very well, and, following the tendency of a critical and parent-judging generation, was inclined to think her frivolous. She imagined that her mother had never sought her affection, and could not understand why the wife of a rising politician should have had so little time to play with her children. It did not occur to her that the separation from this last child — her one little girl — might have been quite as hard for Mrs. Arnold as it was for Christine, and that she had comforted herself then by thinking: "When she is grown up, I will tell her all about it, — the darling, — and being a little woman she will understand."

But Christine was a woman now; and she had not understood. The next morning Ruth came down to the hotel for breakfast, and insisted that Mrs. Arnold should accompany her to chapel afterwards, as Christine was nearly always late.

"Then you must leave her in the reading room, to be kept until called for," said Christine. "She has to go to Economics with me."

"I'm going to Economics too," said Stephen.

"No, you're not, and it isn't of any use for you to cry, because I'm going to let you do something that you'll like a great deal better. Whom are you going to take to chapel this morning, Stephen? Shall I go up and tell her you're coming?"

"I haven't decided yet," answered Stephen, with dignity. "But I'll ask her all right, so you don't need to worry."

Christine's eyes danced, but she said nothing; and

presently Ruth and Mrs. Arnold went off together in high spirits. Stephen set forth with the air of a man who has a mission to fulfil, and Christine sailed past him in an electric car, five minutes after he had started. She reached the college, and vanished under the elms in an incredibly short space of time, and was waiting for him twenty minutes later, when he walked into the Hadley House parlor without a girl.

"Why, Stephen, what's the matter?" she asked sympathetically. "Would n't she go with you?"

"She's in the choir. They both are. Why did n't you tell me?" was the wrathful answer; and Christine laughed until Stephen arose and said that he had an errand down town.

"Come to chapel," she said, holding out her hand. "She's been in the choir for two years, and so has Ardis. Oh, Stephen, there is nothing half so useful, after all, as information scorned!"

They found two places in the right transept, and when the services were over, Christine seized Clare as she came down from her seat on the platform.

"You have n't anything this hour?" she asked anxiously; and Clare said, "No; but, Christine —"

"Then take him and be thankful. He's a blessing, a sunbeam. Oh, Clare, I'll do as much for you some day! I'm late at Economics, as it is. Goodbye." And she quickly disappeared, leaving Stephen to be jostled by departing Sophomores, until Clare took pity on him and bore him off to the Art Gallery.

Christine and her mother arrived at the old Gym just in time to hear Professor Wilmot say that there would be no recitation to-day, but that the class would attend a trial in the Court House, " to serve as a practical illustration of some of the work under consideration."

" I did n't suppose that the girls studied things like this," said Mrs. Arnold, laughing, as they fell into the rear of the long procession, headed by the professor, with a student on each side.

" Indeed we do ! " said Christine, opening her note-book. " We had two cases to work up for to-day. Here 's one, for instance. If a peddler sells you a new kind of potato-peeler, knowing it to be a fraud, and you soon discover that the peeler acts as if it had never met a potato before, what ought you to do about it? "

" I think," said Mrs. Arnold, seriously, " that I should have turnips for dinner."

" No; but suppose that your husband hated turnips, and that they made him sick! It would n't do to back down that way. Neither would it do, mamma, for you to lay violent hands on the peddler, so that he could sue you for assault. No; the only feasible plan would be to detain him, by sitting on his head, until the town authorities could be summoned."

" I 'll be sure and remember," said Mrs. Arnold, demurely. " You know papa says that there 's nothing like a college education to prepare one for the little daily incidents of life. Why, here we are at the Court House now ! "

The case on trial was a new phase of the old struggle, Labor versus Capital.

It seemed that Labor had been doing odd jobs for Capital about his place, cutting the grass, setting out flowers, etc., and at the end of three days it occurred to him that he would like to be paid. Capital put off the payment at the time, saying that he would pay when the work was finished; but Labor returned on the following day to demand payment for the work already done. Capital declined, and Labor, becoming incensed, threw Capital into a cucumber frame, thereby destroying the dignity of Capital, and the glass of which the frame was composed. Capital brought suit against Labor, not for knocking him down, but for using him as a dangerous weapon with which to destroy the cucumber frame. Labor defended himself by saying that he had pulled Capital out of the cucumber frame shortly after having deposited him there, and cited, as a proof of this statement, the fact that Capital was in the Court House now.

Capital insisted that Labor should be made to pay for the cucumbers, in addition to the broken glass; and the question arose in court as to whether an ordinary man could kill a cucumber by falling on it. It was suggested that a cucumber be brought into court, and that some one should fall on it, to settle the point.

But some one else recalled that the cucumbers had been under glass, which might have mitigated the force of the fall, and there did not seem to be any one present who would fall on a cucumber, through glass, to find out. The point under discussion was finally settled by the female domestic of Capital, who alleged that she had removed the cucumbers from the broken portion of the frame, two days ago, to make pickles, and proved her statement by producing one of the pickles from her pocket.

There were very few people in court who seemed to be at all amused by the situation, and indeed it might turn out to be a very serious matter for Labor.

"How much had you agreed to pay the prisoner for work on your premises?" asked the lawyer, turning to Capital.

"A dollar 'n' a quarter a day is what I gin'rally give 'em," answered Capital, "but I don't take much stock in hired help that comes up to you and says, 'See here, mister'—"

"That will do," interrupted the lawyer. "And what is your valuation of the glass that was broken?"

"Wall," answered Capital, slowly, "there was five panes busted clean through, and I set kinder hard on another—" He meditated a moment and then named a price that called forth a murmur of expostulation from the prisoner's friends.

He turned round and hurled defiance in their direction, saying, "You ain't countin' that other one that I set hard onto,"—when he was ignominiously bidden to stand down.

Professor Wilmot did not wait to hear the summing up of the evidence, but ushered his mirthful class out of the Court House, and asked them their opinion of the trial, on the way home. He told them to come to class the next day with a definite idea of how the court should have decided the matter; then they could look up the verdict and compare.

Ruth met her friends on the first corner, and bore Mrs. Arnold off to inspect the attic room at Mrs. Barstow's.

"You see the sun comes in at some window all day long," she said, "and all the girls who are making their own shirt-waists like to come here and sew, because it's so cheerful. We make the girls that can't sew, read aloud until they're hoarse, and then let them take out bastings while they recuperate."

Mrs. Arnold sat down in a low rocking-chair, and picked up a shred of light gingham from the sunny floor.

"Ruth, child," she said, "I wish you could have sent a different answer to the little letter I wrote you. It would have made me so happy, dear."

Ruth slipped down beside the chair, and put both arms around Christine's mother.

"Dear Mrs. Arnold, do you think I could have let you send me through college as you wanted to, and do everything for me that you did for Christine? It was so hard for me to have to hurt you, as I knew I would by refusing; but you can never know how much it meant to me to feel that you wanted to do it."

Mrs. Arnold could not speak for a minute, and only held Ruth very closely in her arms, which may have been what Ruth needed, after all.

"Mrs. Arnold," she said, "you don't think it's wrong for me to be away from home, do you, now that Cousin Isabel is there to help mamma with the housekeeping? You see I'm really not needed just now, and if I don't get an education, how can I help educate the boys?"

"I think it is right for you to be here, Ruth. In making the most of yourself, you are really doing what is best for your family, because a girl with an education can be of use wherever she goes; but without an education she is sure to be handicapped at every turn."

"I want to get a position to teach," said Ruth, eagerly, "and then perhaps I shall be able to send Dorothy through college myself. I want her to be a happy college girl, as her sister was, here among the arbutus and the dear hills and the glorious mountain air. I want her to be a Harland College girl! But oh, Mrs. Arnold, is n't it a pity that she can never belong to the class of Ninety-five!"

Mrs. Arnold laughed, and Ruth talked to her about college and Christine and home, until it was time to start for "Whately." Christine joined them outside Number 6, and was soon deep with the other Juniors in plans for the debate, which began as soon as Miss Carlisle arrived. Mrs. Arnold scarcely recognized her acquaintance of the night before, in this self-possessed little woman, who followed the discussion from side to side and corner to corner, gathering up whole bunches of omitted refutations, and presenting them compactly to each new participant in the fray.

Mrs. Arnold listened in amazement, and told Christine, after class, that if ever a mind seemed to possess fingers of its own, that kind belonged to Miss Carlisle.

"Madame Rigault has fingers of that description, too," said Christine, "but, unfortunately, she has finger-nails as well!"

Stephen rejoined them with a triumphant countenance, having interviewed all the pianos in the Music Building, shinned up a rope in the Gymnasium, and sat in a hammock on the back campus and broken it down. He said that Clare had left him to go to recitation, and being his sister's guest, he thought it no more than decent that he should entertain himself and see that he had a good time. He and Mrs.

Arnold went away that afternoon, most enthusiastic over college and everything connected with it, and Christine hurled statistics after them as the train left the station.

March hurried out as if it were a disagreeable piece on the piano that the player wished to finish, and April came in with two weeks of vacation and rest.

CHAPTER XIV

"PIPPA PASSES"

THE first Monday in Spring term was a soft gray day, full of rain, — the kind of day when one does not wish to move, — and Christine had settled herself for an afternoon's work on her Carlyle paper, when Ardis appeared.

"Come out to walk," she said, shaking the drops from her hair. "If you stay in-doors and try to be original, you 'll die."

Christine laid aside her pile of untouched essay paper with its ominous blue lines, beckoned her rubbers from under the washstand, and put on her waterproof.

"Let's go up and see the river," said Ardis, as they started out merrily under one umbrella; "it is always silver in a storm."

But when they had reached the top of the hill, and stood watching the gray landscape as it shifted unsteadily in the wind and rain, they saw that the river was gray like the rest.

"It is not in a silver mood," said Ardis, a little sadly; "I'm sorry that we came."

"That reminds me of Clare," said Christine. "She's always wondering what the trees and flowers and sky are thinking about."

204

"Clare's in a bad temper to-day," said Ardis, laughing. "She got terribly angry with Maude, and when she is angry she retires to her own room, and rolls off the bed."

"Rolls off the bed!"

"Yes, she thinks it does her good. Clare's such a little tempest, you know, although she does live in a calm and spiritual outward teapot. This morning she rolled off the bed three times, and when I demanded an explanation, she said, ' If I had not rolled off the bed three times, I should certainly have been very disagreeable to her.' Clare detests Maude."

"I don't wonder," observed Christine.

"Why?" asked Ardis, quickly.

"Because I think she is not to be trusted."

Ardis looked at her curiously for a minute, and then said, "Let's go home." And Christine remembered afterwards that she did not speak again until they reached the house.

She worked over her paper until late that night, hoping to finish it in the morning, for Miss Carlisle had gone to Waverly to give a lecture, and would not return in time for "Whately," on the following day. Christine went to chapel with a light heart, for the Carlyle paper was beginning to seem less feeble; it would soon reach the beef-tea stage, she thought; and straggling ideas that had been eluding her for several months, now stood and took off their hats respectfully as she approached.

She was a little late at chapel, and did not notice, until she came out, that there was an unusual excitement among the girls.

"It isn't Monday," she thought, "so nobody's in

a society. What's the matter, Fay? Are you engaged?" she asked, as three enthusiastic classmates rushed up to Miss Bentley and seized her by the arm.

"I'm engaged to be an editor of the 'Prism,' my dear!" she answered with shining eyes. "Why, Chris, did n't you know about it? They were appointed this morning."

"Christine, come into the alcove a minute," said Rachel Winter, taking her by the hand; "there, sit down and wait until the crowd is gone. Why, Christine, did n't you know? Oh, you are so white! Christine, is it possible that you have only just heard? There, it's abominable, I don't care if I ought not to say so. You deserve it more than all the rest of them put together, except Elizabeth Dane, — she's editor-in-chief. And everybody is simply wild with rage and disappointment. I don't see what Miss Carlisle was thinking of, — I don't, indeed."

"Who are the others?" asked Christine, quietly.

"Oh, Rachel," cried a Hillard Freshman, running into the alcove, "let me congratulate you! I think it's magnificent, and we are all so pleased. Oh!" she finished blankly, observing Christine, and retired in some confusion.

"Are you — are you one too?" asked Christine.

"Yes, and I only wish I could give it to you! Why, Christine, I can't write, but then, to be sure, I'm only the business manager, so that would n't mean much to you, would it? But it's an honor, of course. Oh, Christine, I think it's abominable!"

"No, it is n't, Rachel; you know that I'm glad you have it, and — and there is no reason why I should

have it more than any one else, is there? Of course
I should — " she stopped and swallowed valiantly, " I
should have liked it."

" No reason why you should n't have it — when
you are the best writer in our class! Christine, how
can you?"

" Tell me the names of the others."

" Well, Ardis — "

" Ardis! "

" To them that hath it shall be given — yea, everything, from the best seat at Dramatics to the presidency of the class. Grace Reade and Edith Standish
have the Literary department — "

" I 'm glad about Grace," broke in Christine.

" And Faith Bentley the Alumnæ department.
Petunia Blake has the book reviews — I don't remember who she is, do you? But they say that she has done
a lot of scrub work on the magazine, been a kind of
literary charwoman, as it were."

" The no-haired, minnow-brained, crab-gaited! "
said a furious figure, confronting them suddenly;
" oh, Christine, my old honey girl, I 've been smiling
out of one eye and weeping out of the other, all
through chapel, until one side of my face resembles
a rut in the Connecticut River. And it 's myself that
would like to tie those Ninety-four girls up in their
own laundry-bags and hang them out of the window.
Only say the word, and it shall be done."

Christine began to laugh; but laughter of this kind
is not steadying to the nerves, and she jumped up,
saying, —

" Girls, don't sympathize with me, and, above all,
don't let other people sympathize with me. It 's hard

enough to be disappointed, without having everybody in the college know about it!"

She fled into the chapel, and went down the back stairs, hoping to escape further encounters with her friends; but when she opened the side door, there was Grace Reade, studying Chemistry with a class-mate on the sunny steps. Both looked up and smiled as she passed, but it seemed to her unhappy imagination that they did not greet her with as much respect as usual. Everything was an insult in her present state of mind, and she suspected every one of cherishing a secret desire to sympathize with her. She felt that she would like to annihilate the college for knowing of her humiliation. Then she thought of Miss Carlisle, and clenched her hands firmly to keep from crying until she had reached her room.

Some one ran up behind her, and seized her by the hand.

"Christine, I feel like a usurping old villain that needs to be beheaded," said Grace, tempestuously. "We all do, every one of us except Ardis, and she never says what she thinks, anyhow. It is all a kind of parody on the neat little statement that virtue is its own reward. The fact that you are the best writer in our class should be sufficient without further recognition. Oh, what keen intuition, what vast penetration it must have needed to discover signs of literary promise in Petunia Blake! My dear, does n't the very presence of Petunia prove to you that it's all absurd?"

"I presume that Miss Carlisle had the final revision of the list," said Christine, bitterly.

"Don't you believe it! I think that there's some

terrible mistake somewhere, and that Mau — that somebody knows what it is. You see when one girl with a strong will gets hold of a lot of others who don't care enough about anything to fight for it, she is very likely to have her own way. And oh, if there ever was an intellectually knock-kneed set! — Well, I 'm an editor myself now, and have no right to say anything against the ' Prism.' "

Christine's hand trembled a little then, for she could not have said anything against the " Prism." She loved it loyally, and had been proud of it from the day when the first number was issued.

" A person that cared as much as I did might have done — something," she thought. " Why would n't they let me correct proofs, or buy the ink? It would all have been for our college."

" It is the general stupidity and footlessness of everything that annoys me," continued Grace. " If a girl is good in Chemistry they make her Ivy Orator, or if she 's a fine athlete they elect her Assistant Treasurer of the Needlework Guild. Oh, if people knew college girls as we do, they 'd never be afraid that higher education is going to put any too much sense into them ! "

Christine did not cry when she reached her room, but adopted Clare's plan of rolling off the bed, and lay there face down with her head buried in her hands.

" It was my last chance of doing anything, having anything, or being anything at college," she said, " and it 's gone ! "

She put a " Please don't disturb " sign outside her door, and then took it in again for fear that some of the girls would think she had gone into her room to cry.

"But I'm so absurdly helpless before all this," she thought. "And yet no one can fulfil my ambition for me. I must make my own place, and take the responsibility of my own pain. Oh, I wish that I could learn to respect this 'most of the best' that is in me — only because it *is* the most, and God may mean it to be more! Is this lack of recognition due to the fact that I have n't worked hard enough? Or is it really incapacity — a case of $x^2 = 15$?" It would have done no good to tell her that every one must put this same question to himself at some time in his life, and discover whether, being x^2, he cannot still be useful in remaining 15.

" I wonder why it is that young people never have any sense of proportion. This mere loss of a college honor is one of the little things of life, one of the things that we are supposed to laugh at afterwards. And yet how can one's older self laugh at anything that meant so much to the child? There — now I will be my older self, and pretend that this is all in the long ago; I will stand off and look back at it — perspective is never so useful as when applied to a grief — but oh, the child! I can hear it crying still."

She wrestled through a melancholy morning with her older self, which stood rebukingly distant like a phantom, and the living child that wept and wrung its hands.

" After all," she thought, as the dinner-bell sounded, "why can't I adopt Ardis's policy and say that life is too short, as well as too ridiculous, to make a fuss

about little things? If I had every honor in college
bestowed upon me, I don't think that I should make
a fuss about little things, either! What was it that
Clare said to Stephen the other night? 'Thorns are
little steps up to the roses.' Well, I only hope that
when I have scaled up all my thorns, I shall not find
that a fat green worm with creepers in front and
whiskers behind, has devoured my rose!"

When she opened her door, she found a little note
on her threshold, that had evidently been brought
from the bulletin board.

DEAR CHRISTINE, — Will you come to our room at nine
to-night, and help celebrate in honor of the new editors? All
of the clan will be there.

Yours,   SALOME.

"What extraordinary continuity on the part of
Salome!" she thought; "I wonder if she would think
it boded reluctance if I sent a brief note, saying,
'Thanks, I won't come.' But I *will* come, though; I
must, and — thank Heaven for an inspiration, I'll take
the cat!"

The girls at dinner were most considerate, and refrained from talking about the editorial appointments,
at Christine's table; but this shamed her, and she
bravely introduced the subject herself.

Miss Carlisle was expected home early in the afternoon, and Christine decided that nothing would induce
her to meet her professor until the next morning, when
she should have recovered from the first sharpness of
her disappointment. So she went for a long walk
after dinner, and took supper with Ruth that night,

learning her lessons from Ruth's books, and keeping away from the Hadley until it was time to go home and dress for the editorial celebration. Then she stole in at the back door, and having extracted Datisi from behind the kitchen stove, bore him, limp and purring drowsily, to her room. She had just completed his adornment, in the shape of a huge green ribbon bow, when somebody came to tell her that Miss Carlisle wished to see her immediately.

"What can she have to say to me?" thought Christine, as she went downstairs. "Is she going to explain why — no, of course it would never occur to her that I had been hoping for it. She probably wants to tell me that my paper is over-due."

She knocked firmly at the door, trying to persuade herself that she felt perfectly at ease; but when Miss Carlisle said, " Come in," a strange foreboding of something dreadful came over her, and she scarcely dared enter the room.

Much to her surprise, she found the professor talking to Ardis Hathaway, who had just risen to go when Christine came in.

" I think Miss Carlisle might at least have seen me alone," she thought, with a throb of indignation; and then she saw something in Miss Carlisle's face that made her feel cold. Was it a certain hardness that had not been there before, or only a look of unusually firm resolve?

"Please wait a few minutes longer, Miss Hathaway," she said, "and help me explain the details of this affair to Miss Arnold."

" You sent for me — " began Christine, looking somewhat puzzled; and Miss Carlisle said, —

"Yes, I wanted you to understand why it was that you received no editorial appointment this morning."

"She is going to humiliate me before Ardis," thought Christine. "I wonder how much more I shall have to bear!"

Miss Carlisle waited a minute, as if in pity for her, and then said, —

"Yesterday afternoon, when I was on the point of starting for Waverly, Maude Gilbert came to my room, to show me the list of new editors that had been selected by the present board. The list contained several names that I should not have chosen, and omitted one that had a distinct right to be there. But, after careful consideration, I told Miss Gilbert that I approved of the list, with the exception of one person who has absolutely no literary ability, and of another who has not earned the position, and therefore does not deserve it."

Christine looked at Ardis, with terror dawning in her eyes, but Ardis appeared to be quite unconcerned. She even looked a little amused, and watched Christine curiously, as if to see how she would take the revelation to come.

"I insisted," continued Miss Carlisle, "that this last name should be taken off the list, and suggested a certain substitute; but Miss Gilbert brought up the objection that the majority had voted against her. I asked 'What majority?' as there are but seven editors, and Miss Robinson happens to be away. Miss Gilbert said that they had written to her, and although it surprised me to hear that she should have voted against this girl, I had no reason to believe that Miss Gilbert would wish to deceive me. So I decided to take the matter into my own hands, and said, ' Make no changes in the list until I return. There is one name here that must come off at all events, and another that must go on.'

" Miss Gilbert hastened to consult the person whose name was to be omitted from the list, and this person evolved a plan by which her own name might be included at the expense of — the other."

Christine looked appealingly at Ardis for an explanation, but none came, and Miss Carlisle continued :

" The person whose name was to be struck off the list suggested that the Junior appointments be announced during my absence, and formed a plan by which my own words could be so misrepresented to the editors that they would agree to this arrangement. Miss Gilbert told them that I had said I approved of the list, — which, if you remember, was only a part of my sentence. She also told them that I had said, ' Make no changes,' omitting to add, ' until I return.' I also discovered that she had written to Miss Robinson, but that her answer had not yet been received."

Christine had grown very white, but said nothing, and after a moment of silence Miss Carlisle turned to Ardis.

" Miss Hathaway, would you mind telling your friend what name was to have been omitted from the list? "

" Certainly not," answered Ardis, with calm assurance; " it was mine."

" Then perhaps you would not mind telling her the name of the person whose place you are now occupying on the editorial board."

Christine gave Ardis one look that said, as distinctly as if she had spoken: " I trust you in spite of all this. You have only to say that you did not do it, and I will believe you."

The eyes of the older girl darkened, and she turned to Christine, as if they two had been alone in the world.

" Christabel, my darling!" she said, "there is but very little that I can give you now, nothing that you would want to take — nothing that you would care for, dear. You had much better let me go. And yet one's very last fragment of self-respect is of use in a time like this. I can call Miss Carlisle to witness that I have taken the whole blame in this affair, that I have not tried to shield myself. That is something, is n't it, dear? Even a little better than nothing? Oh, Christabel, don't look like that!"

She drew a quick breath, and would have turned away, but Miss Carlisle said: "Wait a minute, if you please! Christine has not yet decided what is to be done with you. As you have obtained this position through unfair means, of course you cannot expect to keep it. To-morrow morning I shall have all these appointments recalled."

" Do you mean," asked Christine, slowly, "that you would take this appointment away from Ardis and — give it to me?"

" It is not a question of giving," answered Miss Carlisle; " it is yours by right. I can easily explain that, owing to my absence, a mistake was made in the appointments, —which would be perfectly true."

"Why did you do it?" asked Christine, turning to Ardis; for the friendly interest that had always led the two girls to investigate each other's motives returned to her then, as if nothing had happened.

" I did it because I knew that I wanted the position more than you did, Christine. You know it is part of my philosophy to believe that the person who wants a thing most, ought to have it."

"Did n't I always tell you," asked Christine, with a faint smile, "that your philosophy would get you into trouble?"

Ardis smiled, also, at the memories that this recalled, and for one moment these two friends went back hand in hand to the old footing of love and confidence; but it was for the last time in their lives.

"You need not wait to hear Christine's decision," said Miss Carlisle, quietly; "that will be known by to-morrow morning."

"I shall know before to-morrow morning," said Ardis, looking into Christine's eyes. "I shall know before you do, Miss Carlisle, because I know now!"

She went softly out of the room, and Christine sat there with the look of a person who has received a mortal blow.

"To-morrow morning," said Miss Carlisle, "this will all be made right again. Try and forget the rest."

"Oh no, oh no!"

Christine buried her face in her hands, and Miss Carlisle saw that she was struggling to regain her self-control. But she knew that this child was strong, and she, too, knew what the answer would be.

It came at last. "Miss Carlisle, the loss of this position means nothing to me now. Don't you see that — that I have lost — more?" And her voice sank.

" But you would like the appointment, would you not? I think it is a position for which you are particularly well fitted."

" Yes, you want me to realize what I am giving up. I understand. Miss Carlisle, you know and I know that this is all over. It will be enough for me to remember afterwards — that you thought I deserved it."

She rose and went to the door, and as she stood there she thought that the little clock tick-ticked loudly, as if in pain. Miss Carlisle came to her, and took one hand in both her own.

" Christine, I will write your father about this. I will tell him that the place belonged to you, that you had earned it, and that you gave it up rather than — I will tell him — " But Christine did not seem to hear, and did not speak until she felt those tears that were not her own upon her outstretched hand. Then she trembled suddenly, as if a ghost had passed through the closed door.

" Miss Carlisle," she said, " she was my friend."

She looked pitifully around the room, as if searching for something lost, and said once more: " She was my friend ! "

Then she went swiftly away, and Miss Carlisle did not see any one else that night.

She thought that she was beginning to realize how a doctor feels when he has lost a patient. The fact that she had distrusted Ardis for so long made the disappointment no easier to bear, now that her fears were verified, for she had hoped against hope that the "possibilities of right" in the girl might prevail. The part that Maude Gilbert had played in the affair made her feel sick, and her heart still ached for Christine.

"It seems to be the main part of my duty here, to inflict pain," she thought. "I have subjected the child to the severest discipline all through her college course, in order that she might be ready for the highest honors in her Senior year. She has had all the drudgery, she has had all the suffering, and her reward is — more of the same kind. I am powerless to help her."

The little clock still tick-ticked loudly, as if in pain. "Influence is something," she thought. "I have had Maude Gilbert for four years. Would not the right kind of influence have prevented this? And yet it is easy to see that the older girl was entirely controlled by her love for the younger. Was Ardis Hathaway put into the world for the purpose of serving it? Is she to accomplish any great good in this dim future for which she is living? Will she always continue to ride down other people in order to gain her own ends?"

She remembered that Ardis had told the truth from beginning to end, and wondered why she should have made a point of this, when she had countenanced so much that was worse.

But Ardis had a reason for everything that she did, and it was "part of her philosophy" to regard lying as an unscientific proceeding. "To lie," she had once said, "is to kill a situation with a sand-bag, when it might simply be held up and passed on."

When Miss Carlisle had discovered that Ardis was

inclined to tell the truth, she confronted her openly with black-balling Christine in her Sophomore year, and asked why it had been done. She was not at all sure that Ardis had been at the bottom of this, but determined to find out, before taking certain measures with regard to the editorial affair. Ardis was silent for a minute, while her mind went back, as it did every day, to a certain business meeting of Phi Delta Kappa which had been followed by a concert at Waverly. She heard once more the music that had leaped like a light through the church, and suddenly the room became suffocating with the scent of roses. She thought that her pain might be less hard to bear, if she could make some one understand how disloyal and dreadful she had been.

"It was all very simple," she answered. "I had only to mention to a few of the Seniors — those who would not take pains to look into the matter — that she had been conditioned, and they did the rest."

"Were you the only one of her friends who knew of this condition?"

"Yes, I think so. I advised her not to tell any one else."

Miss Carlisle thought that this girl was trying to exasperate her, and realized that she must not allow herself to become angry.

"Would you mind telling me why you did it?" she asked.

"For a number of reasons, Miss Carlisle; partly because I wished to gain her respect by having something that she did not."

"And it was immaterial to you whether she suffered or not?"

" I do not think that she suffered. She has plenty of resources in herself, and I thought it would not hurt her to wait a little while."

" Upon what grounds did you consider yourself competent to judge your classmate ? "

" On the ground of my common-sense, Miss Carlisle. I knew that she would be taken into one of the societies this year, and that she would never hear of the black-balling."

"Your calculations went somewhat astray in that direction, for she did hear of it soon after it happened."

Ardis turned absolutely white. " Does she, does she know — "

" No. To tell her that you did it would be unnecessary cruelty. She will have to know enough, as it is."

Ardis rose and walked to the window. Then she turned around and studied the professor's face a few minutes, and said desperately : "What are you going to do with me? "

The victory belonged to Miss Carlisle, but there had been less victory than pain.

" I am going to send for Christine, and allow you to endorse some of the statements that I shall make with regard to this editorial affair."

It was only then that Ardis began to plead, and although she was too proud to speak, it seemed as if her eyes must break the silence.

" I would rather you would kill me than do this," they said again and again ; and Miss Carlisle answered carelessly, —

" But all this must seem very trivial, in comparison with the honor of being an editor of the ' Prism.' "

Ardis made no reply, and Miss Carlisle went to the door. "Send Miss Arnold down here immediately," she said to some one who was passing in the hall; but as she stood there, she thought that she heard a quick sob in the room behind her.

And now, while she sat alone still thinking of it all, the two girls were at the editorial spread together.

"Our Ninety-five cat made us a visit the other night," said Clare, turning his ears inside out. "Ardis and I were cooking oysters in my room, and he dropped in as if by accident. When urged to remain, he looked self-conscious, and said, 'Well, I hardly think I ought, because I'm due at the Hadley now, and they don't know I'm out; but since you press me, — yes.'"

"He has a terrible way of accepting invitations that have not been given," said Christine. "Whenever there is any kind of party on the campus, he invariably turns up, and pretends that I sent him. Strange people rush up to me in chapel, and allude to him as my 'sweet little kitten,' which means that he has been presiding, unbidden, at some private spread."

"We want to borrow him for a little entertainment at our house next week, if we may," said Ardis, gently. "Each performer is entitled to three tickets, so he'll be allowed to invite his friends."

"I think he will accept with pleasure," said Christine, "especially if there are things to eat. He was an usher at our house when we gave 'The Mouse-Trap,' and seemed to enter into the spirit of it."

The supper was over at last, and Christine rushed out into the night air with her long cloak flying behind her, and Datisi struggling impatiently in her arms. He knew that they were going for a walk, and when she put him down, he tore on ahead of her with dancing tail, to hide behind every tree, and spring out at her as she passed.

When they reached the Marston elm, Christine stopped and looked at the one branch that caught the light from the kitchen window. The tree seemed to gather itself up as she stood there, and then to bend towards her with a great sweep of sympathy, as if it would have taken her to itself.

"You see," said a quiet voice at her side, "it understands everything."

"Clare! I did n't hear you come. Do you suppose it really knows that this is a disappointing world?"

"Come and see the breathing tree next to this one. It is in two parts, and therefore not so dignified, but when you 're sorrowful it will put its arms around you."

Christine allowed herself to be led by the soft little hand and pushed gently between the two trees that grew from one root. The wind rushed through the great elm, and at the same time something stirred at Christine's side. It was as if the twin trees had drawn but one breath together, and then they "put their arms around her."

She turned around and felt of them curiously, half expecting to see some witch form glide down into the grass and disappear. But the trees were still.

"Clare, they did breathe! I never felt anything like it before. Do they breathe in the daytime too? Did you discover them yourself?"

"They breathe when the wind is high. Christine, I'm going song-hunting to-morrow morning before breakfast. Won't you come with me, if I stop and call under your window?"

"Indeed I will, little dear. Good-night."

The twenty minutes of ten bell rang along the Marston House corridors, as Christine sped on her way, and in her haste to reach home she nearly upset a number of Astronomy students, who were staggering about in front of the Observatory with upturned faces, and notebooks that contained mysterious dots, pencilled one upon the other.

"I wish I could have taken Astronomy!" she thought; and then she remembered how she and Ardis had always talked over their Electives together. "Everything is associated with her. Nothing can be complete any more, not even the memory of what little I have accomplished. I can have no memory that is free from her."

She did not light the gas when she reached home, for fear that some of the girls would come in to see her.

"Why couldn't there have been one person who was absolutely beautiful?" she thought. "No, not perfect, but beautiful to look at and beautiful to know. I suppose that a person like that could not be allowed in a world so full of incompleteness. Because she came so near — so near to the truth, her nature must of course contain a lie. Only because she came so near to being a perfect thing with her wonderful mind, her beauty, and her gifts, she must needs be dishonorable to maintain the balance."

There was not much sleep in Number 2 Hadley

that night; but when morning drew near, Christine found herself wandering hand in hand with Ardis through beautiful places; and then came the cry of waking day to tell her that it had been all a dream. She sat up and threw off the blankets, because they seemed so heavy, and then she realized that the weight was on her own heart.

"How silly of me!" she thought. "Why does n't Clare come? But no, it is too early."

She pulled aside the curtain, and looked out at the sky which held all the possibilities of a day. It was faintly pink and mysterious; the birds had not yet begun to sing.

"That sky holds all the past of yesterday and the future of to-day! Why does n't Clare come?"

She felt greatly in need of the help that Clare might give, but knew that she could not ask for it, because Clare must never know what had happened.

"I believe it would kill her," she thought. "My one comfort will be that I can save her from all knowledge of — of what Ardis really is."

She lay down on the bed and fell asleep for a few minutes, dreaming, as people often do, that what she was expecting had come to pass. She and Clare were walking through the sunrise, and Clare had said, "Tell me everything; I shall understand." And the desire for sympathy was so great that Christine could not resist it, and told her everything. Then she awoke with a start and thought: "Oh, I have told her — I have told her, after all! No! I have been asleep. But how could I be so weak as to tell her, even in my sleep!"

She dressed hurriedly and sat down by the window

to wait for Clare. The birds were awake now, and a
few early sunbeams were drawn through the tree-tops
like the strings of a harp. The leaves were shaken by
a sweet, melodious clamor that came from invisible
throats; and as Christine listened she heard another
song climb towards her through the yellow morning.

> "The year's at the spring,
> And day's at the morn ;
> Morning's at seven,
> The hill-side's dew-pearled."

She took her hat, and crept down to the front
door, while the song came nearer still.

> "The lark's on the wing,
> The snail's on the thorn ;
> God's in his heaven,
> All's right with the world ! "

The song was hushed now, as the singer stopped
under a side window of the Hadley, and called softly,
"Christine ! "

"Good morning, Pippa," was the unexpected answer. "Where did you find that melody? It sounds
as if it might have been hidden in a flower."

"No, I got it from the birds," said Clare. "That
last chord — it is a chord in my mind, you know —
was hard to find, because the birds wouldn't stop
singing a minute. They seemed to know I wanted
to finish the melody, and only sang the faster; but
suddenly an old brown bird plumped down on the
breathing tree, and gave me just the note that I
wanted. It made a chord with all the others, and
I must write it down soon, or it will fly away when
the singers do."

"Let's go up and visit our guardian angels," said Christine. "I have always thought of them as guardian angels, since that first night at college, Clare."

"And why should n't they be? If Michael Angelo thought that every block of stone is the prison of some grand form, he might have been able to show us Mt. Waverly and Mt. Gwynn as they really are, — two mighty creatures resting on their swords, dressed all in green, with hair blowing yellow in the wind."

"Clare, why did you want me to come out with you this morning?" asked Christine, suddenly.

Clare laughed. "Why must I have had a reason? You are my friend, are you not? And the day is very beautiful."

But there had been another reason for bringing Christine out into the morning, although she knew that nothing could make the editorial disappointment any easier to bear. She felt that Christine must be taken to the out-of-door friends who understood her best, and who were themselves the "Everlasting Yea," in a world of question and of doubt.

"The arbutus will be out soon," she said, as they reached the grove opposite their old boarding-place on the hill.

"I am glad the bloodroot is gone," said Christine. "The first flower of the year would naturally suffer more."

They crossed Mrs. Hemp's yard, and sat down at the top of a long flight of steps which led down the hill on the other side.

The watchers over Harland were still gray in the shadow, like pussy-willows, but in the sun they were bright with delicate slants of green. Wandering melodies were afloat in the air.

" How strange it is," said Christine, " to be outside of the sunshine. I can see that it is here, and I can put my hand into it, but I do not feel it at all."

" I am going to leave you alone now," said Clare. " You can talk to them better if I am not here, and I must write down my bird song before it is gone. Good-bye, dear, and don't forget to come home in time for breakfast."

She went away, and Christine was left alone with the shadow of the friend she had lost. It was because of this shadow that she could not feel the sunshine when she stretched out her hand. She knew that the mountains were listening to hear what she would say, but there was nothing to tell them that morning. The sunbeams stole up, and touched her with joyous fingers, then drew back, as if wondering that she was no longer one of themselves.

" I cannot bear it!" she cried, and sprang to her feet; but at the moment when she found that she could not bear it, something broke like a song from the mountains, and, rushing over the meadows, wrapped her in a strange new sweetness and strength. She felt that it was coming, and now it was here, — the great nearness that she had never known before.

The birds began to sing again, and a flower that had been waiting in the grass grew suddenly sweet. She put her hand out into the sunshine, and felt that it was warm.

" That was God," she thought, as she turned towards home. " I wonder why it was that I never understood before!"

CHAPTER XV

CLARE and Ardis Hathaway were sitting in a hammock on the back campus, frankly and undisguisedly discussing men. It was fitting, and altogether desirable, to be discussing them now, when the Prom was only three weeks ahead, and every one understood that the subject would be dropped conscientiously later on.

People were already waylaying each other in chapel to ask with bated breath, "Have you got him?" and severe, indeed, were the epithets applied to him who would not come. Nobody was supposed to have more than one invitation; but the girls who wished to invite a large number of men overcame this difficulty by distributing them generously among the people who had no men at all.

"I wonder if I ought to ask Stephen Arnold," said Clare, doubtfully; "he invited me to Class Day, and Mrs. Arnold arranged to have me go up with Christine and Ruth, and stay with them all in Cambridge. But somehow I don't feel — and of course it is n't certain that I 'll go."

"What don't you feel?" asked Ardis, amused. "You ought to have a number of feelings."

"I don't feel as if I knew him well enough to ask him to the Prom."

228

" He knew you well enough to ask you to Class Day."

" Yes; but men are different."

" No, they are not — except that all the faults they laugh at in women, they have to a worse extent themselves."

" I never knew anything about men," said Clare. " The men at home are all Ethel's friends, not mine."

" It 's time that you had some, then. There is a masculine side to every woman, just as there is a feminine element in every man, and I think that we need both influences in our growing up. But I was brought up too much by men; I — "

" What were you going to say? " asked Clare.

" Nothing; only if a woman has got to be, I think it 's a good plan to have another woman around, who got there first. A woman's feelings are like a cat that shoots across the street and squeezes through an impossible hole in the fence to get away from the dogs. Feelings are sure to be barked at, if they show themselves in public."

" I don't think that the college girls bark at each other," said Clare. " Feelings are, after all, such universal things; we all have them, and the feelings that we girls have at this stage in the game are pretty much the same. So what is the use in trying so hard to conceal them? "

" Women *do* understand each other abominably," said Ardis. " Who was it that said ' Women understand one another in flashes '? "

" Elizabeth Stuart Phelps — who knows. Ardis, who are you going to ask to the Prom? I told you who I was going to have."

"I thought you did n't know him well enough. Well, I'm going to ask some one that I know very well indeed — George Slater, of Wyckham — Ninety-four. You've seen him up here."

"Yes, and I was hoping that I would never see him again."

"Why, why!" said Ardis, laughing. "What have you against George?"

"Don't call him that."

"I'll call him what I please. Who has been talking to you about him?"

"No one. He is not the kind of man that people like to talk about."

Ardis looked dangerous; but when Clare was roused, she possessed the often undesirable quality of fearing nothing.

"The great disadvantage of inexperience," said Ardis, crushingly, "is that people believe everything that they are told."

"What is the use of talking nonsense?" asked Clare. "Everybody knows that Mr. Slater is wild, and that he was expelled from another college before he came to Wyckham. I should n't think you would like to ask a man that other girls don't want to dance with!"

"He is a very good dancer," said Ardis, smiling, for she was not accustomed to being angry with Clare, and thought that it would be easy to laugh her out of this new prejudice.

"Don't you think it is better to look for what is good in people than what is bad?" she continued. "If Mr. Slater has a fine mind and rather unusual gifts, why should I refuse to know him? His private character does not concern me in the least, any more than mine does him. It's none of my business."

Clare said nothing.

"If a fine musician or a fine actor is known to be morally uncertain, does it prevent people from going to see him? Is n't it better to take people for what they are, than to berate them for what they are not?"

"You do not make a friend of any actor or musician simply by going to hear him," said Clare. "He merely represents his art, and you never know any other side of him. But you evidently believe that the best way to avert evil is to ignore it. I do not!"

"Well, you certainly can't say that I've ignored George! He's been up from New York three times this year already."

"If there was a case of small-pox in your vicinity, I suppose you would advise any one not to try to avoid the small-pox patient, if he or she happened to be a very gifted person! Your arguments might possibly be listened to, until you caught the small-pox and died of it."

"Not if you were vaccinated!" said Ardis, seriously. "Would n't it be great to have a hospital for that kind of inoculation! Ward No. 1, for conceit and its moral complications. Ward No. 2, for self-ishness in its most violent form. Ward No. 3, for falling in love. It would be rather fun to inoculate people with the wrong thing now and then, and they could n't get back where they were before, because their point of view would be entirely changed."

Clare struggled slowly out of the hammock, and walked away.

"Good-bye," called Ardis, cheerfully, but she did not answer.

That night Ardis went into 18 Marston, and found Clare sitting alone by the window. The room was dark, and outside one could hear the soft talking of trees.

" I came to tell you that I won't ask him," she said, " and I want you to promise that you will never look at me again as you did this afternoon."

She knelt down beside the chair and put her arms around Clare's neck.

" I — I will promise," began Clare, and then a large tear fell down and splashed unceremoniously upon Ardis's nose.

" And you do love me, don't you? "

" Yes."

" Ever and ever so much? "

" All the much that there is."

" Good-night, little Clare."

" Good-night, my dearest! "

The Prom was even more successful than any one had anticipated. The Juniors and Seniors were able to dance without being demolished by their neighbors, and the Sophomores, who had decorated the Gymnasium, danced on the concrete walks outside, while the festivity went on. The Freshmen waitresses revelled in three different kinds of ice-cream, and were caught by the Refreshment Functionary from down-town, while trying to smuggle salad through the windows of the basement to friends on the lawn. The orchestra was obliged to repeat the last waltz three times, in response to the enthusiastic encores; and it was not until the musicians had folded up their instruments in funereal dark cloths and the lights had been turned down, that the company was willing to disperse. Then the few nocturnal spirits who happened to be gazing out of their windows upon the moonlit campus, saw visions of dainty ghosts in evening wraps, each accompanied by a stalking black shadow, who faded away into nothingness when the night-watchman came along and hustled the ghost into the house. In the morning everybody went to chapel, and the 10.50 train for New York carried off more select dress-suit cases than had assembled in South Harland for some time.

The upper-class girl smoothed the wrinkles out of her best gown, and laid it away with a regretful little sigh. There was something so irrelevant and yet so fascinating about that evening dress, tossed over a chair that tilted back among the Greek and Latin lexicons! It seemed like a gay and frivolous self come back to laugh at her. There was something annoying, also, in the sight of that one satin shoe, planted impudently in the middle of the floor, where it had no business to be. And yet the Senior had not liked to put it away the night before, because there was so much music in it! She looked at the low-necked dress again, and wondered if it knew that she had not learned her Psychology lesson. Then she shook it vigorously, and carried it back to a trunk in the attic, together with the long white gloves, which she knew could not be cleaned. Coming back to her room, she gazed at the bowl of fading roses on her desk, put a little mark under one of the names on her dancing-card, and — took up her Psychology.

Christine went over to Clare's room soon after recitation and said, 'Well, how did you like it? And *have* you heard from your mother yet about Class Day?"

"Yes, I have," answered Clare, who held an open letter in her hand, " and she says I may go. Oh, Christine, my sister Ethel is engaged to be married! and — I think she might have told me she was going to."

"People do not generally divulge their plans in that direction, Clare. How fresh your flowers are!"

" Yes, your brother said that he was going to divide the bouquet into two parts, so that one would be fresh for this morning. I thought it was a beautiful plan; but last night there was a great bunch of roses, and this morning as many lilies of the valley, and I don't think it's quite fair, do you — when I'm only one girl?"

"Stephen knows how much you care for them," said Christine. " I love them too, and he sends them to me very often, when we are anywhere near each other."

"I should think you would miss him, Christine. I don't mean in connection with the flowers."

"I do miss him, every day of my life!"

"I wonder if my Prom dress will be suitable to usher in," said Clare, referring to her letter. " Mamma wants to know. What shall you wear to usher in at Dramatics, Christine?"

"I am not going to usher; Ardis has not appointed me."

Clare looked absolutely aghast.

"Not appointed you — when you ran against her for President? Why, that could n't be! No one ever heard of such a thing. Are you sure that she has n't appointed you?"

"I should have been likely to hear of it if she had," said Christine, smiling. "When is your sister to be married, Clare?"

"Next winter, and I shall insist upon having mamma spend the rest of the year with me, for she 'll be all alone. Oh, Christine, it 's terrible to have your sister engaged, — simply terrible! And I 've been wondering all the time why she would n't come up and see me, and now I know it was all because of that *man*."

"I should like to meet your sister," said Christine, trying not to laugh. "Is she anything like you?"

"Not in the least," said Clare, indignantly. "*I* would n't get engaged."

The Leader of the Glee Club came in at that moment, to ask Clare about some music that they were transposing for the next rehearsal, and Christine went away; but Clare was so disturbed over what Christine had told her about the Junior ushering, that she frequently wrote the second alto parts in the first soprano, and had the pleasure of rubbing them out afterwards, stems and all.

It is desirable to be a Junior usher for several reasons: First, because one officiates, in a becoming gown, at all the Commencement exercises; secondly, because it is a great compliment to be one of a limited number, chosen by the Junior President to represent her class. As one of the uninvited once said: "There are four kinds of Junior ushers, — the popular girls, the pretty girls, the well-dressed girls, and the girls that no one but the President would have thought of." We all know by experience that the uninvited have a clever way of saying things, and that some of the things they say are true!

Clare could scarcely believe that Ardis had intended to omit Christine, for Ruth had been appointed, and Kathleen, and Rachel, and all the others of "the clan;" so she determined to find out, if possible, where the trouble lay.

"Ardis," she said that evening, "have you appointed all the ushers yet? We want to know how many there are to be, so as to order our hoop-sticks in a body and save expense."

The ushers' wands were usually made of hoopsticks, or pieces of flag-staff, wound with white satin ribbon.

"The list of names is up in my desk somewhere," answered Ardis, carelessly. "I had five more than usual this year, because the Seniors say there are never enough at Collation."

"Has Christine told you what she is going to wear?"

"No, I don't think so. Has she told you?"

"No; in fact I heard this morning that she had not been appointed, but thought it must be a mistake."

"It is well to be able to recognize a mistake when you hear it," said Ardis. "I suppose that the overtones of a mistake must be out of harmony with the C major of principle. You see, I use a musical analogy, because it is one that you are likely to understand."

Clare looked puzzled, but, remembering her Logic, reasoned that because she could understand a musical analogy, it did not necessarily follow that she would fail to understand another kind!

" Well, I'm glad that you've asked her, anyway,"
she said. "I knew, of course, that you would."

But she also knew that Ardis had not given a definite answer to her question.

That evening she happened to be passing Lincoln
Hall when meeting of the Symposium broke up, and
Mildred Wyman overtook her before she reached
the house.

" Did you know that a committee from the class
has called upon Ardis, to ask her to appoint Christine? " she said. " We were talking about it this evening, and the girls think that it's simply unpardonable,
—when Christine practically gave her the presidency!
Ardis yielded a little; at least she told the girls they
might take the message, and they did, and probably
have it now, for Christine declined to receive it. I
don't believe that I should have accepted it in that
way myself."

" Oh dear, I thought — I hoped that she had been
appointed," said Clare. " What will Ardis say? "

" Well, I don't know as I care! " said Mildred,
indignantly. " There are a great many people in
Ninety-five who think that our pretty class President
is not a paying investment."

Clare was much disappointed in Ardis, but knew
that there had been some trouble between her two
friends, and thought that Ardis might have had more
excuse for her conduct than any one imagined; there
were always two sides to a story, no matter how
one-sided and convincing the story might appear.

To do Ardis justice, she had fully intended to
appoint Christine; but Christine had ignored her so
completely, since the night of the editorial supper,

that she had found no opportunity. She thought of writing her a note, but feared that if she did this, Christine would think that she was afraid to speak to her. She was still wavering, and undecided what to do, when she was waited upon by a committee from her class, and their interference filled her with humiliation and wrath. She was also much annoyed that Clare should have spoken to her about Christine, and thought, when the committee came to her room, that Clare must have had something to do with it. Having learned to distrust herself, she found it difficult to trust other people, and because she had lost Christine, imagined that Clare had deserted her too.

Clare, who was thoroughly distressed by all this, tried to make Christine relent, and accept the appointment, saying that the misunderstanding had been going on too long. "Clare dear," said Christine, sorrowfully, "I wish that I could — if only to please you. But it is true, as you say, that — this misunderstanding has been going on too long!"

Clare knew by her face that nothing more could be done, and went away thinking, "I am of no use to any of my friends, I am of no use to myself! Question: why was I born?"

The possibility that she might be of use to her class never entered her mind until the night of the Glee Club elections, when she was made Leader by a nearly unanimous vote. Then she knew that at last they had made a place for her — little Clare — in the dear college world, and that it was the place of all others she would have chosen to fill.

"Ardis," she cried joyously, — "Ardis, do you know what this means to me?"

But Ardis did not reply. She herself had been elected Manager, and was wondering if she could not have managed Clare better, if their positions had been reversed.

Several of Clare's friends were outside on the steps, applauding, and it seemed that every one had known all about it beforehand; so nobody was surprised except Clare. The Glee Club escorted their new Leader to her home, and sang to her all the way, although she herself could not sing, for fear that she should cry; and when they reached the Marston, the girls who had been following the club across the campus, gathered around and said, "We are so glad, little Clare!"

The singing had never sounded so beautiful to Clare as it did that night, and she thought as she went to her room, "They are mine — my own, my very own!" Then she spent two hours trying to forget that Ardis, too, had not said she was glad, and found herself crying, after all.

Christine Arnold was a quiet observer of everything that went on, and pretended that she was like Teufelsdroeck in "Sartor Resartus." She remembered that Carlyle had a gray cat, something like Datisi in appearance, and thought that very likely Teufelsdroeck had one too. She had determined not to feel, and accordingly devoted her entire attention to study, reading all the references that were given out in class, and vanquishing her soul with the "law of diminishing returns." She declined an invitation to the Storey dance, and stayed at home from the Wyndham Dramatics. Then she changed her tactics, and appeared at every festivity with a cordial smile,

" To avoid seeing people is not the way to avoid being hurt," she thought. "It's like being shot in the back!"

She occupied her spare time in getting up a delightful " farewell meeting " for the Seniors of Phi Delta Kappa. Theresa Robinson, the head of the Executive Committee, was the only Senior who could know beforehand what the entertainment was to be. They were to have scenes from " Pippa Passes," which had been suggested by Clare's melody for "The year's at the spring;" and Clare herself was to be Pippa, although she insisted that she could not act at all. " Isabel will sing ' The year's at the spring,'" said Christine, " and you must write some music for ' Overhead the tree-tops meet,' — a little lower down, you know, for Ardis."

"I know the range of Ardis's voice," said Clare, delighted, " and I think the song will be better if I remember that she is to sing it."

She worked over the music until the day before the meeting, and then carried it to Ardis, hoping that she would want to try it over immediately, for an unsung melody is like a sensitive plate that has not been developed.

Ardis was sitting at her desk, taking notes on the " Areopagitica," in a savage-looking blank book with ink-spattered covers.

"Who asked you to write this music, Clare?" she asked.

"Christine," said Clare, looking a little surprised, " but of course Theresa told her to. Hasn't Tess said anything to you about it?"

"Yes," answered Ardis, turning to her work again, " but I don't think that I care to sing your music."

Clare could scarcely believe that she had heard her aright.

"Do you really mean that, Ardis? Of course the music is n't much in itself, but — it was written for you."

"I 've been looking up the words," said Ardis, carelessly, "and find that they have been set to music by a man in Boston; so I sent for the song, and expect it here to-night. I 'm sorry that you should have had the trouble of writing another, but of course you will admit that professional work is a little more desirable."

Clare took up the poor little manuscript, and went back to her room, too surprised and hurt to say a word.

"*I* did n't offer to write that music," she thought indignantly. "They made me — they made me! It 's unfair to humiliate a person who has n't any confidence, to begin with — it 's unnecessary. It 's like ironing a book-mark. It 's abominable!"

She seized the rejected sheets of music, and tore them into small pieces, scattering the fragments over the floor; then she raged around her room for half an hour, calling herself names.

She had not written her Milton abstract for the next day, and was obliged to do it that evening, while a brass band was playing on the campus, and everybody was out. Theresa Robinson came in, flushed with dancing, and asked Clare if she had finished the song for to-morrow. Clare pointed to the wastepaper basket, and said that Ardis had declined to sing it.

"That girl is getting more insufferable — " began

Theresa, and abruptly left the room. But in a few minutes she returned, saying: " Ardis prefers to sing the song that she has selected; so I told her that we could dispense with her services more easily than we could with your music, and asked Faith Bentley to sing it. Of course her voice is not like Ardis's, but if she's on the Glee Club she can do it well enough, and she is at least obliging."

"I am afraid that nobody will sing it now," said Clare. " There did n't seem to be any need for the music, so I tore it up."

" Tore it up! Why, Clare, how unlike you! "

" Why is it unlike me? You don't know what I'm like at all."

" I don't wonder that you were angry at Ardis, but I think you might have had a little more consideration for the society."

" I think the society will survive."

" Could n't you re-write at least a part of it, so that the programmes would not be spoiled? We made such a point of this new music, written by Pippa herself for this occasion."

" I could re-write all of it if I chose," said Clare, "but I don't intend to."

" You poor little thing! It's a shame that you have been treated so. But I can't see that I'm to blame, or the society either, and I was so hoping that there would be no unpleasantness at our farewell meeting."

" The music was written for Ardis, and if she won't sing it, nobody shall."

" Well, you *must* have been badly treated to make you behave like this."

"I'm not 'behaving,'" said Clare, indignantly. "What do you mean?"

"That's what I mean," laughed Theresa. "You've stated my point exactly."

Clare made no concessions that night, but the next morning she was up early, re-copying the music. She may have understood how Dante felt, when, having quarrelled with his friend Can Grande della Scala, he could not show him the last thirteen cantos of "Il Paradiso," and therefore determined that nobody else should see them.

It took a long time to re-write the music, but at noon Theresa found this note on the bulletin board:

DEAR TESS, — I was all wrong, as usual. There is nothing but wrongness in me. Faith has a copy of the music now.
CLARE.

The Sigma, being the older society, was to hold its farewell meeting in the reading room, and Phi Delta Kappa was ignominiously banished to Music Hall. But it turned out afterwards that Music Hall was the very best place for a musical meeting. Dr. Page's room, opening out of the hall, served as a dressing-room, and the tiny window over the platform was just the thing for Pippa's bit of sky.

The little mill-girl looked very sweet in her simple Italian dress, with her brown curls falling over her shoulders, and the brown eyes full of earnestness. It was true, as she had said, that she could not act; but her great love for the words may have helped them to tell their story truly, for when she knelt down, at the last, beside her little bed, there were tears in the eyes of many who saw her.

There is a certain kind of voice that invariably distracts the attention from what it says, because of a sympathetic quality that acts upon the mind of the listener like music, and steals it away. The Juniors who heard " Pippa Passes " thought of the deeper responsibilities that awaited them next year. The Seniors thought of their college bell, and of the ivies that were rustling outside in the night. But little Clare thought, " All service ranks the same with God — . . . there is no last nor first."

The Seniors were delighted with the new music, and said that they valued it all the more because it had been written for them.

" But it was n't," thought Clare, " it was written for Ardis. Dear me, what a bad temper I've been in ! "

The days were growing warmer now; the Seniors were practising the Ivy music every night, and examinations were drawing near. There had been a merry party on the Storey House steps one afternoon, when the ushers assembled to make their wands.

The Junior-Senior reception took place in the Gymnasium, and the first arrivals were mystified by finding three huge bowls of roses standing on the platform among the evergreens and palms; two hundred roses talking to each other, and no one who understood their language sufficiently to ask where they came from.

But the secret was revealed before the first dance began, for silence was called in the hall, and Ardis read the few simple words that had come with the flowers: " To the Class of Ninety-five, with love from the Class of Ninety-three."

JUNIOR USHERING

The girls of Ninety-five were impulsive as a class, and if many of them did not speak for a minute, and turned away their faces from the Seniors who were with them, there was no one in the hall who was old enough or wise enough to blame them. Ardis and the Vice-President pulled off their evening gloves, and distributed the long-stemmed flowers among the Juniors, who applauded and sang by turns. They always sang whenever there was the slightest excuse for doing so, and the other classes said that they sang oftenest when there was no excuse at all!

Each Junior presented her rose to the Senior whom she had invited, but kept the love that had come with it for herself.

The advent of the crimson roses was particularly auspicious on this occasion, for Ardis had incurred the wrath of both classes by refusing to take the Senior President to the reception. College etiquette demanded that she should do so, and college etiquette had been most unpleasantly defied. Ardis insisted that she had invited Maude Gilbert long ago, and that somebody else should take Miss Keith. Of course the President of Ninety-four had made no other arrangements, and one of the Juniors was obliged to give up her own Senior at the last minute, and take her to the reception. Miss Keith was a most charming girl, whom any one would have liked to invite, but she could not help feeling a little hurt at the treatment that she had received. Ardis was in general disfavor at this time, having neglected her presidential duties for work on the " Prism," while trying to exercise her presidential authority over the editors' themselves. She had attempted to "run" the Athletic Association, but was politely informed that her services were not required, whereupon the name of Leonora Kent, Vice-President of the association, was struck off the ushers' list. She never rewarded a service, nor forgot a slight, and if she had been an Empress instead of a Junior President, her subjects would have had reason to tremble for their lives!

Clare, who loved her best, saw in all these strange things merely symptoms of a mournful unrest that was trying to forget itself in work. Ardis had been particularly considerate since the episode of the song, and Clare had comforted herself by thinking that she did not mean to be unkind; but her own day of reckoning was to come.

When the ushers went down to have their places assigned in the Opera House, Clare was put up in the highest and most undesirable part of the gallery, where it was necessary to go up and down stairs, to seat the people. It was undeniably the worst place in the house, and Clare knew that somebody must have it; but she had never been strong enough to climb many stairs, and was very likely to take cold if she became physically exhausted.

"It is n't that I deserve a better place," she thought, "for I don't; and it's doing as much for my class to usher up here as it would be downstairs — but I wish I had a different kind of back!"

She stood the first night of Dramatics very well, for people came early, and another usher had time to help her; but on Saturday night there was a greater crowd. Fathers and mothers blundered into the wrong places, and could not be made to understand why they should move. Aunts and cousins had omitted to provide themselves with programmes, and wanted messages taken to friends downstairs. Clare felt as if she had walked miles over those ladder-like steps, and before all of the people were seated, she suddenly became very faint.

Christine Arnold was in one of the balcony boxes with Marjorie Drew, and had been furtively keeping one eye upon Clare. In a minute she was around at the gallery entrance, and had taken Clare out upon one of the iron platforms of the fire-escape. The fresh air revived her immediately; but while they were there, the lights in the house went down, and the curtain rose on the first act.

"I must go back," said Clare, in alarm. "Thank you so much, Christine. Oh! it is so humiliating, so absolutely degrading, not to be strong — to be found lacking in everything that is asked of one in this world! Let me go, dear. You see there is no one to tell those two old ladies where they are to sit."

Christine intercepted her, and Clare found herself walking down the balcony stairs instead of up to the gallery entrance. "You are well enough to go home alone," said Christine, "and the college is only two minutes from here. Give me your wand; I will take your place to-night;" and before Clare could raise any objections, she was gone.

Clare knew that she had taken cold, and having reached the end of her strength, was only too glad to go home. She began to realize that she had made a mistake in accepting this position in the gallery at all; but it would have been unheard of to ask any one to exchange with her, and to give up ushering

ACROSS THE CAMPUS

for those two nights meant giving it up for the whole of Commencement. There was Baccalaureate to come, and Ivy Day, and the final graduation exercises on Tuesday, with a collation at the campus houses afterwards. It was scarcely wise to risk her health for things like these,—but she was very young!

Christine took her place on the top steps, and stood there, tall and beautiful, like an avenging angel in a Donovan gown. She was so angry with Ardis that the color had come to her cheeks and the light to her eyes, and she heard one of the alumnæ ask an undergraduate, "Why is the most beautiful of the ushers up here on the gallery steps?"

The next day Clare was sick in bed, and two days later her mother was sent for. The cold had developed into bronchitis, and all thought of ushering or of Harvard Class Day was at an end. It was a dismal time to be sick, for nearly every one was too busy to come and see her, and the sound of the Glee Club singing on the campus drove her wild. It would have been so pleasant to wander around with them, and be pointed out to visitors as the new Leader for next year. Clare was not unreasonably egotistical, but she was human.

Her mother had stopped sewing on the Class Day gown, and it hung limp and forsaken in the closet. Then came a night when she struggled and struggled for breath, and wished that "this time might be the last;" for it was an old enemy that had overtaken her, and she was very tired.

But one morning the pain was gone, and she lay with a white rose on her pillow, looking at the square

248

of sunshine that quivered on the floor, and leaped sideways across the bed. Her mother sat sewing by the window.

"How cowardly it was in me to wish that this time might be the last," she thought. "This is a beautiful old world!"

Christine had been obliged to go to Class Day without her, but she had written Clare all about it, and a beautiful box of roses had come from Mrs. Arnold and Stephen. Ruth had sent Clare's ticket of admission to the tree exercises, and a tiny spray of the flowers that Stephen and Mr. Packard had pulled down for their friends.

"But it is only the well people who can be young," thought Clare. "Oh, I hate to be weak, I hate to be weak! There is no place for the weak people in this world, and I, who wanted to do so much, can only be an 'almost,' like poor Quasimodo, or, at best, a 'might have been.'"

"Clare," said her mother, as if she had been reading her thoughts, "I have something ever so nice to tell you — a secret. Guess what it is."

"I can't," said Clare, smiling. "Is it that you love me? But that's no secret, you know." She and her mother were so near of an age that Clare invariably alluded to her own childhood as "that time when we were little."

"Yes, that's it," said Mrs. Deland, "but there's more to it too. You know Miss Taylor's on Elm Street where Ruth and Christine are going to board next year?"

"Yes, that's where Ardis used to live. It's a homelike little place. And isn't it fine that Dr.

Burritt has got back some of his money, so that Ruth won't have to work any more, — except on lessons of course. My dear old Ruth! I'm so glad that she let Christine write me about it."

"There is another room at Miss Taylor's," continued Mrs. Deland, — "a little single room with two windows and lots of sunshine. And who do you suppose is going to have that?"

"I don't know," said Clare, who was beginning to forget how it feels to be an "almost" in the world. "Tell me."

"Clare Edmonds Deland."

"Mamma, you have n't engaged it without asking me!"

"I certainly have, dear, and Christine and Ruth agree with me that it is best. I have felt for some time that the nervous tension of these campus houses is too great for my little girl, although it may not be bad for even moderately strong people. Of course the campus life is a very important part of your college experience, but you have already had two years of it, and that is enough! You have gradually allowed yourself to become excited over trifles, and to worry over things that are not worries at all. So, if you want to be a Senior, and Leader of the Glee Club, it will be necessary to make some change."

"But to leave the campus, mamma! Why, you don't know what it means to us all."

"I think I know what it means to your mothers," said Mrs. Deland, with a smile. "Your letters are few and far between, and you never bring home any of the handkerchiefs that you took away. If you would exercise a little more judgment in the other people's handkerchiefs that you select, I would not complain, — but just look at this one!"

"Miss Taylor has a pug dog with a tucked stomach," said Clare, dismally. "And I don't like to think of leaving the campus, because that will mean leaving Ardis too."

"I think it is just as well for you to be separated from Ardis for a while. And if she is to be Manager of the Glee Club next year, there is no doubt but that you will see enough of her!"

Mrs. Deland had wisely refrained from expressing her entire opinion upon the subject of Ardis, although it might easily be inferred that she had one.

She went out that afternoon, and when she returned, brought Clare a note from the bulletin board.

"I always like to walk through the college whenever I go anywhere," she said. "Buildings have a personality of their own, and this one is so young and enthusiastic that I feel like dancing as soon as I open the door. It is not so bad to meet a ghost, if it is the ghost of a happiness! And I always pretend that I am you, going to recitations. To-day I looked for an imaginary note on the bulletin board, and behold, it materialized before — Why, darling, what's the matter?"

Clare had read the note, and laid it down suddenly, with a new look on her face.

"The note itself is not so much," she said, "but somehow it makes me think of all I want to do — and to be."

It was from the Leader of the Glee Club.

ACROSS THE CAMPUS

My dear little Clare, — I have been so hurried that I did n't come to say good-bye, but it may have been partly because I could not bear it.

I like to think that you are to take my place. You will enjoy the work more than anything or everything else in college, because there is something about it, beyond or above — I don't know what it is. But don't let them forget me, Clare, don't let them forget me !

Your friend,   Celia O. Howard.

Clare kept the little note warm in her hand all day, and knew that her Senior year had begun.

CHAPTER XVI

SENIOR RESPONSIBILITIES

THE Seniors were assembled in front of the Hillard House, waiting for their class group to be taken, and the photographer had just said: "Will that last young lady on the right, in the green skirt, move a little this way, and the one in the pink waist set down?"

All the under-class girls who were pointing their little Kodaks at the group, waited expectantly for the critical moment to arrive; the photographer withdrew his red face from under the focussing cloth, said, "Now, don't nobody smile!" and was about to squeeze the rubber mystery at the end of the long tube, when two girls dashed out of Lincoln Hall in their chemistry aprons, and tore breathlessly over the lawn.

"Hurry up, Freda!" "Where have you been, Mildred?" "Oh, you lunatics!" came in jeering comments from various parts of the picture, and the funereal expression that had pervaded the group, vanished in an instant.

"If the two new young ladies would kindly remove their pinafores," said the artist, deprecatingly, and the blue checked aprons were immediately pulled off by officious friends in the foreground.

"Three cheers for the President of Ninety-five!" called Kathleen Carey, as the long-suffering man raised the tube in his hand.

"Rah, rah, rah, *Ruth!*" came the unanimous reply; and as the photographer again waved the tube in desperation, Kathleen added, "Burritt!"

But the picture was taken at last; and as the class group scattered, to make room for the Juniors, Christine dashed over to College Hall after her notebook, calling out to ask Kathleen if she was not going on the Geology trip.

"I want to stay and be taken in the Freshman picture," shouted Kathleen. "You can tell him I'm ill!"

But three minutes later, when Christine emerged from the street entrance of the Music Building, Kathleen was already there upon the steps, singing "Way down upon the Suwanee River," to an admiring audience.

A wagonette was waiting at the door, and the whole class scrambled into it with much agility and laughter, while Professor Saunders sat at one end, waving a blue cotton umbrella. Heads popped out of several windows in the Music Building, and the composite pandemonium became audibly less.

"We ought to have a horn," said Grace Reade, as the drag started. "Oh, Professor Saunders, can't we stop somewhere and get a horn?"

"My dear young ladies," answered the professor, beaming upon them from behind his blue glasses. "this excursion takes the place of one of your regular recitations."

But he enjoyed the fun immensely, for all that, and

stopped the wagonette several times on their way out of town, to investigate the formation of certain apple-trees.

The object of the excursion was to trace old river-beds, and Professor Saunders stood up now and then to point out some especially fertile pasture that had once been the bottom of a lake.

" You can generally tell where water has been, by observing where the townspeople locate their ceme-teries," he said. " Rocky formations are never con-venient to dig in."

The wagonette left the road now, and bumped cheerfully over the corn and grain stubble to a high bank overlooking the river.

" Out, every one of you ! " said the professor, clos-ing his umbrella. " A few thousand years ago the Waverly River flowed into the Connecticut at the point where we are now standing. If you will follow me down this bank —"

It was rather a steep bank, and several of the stu-dents descended more speedily than they had planned ; others were obliged to sit down and slide, with a hail-storm of little stones rattling after them. But the charge of the blue umbrella inspired fortitude in the hearts of all, and even the most timorous " took " the bank without flinching.

The professor walked slowly along, thrusting a stick into the yellow earth of the embankment, until he stopped, triumphant, and picked out a little knot of plastered leaves and twigs.

" This was the ancient bed of the river," he said, "and we shall never know by what upheaval it was forced to change its course."

"Perhaps it reformed!" whispered Grace; and Kathleen added, "Probably its father knew something about it."

"Is n't it strange, Professor Saunders," said Leonora Kent, "that we can find the childhood of a river in one place, and its manhood in another, and yet they 're both going on at the same time."

"Yes; but the manhood of the river can never return to its childhood," said the professor, "and in that it is not so unlike ourselves. Young ladies," turning to a knot of girls who seemed to be fishing for something in the water, "have you found anything of interest among those logs?"

"Clay!" was the jubilant answer, as Kathleen raised two sticky hands; and Rachel Winter prepared to roll up a huge ball of the clinging substance in her handkerchief.

"Might I ask what you are going to do with it?" inquired the professor, doubtfully; and Kathleen answered, "Make a hair-pin box."

"I shall model my room-mate's head," said Rachel, glancing towards Salome, who was busily taking notes on what the professor had said.

"How clever in him to fathom the dissimulation of that river, after it 's been out of its old bed so many years!" said Christine. "It may try to look innocent, and say that it was never there, but you have only to rake out a few of these old leaves and sticks, and say —"

"Pardon me, but you 've dropped something," continued Kathleen. "How do you account for these, old boy, if you 've never slept in that bed? Oh, you 're a sly one!"

The wagonette crossed the ferry on its way home, and several of the girls jumped out to stand by the railing, or trail their fingers through the sunset in the water. Under the boat were pink ripples and pink clouds, but near the banks was a gentle green twilight, where the reflection of growing things plunged face downwards into the water.

"Do you remember how proud we used to think we'd be when we were Seniors?" asked Grace, "and now we don't think about being Seniors at all, but only of what we have to do!"

"When we were Juniors, I think we felt the importance of our position," said Christine, "and when we were Sophomores there was no living with us. But now —"

"We are altogether desirable. Is that what you were going to say?" asked Grace.

"No; I was only thinking — Where do you suppose we had better spend our last Mountain Day?"

"Stop it, sir!" shouted Kathleen, indignantly, seizing her by the arm. "You stop it now. 'Last Mountain Day' indeed! What do you mean by mentioning the word 'last' in my presence?"

Grace's eyes had filled suddenly with tears, but she laughed through them, as Ninety-five was wont to do, and said, "What a comfort it is to remember sometimes that we can't do any more than we can!"

"It *is* a comfort," said Christine, "because we are always blaming ourselves for not being able to march serenely past our own possibilities."

"I've taken what seemed to be the best road at every turn," said Grace, "and yet I've so often landed in an alley or a back yard. But that decision for what I thought was the best was all that could possibly lie in my power. And yet what have I to show for it?"

"You have us," said Kathleen, cheerfully. "We show up on all occasions."

"Yes, thank Heaven!" said Grace. "The girls of Ninety-five will always be reason enough to each other for having come to college, even if we can't often remember why xy would n't have been z, if it had n't been not-zp."

"I turned that syllogism round in the exam, and made it into an A," said Kathleen. "I find that you can make anything into an A, if you cut it over carefully and let out the under-arm seams."

"Was it right?" asked both girls, eagerly.

"No!"

When the wagonette reached home, the supper bells were ringing over the campus, and the baked apples on Miss Taylor's table were smoking hot. Baked apples are not bad after an afternoon's drive; neither are gingerbread and hot rolls.

"Oh, where did you find those autumn leaves?" asked Clare, as Christine tossed the tangible results of her excursion on the hall table.

"They 'held us up' on the way home. Just one big, beautiful branch — the first of the season. Oh, I do feel so disreputably dusty and wind-blown and *young*. 'Hey, Robin, jolly Robin, tell me how your lady does.'"

"Why, Christine, I did n't know that you could sing," laughed Clare, as they went to supper. "I'll take you down to rehearsal to-night."

"Do you suppose they 'd put me out if you did?"

" You 'd be much more likely to put *them* out. Oh dear, I wonder if that little Gladys Campbell will remember to bring back my copy of the Waltz Song ! "

" Gladys Campbell is interested in you, Miss Arnold," said Miss Sabin, the young Greek assistant, who sat at one end of the table. " She asked me the other day how old you were."

" You can tell her that I 'm just twenty-one," said Christine, holding her roll in mid-air. " My parents can no longer claim my earnings."

" Oh, Gladys ought not to say such things," said Clare, looking disturbed. " People will think that she is fresh."

A laugh went round the table at this, and Ruth said : " Clare has a feeling of responsibility about Gladys, because she is Edith Campbell's cousin, and the youngest Freshman on the club. Is n't that it, Clare ? "

" Those are two reasons why I ought to be interested in her," said Clare, " but I care about her mostly, because she is a dear, loving child."

" Miss Deland thinks that every young person is a bundle of promises," said one of the Juniors, " and that the faith of our friends is what enables us to fulfil them."

" Or break them entirely," said Christine. " But I don't think that we ought to be too dependent upon outside approbation, or let ourselves be too often influenced by what people expect; because if we did that all the time, we should soon cease to be facts and become mere inferences."

" And then if two people happened to hold exactly opposite opinions of our character, we should cease to exist altogether," said Clare. "May I be excused, Miss Sabin?"

She did not take the conventional path to the college, but crossed over to the Methodist church-yard, and went through the "hole in the fence." This hole opened on the campus, and the displaced slats were nailed back at intervals; but the hole always re-appeared again in due season, looking none the worse for its enforced absence. A group of Ninety-eight girls were playing "snap the whip" on one of the tennis courts, and a light breeze made all the hammocks look as if ghosts were swinging in them. The apples were stacked in gold and crimson piles under the trees, and one belated ripe one dropped down with a cheerful thud at Clare's feet. She picked it up and laughed, for it seemed exactly as if the apple had done it to startle her.

When she reached the front campus, the Glee Club girls were wandering towards the Music Building in knots of two and three. Gladys Campbell was sitting on Lincoln Hall steps with May Church-ill, one of the Glee Club Juniors, and Clare looked at them uneasily as she passed, for May Churchill was the very last girl that she would have chosen as a friend for little Gladys. But " little " Gladys, as Clare loved to call her, was really not little at all. She was tall, and beautiful to look at, and one could tell at a glance just what kind of a mother she had at home, what books and pictures she had seen, and what music she had heard. One knew that all had been right with the child.

"I wonder if they know it's nearly six-thirty,"

Clare thought. "I'll wait a little, and see if they don't come."

Ardis had not returned yet, and Clare had been obliged to re-organize the Glee Club alone. The responsibility was great, because there was so much besides musical ability to be considered in the selection of new members. Strength of character and high principles counted here, as in everything else, and Clare knew that the girls who were faithful to their studies would be faithful to their club.

"Let me see," she said, as she joined the group in front of the Music Building, "we're all here now, except —"

"I'll go and get them," said Isabel Bovey, indignantly; "it's terribly mean of them not to come."

"Thank you, Isabel," said Clare. "No, I'll go myself. They'll understand better that way. Thank you, dear."

She walked down to Lincoln Hall steps, and said brightly, "Oh, May, won't you and Gladys please come to rehearsal? The Glee Club can't get along without you at all, and neither can I."

"Aren't you ashamed to forget rehearsal?" asked May, turning to Gladys, "and you a Freshman! They'll bounce you from the club."

"No, they won't," said Clare, taking Gladys by the hand. "We need her on the club!"

"It was you who forgot to go, Miss Churchill," said Gladys, shyly; "you're a Junior, and *you* ought to be ashamed."

"I think you ought both to be ashamed to forget me, when I'm always thinking about you," said Clare, laughing. "If you're not careful, my feelings will be very much hurt. Now do come, or the girls will think we've deserted them." She slipped her other hand into May's, and the three went back to Music Hall together.

Clare knew that May had kept Gladys away from rehearsal on purpose, but chose to ignore that fact, rather than let May think for an instant that she was distrusted. She had her own theories with regard to this Junior, who was so pretty and so talented that it made all the rest of her seem like such a mistake. In the first place, May rarely, if ever, knew her lessons, and in a woman's college one does not respect the people who do not study. In addition to this, she smoked cigarettes, and drank a great deal of champagne, — two undesirable facts which had caused her to be instinctively shunned by the refined element in the college. The upper-class girls did not see fit to engage in any violent discussion with regard to the propriety of smoking, for women. They understood that it is not a matter of conviction, but of repulsion, and simply left May alone.

Some of her friends would have stood by her for better or worse, — as college girls know how to do, — if she herself had not proved inconstant and unreliable. But, as it was, she preferred to have a large following of under-class girls, who were either too young or too ignorant to understand her lack of moral fibre — to entertain them lavishly, and offer them everything in her possession, from the cigarettes to the latest and most approved methods of evading one's duties.

Clare had evolved a comparatively new plan with regard to the management of May, and was waiting hopefully to see if it would succeed. It was a very simple way, after all; she was going to trust her.

As she led the singing that night, she felt that the wide meaning of it all was broadening out before her, like a road that ends in a sweeping beach of sand. Beyond that was the ocean, and beyond the ocean was — God. And yet people would not see that there might be a sacred side to this musical work, this perfect union of the Leader in her girls, and of the girls in the Leader that they had chosen for themselves.

Clare had decided that they should sing better than any Glee Club had ever sung! It was not a " Glee Club," after all, but an unusually fine choral society of trained voices, and why should they not sing the very best music, in the way that such music should be sung?

" I will hitch my wagon to a star," she thought, " and then if — I fail, I shall at least have had the little path of starlight to ride in ! "

But every time that she heard those fresh young voices, with all their possibilities of laughter and of tears, she knew that the little path of starlight must lead up to its star at last.

Rehearsal went well that night, and after the Assistant Leader had put away the music and received her instructions for the next few days, Clare went into the old organ-room, where she and Ardis had first practised together.

She had not been into that room since the day of the Glee Club elections in June, and there were many things to tell the organ that it had not heard before. She made shepherds' pipes and their echoes upon the different banks of keys, pretended that she was a melody going on a journey through the world, and ended, as she always did, with "The Lost Chord." "It may be that death's bright angel" — the Vox Humana sounded very human that night, "will speak in that chord again. And it may be that only in Heaven — " Clare jumped down from the organ-bench and threw open the door in wild delight, crying, "Ardis, Ardis!"

In a minute there was a warm, sweet arm around her neck, and her cheek was pressed against the cool heads of the little violets that Ardis wore in her dress. At first she was too happy to do anything but sit still, while Ardis kissed her forehead and her hair, and even her hands, with the dusty remnants of "shepherds' pipes" between the fingers. Then she said, "When did you come, and why did n't you tell me you were coming, and why did n't you come before?"

"I came here straight from the train," replied Ardis, "remembering that it was rehearsal night, and the first thing that I heard was 'The Lost Chord.' Why did n't you write to me this summer, Clare? I 've missed your letters."

It never occurred to her to connect Clare's silence with the Junior ushering trouble in the spring, any more than it occurred to Clare that she might think so. For Clare understood that Ardis had not intended to make her ill, and Ardis even felt aggrieved that her delicately intended slight should have had so tragic an ending.

"Well, there was something that I wanted to tell you," said Clare, "and did n't like to write it; so I thought that I 'd rather wait — "

"Good heavens, little ones, you're not engaged?"

"No, no; one in the family is quite enough. But speaking of engagements, did you get Louise Burritt's wedding cards?"

"Yes, and I've met the man too. What was it that you wanted to wait and tell me?"

"About my not going back to the Marston this year. I'm up at Miss Taylor's with Christine and Ruth."

"And left me all alone? Oh, Clare!"

Ardis· looked very much hurt, although Clare explained over and over again her reasons for leaving the campus. "It was only so that I could be more quiet," she said.

Ardis went to the window, and looked out at the twinkling lights of the Storey House opposite, and at the long, mysterious shadows that made the concrete walks take unfamiliar turns. Then she tried to speak and stopped, and Clare saw that the slow, unaccustomed tears had gathered in her eyes.

"'From him that hath not,'" she began. "There, don't be alarmed at my quoting Scripture, Clare. I've been car-sick, I believe. Whom have you taken on the Glee Club? Any one that I know?"

Clare told her all the Glee Club news, and walked down with her to the Marston, when the janitor came to shut up the Music Building.

"You will miss that old elm-tree of yours," said Ardis, as they said "Good-night" on the steps.

"Yes; but I think that I could get along without the elm, if I had you. It's rather hard — not having you, Ardis. I don't believe you understand just how hard it is."

265

Two memories flashed through the mind of the older girl as Clare said this, — one, of a song that was not sung by the person for whom it was written; and another, of a weary little usher alone on the topmost gallery steps. But Clare had forgotten!

"We will see each other in choir and Glee Club," Ardis said.

"We sha'n't see each other in choir any more, because they banished all the Seniors yesterday, before rehearsal. But we can go to chapel together. And won't it seem funny to be sitting with our class again!"

"Being put out of the choir seems like the first step towards being put out of the college, does n't it?" said Ardis. "After all — I'm fond of this place."

"We have one more of these dear, happy years before us," said Clare. "We must help each other to make the most of it!"

"Good-night!" called the matron cheerfully, from her window; and both girls laughed, as Clare wrapped her cape around her and started for home.

The social side of college life is composed of incidents which have absolutely no connection with each other; and while the centre of the circle is the intellectual life, which grows steadily, beautifully, and well, the tangents may be anything, from blue prints to sociological reforms.

"I think that the many-sidedness of the college girl may account in a large measure for her happiness," said Professor Burton, the next day, as he came out of Lincoln Hall with his friend Dr. Comstock. Professor Burton was taking his mid-day

meal at Miss Taylor's that year, and Dr. Comstock
often dropped in to walk up with him. This morning they had been discussing germs, and, incidentally, the subject of the college woman. ·

" Then you don't think that this many-sidedness,
as you call it, tends to make them indifferent to the
old-fashioned womanly interests that — "

His sentence was never finished, for at that precise
moment he and his friend were run into from behind by a baby carriage coming down the Hillard
House walk at full speed. The carriage was pursued by half a dozen students in riotous spirits, who
had made up their minds that the baby must be
captured at all costs. They had been down town
foraging, and as they waved various ungainly parcels
in the air while running, it was not strange that
the little nursemaid should have thought her last
hour had come.

"Whoa there, hold on, you'll capsize your pas-
senger!" said the doctor, laying a detaining hand
on the little vehicle. " Don't you know better than
to bounce a year-old baby over the ground at that
rate? "

" Them ladies wanted to steal her! " said the
child, looking around apprehensively at her pursuers,
who were drawing near.

" No, they don't. You must n't be a lunatic, you
know," said Professor Burton, reassuringly. " We
have n't the proper appliances for dissecting babies
in our laboratory."

The girls came up, laughing and breathless, and
after much persuasion bargained with the little maid
to let them have the baby on the Storey House steps

for ten minutes, in exchange for two bags of peanuts and one of Mrs. Flannagan's chocolate cakes. The girls who were going home from noon recitation stopped and gathered around this serene atom of humanity, who seemed quite unconscious of the fact that she was the temporary property of Harland College. She did not realize what it meant to be legally " hired out " to a starving and babyless community, which had been willing to exchange good peanuts for her services.

Christine Arnold sat down with the baby on the Storey House steps, and the other girls regarded them both in awed and worshipful silence.

" I did n't know that you cared so much for children, Miss Arnold," said a little Freshman, who was quite absorbed in counting the three white buttons on the baby's shoe.

" All women do," answered Christine, sternly. She was wishing that every one would go away, so that she could cuddle the baby as much as she wanted to.

" Oh, but I 've known some women that have n't," said the Freshman, timidly, " and I can't understand it, either."

" I said — all *women*," re-emphasized Christine; " there may be females who do not ! "

The baby must have found out and understood some side of Christine that other people did not often see, for when she was ceremoniously returned to her carriage and fastened in, with an absurd knitted strap, she put out two little hands and cried to come back.

" Higher education does not seem to have interfered with their maternal instinct, at all events," said

SENIOR RESPONSIBILITIES

Dr. Comstock, laughing, as he and Professor Burton walked on.

"Good heavens, no! I have decided, from my own observation, that the college life tends to increase womanliness in women rather than to diminish it. Anything that teaches a girl to distinguish between the realities and artificialities of life cannot fail to make her understand what, for her, must be the greatest reality of all! I think that the college girl is always more womanly at the end of her four years' course than she was at the beginning — for the simple reason that there is more of her to be a woman with."

"Would you care to marry one of them?" asked Dr. Comstock, thoughtfully.

"Well, I'm not particularly anxious to 'appear out bride;' but statistics have shown that a man who spends his life in studying one kind of bacteria is sure to perish by it in the end."

"How would the young ladies like to hear you refer to them as bacteria?" asked Dr. Comstock, as he and Professor Burton parted company.

"They did n't hear me," answered the professor, pulling open Miss Taylor's screen-door.

"I did," said Christine Arnold, coming out of the parlor, satchel in hand, "but I won't tell anybody."

"I don't believe that you did," said the professor, "because I have a low and gentle voice — an excellent thing in man. But no matter what you may have overheard, you may rest assured that it is nothing to what I could say if I chose."

"We all understand that," said Christine, gravely, "especially since that day when you informed the assembled table that you had to pay insect-collectors more for catching wasps because of the 'personal element' in it."

"It is the trivial things like that which live after a man is gone," said the professor, mournfully. "The really great facts of his life pass by unnoticed."

"Speaking of passing, was there a car in sight when you came in?"

"There was, but I think it was n't going your way, although, of course, it is not for me to say which way you intended to go."

"I'm bound for Worcester — to spend Sunday with my friend Marjorie Drew. The fact that I'm an intimate friend of the Senior President and of the Glee Club Leader convinces me that I need to accumulate strength for the coming year. Have you any message for Miss Drew?"

"Give her my love," said the professor, imperturbably. "Are n't you going to have any dinner?"

"I have a luncheon to eat on the train," explained Christine, laughing. "Here's my car. Good-bye;" and off she went, leaving Professor Burton to draw a mental contrast between a certain Sophomore with a green '95 on her Gym suit and her hair in two long curly braids, and the beautiful young woman whom he had seen on the Storey House steps that morning, with a little child in her arms.

"Wonder how she got home before I did," he meditated. "Oh, I know. Hole in the fence."

Worcester was about two hours from South Harland, and when Christine had finished her luncheon, she took out her James's Psychology and learned the lesson for Monday.

Marjorie met her at the station, and bore her off triumphantly to the little rooms where she and Harriet Keith kept house. Marjorie was teaching in a college preparatory school, and Harriet had a very good position on a newspaper.

"You can't imagine what fun we have," said Marjorie, as she helped Christine out of her wraps. "We cook our own breakfasts and suppers, — that is, make coffee in the morning, and warm up a cold bean at night; but we are very swell at noon, and have dinner tickets at 'Mrs. Hooper's Ever-Ready Luncheon!'"

"And does Miss Keith still have theatre tickets galore, and all the latest books to review?"

"Yes, in certain directions, Harriet has what might be termed a 'snap;' but she has to pay for it by losing most of her sleep. Sitting up nights, in an office full of tobacco smoke, is not quite so amusing as interviewing an Irish wedding by day, and being presented with a piece of jelly-cake wrapped up in a fragment of your own newspaper!"

Harriet herself came in before long, and welcomed Christine with enthusiasm.

"I have tickets for 'Samson and Delilah' to-night," she said, "and I'm going to try to get off to-morrow afternoon, so that we can go to some matinée together. Now do tell us all the college news. We don't even know the class elections."

"Except Ruth Burritt's," said Marjorie. "Who is your Ivy Orator, Christine?"

"She's not elected yet, but there's not much doubt that Edith Standish will get it. We have a class meeting to-morrow."

"How is my poor little Elsie getting on without Ruth this year?"

"Oh, she's busy with her 'Prism' work and her tutoring. She takes her dinner at our house now, so we have very festive times together."

"And is Miss Deland doing well with the Glee Club?" asked Harriet.

"Yes, finely! But I really think she cares too much about it. When there has been a poor rehearsal, she comes home and goes to bed."

"Do you still sport that emaciated cat of yours?" asked Harriet, disrespectfully. She was one of those unexplainable, inexcusable people who don't like them!

"No, poor Datisi! Miss Taylor has an abominable, loose-skinned pug-dog, with a bulging eye, and accordingly Datisi had to go back to his mother's people. I took him there myself, wishing to witness the maternal joy on his arrival; but education had created a barrier between parent and child. Datisi was greeted with a fierce triangular spit, and fled under the barn, with a tail of increased proportions. I have n't seen him since."

"Have there been any brilliant recitations among the Seniors this year?" asked Marjorie, changing the subject. "I shall never forget that time in Ethics, last Spring, when Professor Harding asked Nathalie Rollins what she meant by free-will, and Nathalie answered, 'I think that every woman has a right to live and be loved'!"

"Nathalie was the person who thought that it was never right to tell a lie," said Harriet, "not even to save a dear friend from being murdered."

" 'Not even if it were the lesser of two evils,' " quoted Marjorie. "I became suspicious of Nathalie from that moment, and have not believed a word that she said since."

"Of course there are certain circumstances under which it is highly commendable to lie," said Christine; "for instance, I think that every woman is expected, to say ' No,' when questioned about any man."

"Unless it's the man himself who happens to question her," said Harriet, thoughtfully; and Marjorie gave a wail of despair.

"There is a certain young reporter," she said, "and Harriet is only twenty-one — not that there is any connection between the two facts, however."

"Of course not," said Harriet. "But seriously, Marjorie, college girls do *not* lie as a class. We've heard people speak of that more than once."

"Miss Carlisle says that untruthfulness is a habit, like everything else," quoted Christine, "and that the average college girl does n't lie, because she is used to thinking and searching for the truth. Four years' training in accuracy makes truthfulness the first instinct, at all events, and — "

"I 'm sorry to break in upon this discussion," said Marjorie, rising, "but, Harriet, did you remember to bring home the bananas? "

" Yes."

" And the cheese for the rarebit? "

" Yes. Don't you want me to make the toast? "

" No, you 're tired; stay here and talk to my company while I get supper. To-morrow morning we 'll take Christine over to see Hester, won't we? Poor Hester, she is n't as happy as we are."

18   273

"Is that Hester Morris, who was in your class?" asked Christine. "I heard that she was down here teaching, or something."

"She's lecturing on stuffed beasts, in the museum where they reside," said Harriet, "and when she was at college she specialized on Political Economy and French."

"That illustrates the versatility of the trained mind," replied Christine, gravely. "Oh, by the way, girls, I have a pot of Dundee jam for you in my bag."

The little visit with Marjorie and Harriet came to an end all too soon, and Sunday afternoon found Christine on the train bound for South Harland. As the cars swept along beside the river at dusk, she watched eagerly for the first glimpses of Mt. Waverly and Mt. Gwynn. They had become very dear to her in the three years that she had known them, and it was a comfort to remember, every night when she closed her eyes, that the watchers over Harland were watching still! She imagined that vespers must be nearly over now, and wondered what hymn they were singing. Then she thought of Ardis, and was thinking of her still when the train drew into the station.

Ruth and several of the others were there to meet her, and, as soon as they had boarded an electric car, announced to Christine that she had been elected Ivy Orator by a large majority at class-meeting the day before. This was the greatest honor of Commencement, and at first Christine feared that she was the subject of a jest; but after she had received the congratulations of the younger Faculty at Miss Taylor's, and of about twenty students who dropped in during the evening, she began to realize that greatness had, at last, been thrust upon her.

" I telegraphed your family yesterday," said Ruth, " and here's an answer that came from your father last night. I thought it was safer to open it."

The telegram read, —

" Magnificent. Will be there to hear you spout.

ARNOLD."

On the following Wednesday night the S. F. D. C. gave a farewell dinner to their President—and disbanded!

CHAPTER XVII

"IT CAME UPON THE MIDNIGHT CLEAR"

OCTOBER came, and the dusk was reddened by the falling leaves. Then it was November, — a time when the sunshine that is in one has all that it wants to do.

Once it rained steadily for four days, and the college dressing-rooms were pervaded by an atmosphere of damp and resentful rubber, while long streams of water from the umbrella-tips meandered across the floor. At the beginning of the fourth day everybody was discouraged, and Clare walked down to chapel with the firm conviction that she had not a friend in the world. Her spirits were always affected by the weather, and when the trees wept, she felt like shutting herself up in her room and weeping too. Her state of mind was not improved by finding a note on the bulletin board from Margretta Nolenski, the Assistant Leader of the Glee Club, saying that she had been called home the night before by the sudden illness of her mother.

"It will be doubtful whether I come back this term," she wrote, "and then perhaps I sha'n't want to come at all. Oh, Clare! The music is all in order, and I left that second-alto part that you wanted, inside your score of the 'Meistersinger.'"

"IT CAME UPON THE MIDNIGHT CLEAR"

Clare was desperately sorry for Margretta, and yet she felt conscious, at the same time, of a vague, unreasoning rage at any one who would be so pathetic on a wet day. There seemed to be nothing in the atmosphere to fall back upon.

Ardis came through the corridor at that minute, and Clare told her about Margretta, adding: "I suppose that I ought to appoint a temporary Assistant, but the girls are all so busy — I hate to ask them."

"Come up to chapel and talk it over," said Ardis. "Let's see: there's Belle Bovey, — but she's Junior Councillor, and on the Executive of Phi Delta Kap, and Secretary of the Biological Society. Kate Dervish would be too difficult. No, I'll tell you what — I'll do it myself. It wouldn't be much more work in addition to the management, and it will be easier for you to have some one that you're used to."

"Oh, Ardis, will you really?" asked Clare, delighted. "If it won't be too hard — only till Margretta comes back? There isn't so very much to do, you know, and it would be lovely for us to work together."

"I shall consider myself duly appointed Assistant Leader until Margretta comes back," said Ardis, gravely. "That condenses the responsibility, and makes things simpler all round."

"And will you come up this afternoon, and hear a beautiful plan that I've been wanting to consult you about for some time?"

Ardis said that she would, and when the Seniors filed out after chapel, Clare was so happy that she quite forgot to be alarmed, as she generally was, at

277

the size and dignity of the Freshman class. She had not yet become accustomed to walking solemnly down that long middle aisle, with rows upon rows of strange faces before her, and a feeling of insignificance about her own knees.

She hoped that Ardis would come soon after dinner, and hurried through her studying so that they might have time for a good long talk. But just as she had finished her twentieth page of Bosanquet's "Æsthetics," Ruth came in with her fancywork, saying that she and Christine were too cross to study any more. They were going to make candy, and tell funny stories, and have as good a time as they possibly could, while the weather was so limp.

There was a cheerful rattle of pans in the hall, and Christine came in with " Plato and Platonism" over her arm, and a bar of chocolate in one hand. She threw down the pans, placed the bar of chocolate very carefully in the " Plato" for a book-mark, and went downstairs after butter. When she returned, she found her two friends engaged in what appeared to be an altercation.

" Ruth thinks that I'm a Pantheist," said Clare, resentfully, " and I *know* that I'm not, because Pantheism attributes actual divinity to everything in nature, and I never thought that anything less than the human soul could be divine, although it does seem sometimes as if music — "

" Music is caused by the motion of material things," interrupted Christine, with a flourish of the butter-knife.

" Don't you suppose I know that, silly? But music comes nearer to suggesting its divine meaning than

"IT CAME UPON THE MIDNIGHT CLEAR"

other materials do, and that's why there is so much music in the world."

"Too fat an *à priori* to get through an ordinary door! Turn it round sideways, or pitch it overboard, and bring in a good practical reason."

"Certainly. The universe is built according to certain ratios, measurements, and numbers; and music is the speech of numbers. Everything that grows sings, and has a note of its own."

" Yes," said Christine, "*I* have; and so has Ruth."

" Clare meant the things that grow out of doors," explained Ruth, reproachfully.

"Well, I grow out of doors some of the time. You can't expect me to stay in the house all day. You're like the man who told his clerk that if he wanted to raise a mustache, he'd have to do it out of office hours."

"I was going to say," continued Clare, after stopping to "land" Christine with a sofa-pillow, "that when the petals of a flower are written in regular intervals, it makes of the flower itself a melody. For instance, every pansy has a little peal of five bells, while a daisy often contains the whole chromatic scale."

"Nevertheless," repeated Ruth, "I do think that you are a Pantheist."

"I'm not a Pantheist," said Clare, indignantly. " You're a Pantheist yourself! "

"Children, children!" said Christine, severely. " Ruth, you must not call Clare a Pantheist, because I know for myself that she is not one; and, Clare, you must not call Ruth a Pantheist, for the reason that she happens to be a straight descendant from Heraclitus

279

— especially when she clears up my top bureau-drawer. Her motto is, 'Everything passeth away; nothing remaineth!'"

"Don't mention philosophy," said Clare. "I can't understand the Plato for to-morrow at all."

"I don't exactly see how he can think abstractions are real," said Christine. "Why, just suppose that you should meet one! What in the world would you do? I think that I should say 'gyt naebbe gae geleafan,' out of my Anglo-Saxon Reader, and then it would go away."

"Things can be real without being tangible," objected Ruth. "A thing does n't need to have two legs and two arms in order to be real."

"No," said Christine, thoughtfully. "Consider the hen."

"I suppose you meant that for a joke — about meeting an abstraction; but your jokes are often so complicated that one cannot disentangle the point at all."

"Dear me," said Christine, "you can't expect the same person to provide both the joke and the brains to appreciate it!"

Ruth was trying to think of something annihilating to say in return, when there was a loud knock at the door, and two waterproofed figures rushed into the room, dragging their umbrellas over the floor.

"Den of knaves and conspirators!" said Kathleen, breathlessly. "I smelled it from away over behind the Episcopal Church — in front of the Wyndham."

"Sit down, sit down!" said Christine, carrying off the umbrellas to drip in the bathtub.

"It is nice to see you up here again, Grace," said

Clare, removing her friend's gossamer. "The 'Prism' has all that there is of you nowadays."

"I say, is n't it done?" asked Kathleen, peering into the simmering brown mass, which Ruth was slowly manipulating with a spoon.

"No, go away, Kaddy; you'll upset it. Look over the banisters, and see who it was that just came in — that's a dear."

"That's a deep-laid plot," said Kathleen, knowingly, "but I'm no chicken. You can't persuade me that any one else has a far-sighted enough smell to have spotted that P. F. already. Oh, you sly old dog, you!" she exclaimed, as Freda Hastings appeared in the doorway. Everybody became more hilarious now, for who could help forgetting to be blue when there were six of them, and they all belonged to the class of Ninety-five!

A bird flew up against the window and darted away again, shaking the gray drops from his gray wings.

"Poor little fellow!" said Ruth, "I think it frightened him to see you so close to the window, Clare. Move away, and see if he won't come back."

"No, he knows me — he has been here before," said Clare. "I like to think that he is a wandering spirit, and has some message to communicate when I am in the right mood to receive it."

"Perhaps he is really a spirit," said Freda. "Some of the Asiatic Indians believe that the spirits of their relatives come back to the earth in the form of snakes, and why not as birds?"

"Dear me," said Christine, "what a splendid chance to get even with your ancestors!"

ACROSS THE CAMPUS

"I'd like to catch the snake that contains whoever gave me such a bad temper," said Clare.

"What would you do with him?" asked Christine.

"What *could* one do to really embarrass a snake! I think that I would paint mine in alternate stripes of pink and green, and then leave him around where he could hear what other reptiles said about him. And then I would give him all the things to eat that he did not love."

"They like toads," said Freda, scientifically.

"Well, then, everything that was not a toad he should eat; and when dying of repletion he would regret that he had left me all his bad qualities, and sob out, 'Better to have bequeathed them to a hospital or a charity kindergarten — to any one rather than to you!'"

"Edward Bellamy says," observed Ruth, seriously, "that 'the lives of the unborn are in our hands; as we deal with them, so may God deal with us.' Now, it seems to me that if this is true, it must work both ways, and the people who are dead are just as responsible for our failings."

"Very likely they are," said Christine, "and in that case our ancestors are being what Bellamy would call 'dealt with' now. I feel sorry for some of mine."

"In faith, so do I," said Kathleen, "and it would n't be fair to make any one ancestor responsible for the whole of me. I'd have to be divided up between them. — Ruth, why did n't you tell me the butter was on the window-sill before I leaned back here?"

The front door slammed again, and somebody came upstairs.

"Herein!" called Clare, before the knock came,

for she had recognized the step, although the others did not.

"Why, if it is n't our good friend Epicurus," said Kathleen, "and he has on his new blue and yellow changeable silk gossamer. Come in, Epicurus, and have some P. F., for we 've all got to die some day."

"I 'm afraid I can't stop for P. F. this afternoon," said Ardis, smiling. "I came up to see Clare on business and by special appointment."

"You can take some P. F. and your appointment into our room, Clare," said Christine, "seeing as we 've appropriated yours."

"Thank you, I was intending to. Now, about the business, Ardis," she said, as soon as they were alone. "It is n't business yet, but it 's got to be business before it 's over, and I want your advice and encouragement. What do you think of giving a concert, a nice big one, in December, for the benefit of the children at the College Settlements?"

"I think it would be a most insane and unbusinesslike proceeding," said Ardis, in astonishment. "What put that into your head?"

"Playing for the H. A. C. W. the other night. It occurred to me that it was doing very little for them only to play hymns, and I wondered if, being the Leader of the Glee Club, I could n't help them a little more."

"So you thought of turning the Glee Club into a second 'Harland Association for Christian Work,' did you? I would n't do that if I were you; because you know the original object of the club was to sing, and not to overcast undergarments or scallop babies' petticoats."

"You are confusing the H. A. C. W. with the Needlework Guild, I think," said Clare, "and you have entirely misunderstood my plan with regard to the Glee Club. We all know that the primary object of our club is to represent the best musical work of the college; but we also know that from a financial point of view we are the most important organization here. And as long as we can make money so easily, it seems a pity not to employ our musical powers for some charitable ends."

"But do you realize that if we give a concert in December, we shall not be able to fill the house again this year? Our annual winter-term concert has become traditional, and, being the manager, I do not care to have it turn out a financial failure."

"I think that we could fill the chapel twice," said Clare. "Of course the size of the audience that we have at the Easter concert will depend upon the way that the girls sing at the Christmas one, and if they sing well — Oh, Ardis, they sing divinely already! You know that they do."

"You are terribly unpractical, Clare," said Ardis, impatiently. "Who ever heard of getting up a big concert out of hand like this? In the first place, the girls won't be ready, and in the second, it will cost a tremendous sum."

"No, it won't," said Clare, eagerly. "I've thought all that out myself. Programmes will be five dollars, tickets a dollar and a half, and holly three. I suppose we could get along without the holly, but somehow I don't think we'd better. And it will amount to very little, in comparison with what we'll take in."

"Yes, you'll take in your money now, instead of at the end of the year, and having given it all away, will land the club in a state of philanthropic bankruptcy. Clare, I must congratulate you on your business foresight in this matter."

"Don't speak to me like that, Ardis," said Clare, turning her face away. "It is n't necessary."

"I'm sorry, little one. I don't mean to be unkind; but you must understand that this plan of yours is a very impossible one, because you have no right to run the club into debt in order to help other people out."

"Then you won't bring it up before the club?" asked Clare. "You know it is the business of the Manager to conduct matters of this kind."

"Pardon me, but not of this kind. I prefer not to bring up anything for discussion that obviously cannot be done."

"I'm sorry that you think it cannot be done," said Clare, "because, Ardis, I suppose I ought to tell you — I've made up my mind that it's going to be done."

"Then why did you do me the honor of consulting me at all? You seem to be quite capable of conducting the whole affair yourself."

"Because — Oh, Ardis, don't speak to me like that! You are the Manager of my club, and does n't it count for something that you are my friend, — that I've always wanted to consult you about everything? I thought that you would approve, that you would help — Oh, I am so disappointed!"

"There is a rehearsal to-night!" thought Ardis; and she suddenly rose to go.

"What are you going to do?" asked Clare, anxiously.

"I am going to stop this foolishness of yours before it gets any farther."

"No, no!" cried Clare, running to the door. "You must wait a minute. Ardis, Ardis, do you hear? You must n't say anything to the girls about this, before rehearsal to-night; it is n't fair. I have n't spoken to any of them, because I was waiting to consult you first, and I think that the consent of the club should be asked from the club as a whole, and not from individuals who have been prejudiced beforehand. No, Ardis, you shall not go. No, no, — *wait*."

"I shall be obliged to take you away from that door by force, if you don't let me out," said Ardis, impatiently. "Clare, you 're acting like a fool!"

"Then you can go," said Clare, standing aside. "You can go, because I don't think that I should like to have you hurt me. And you can say what you like to the girls. I don't care what you say, as long as I have the right on my side."

"You may have what you think is the right on your side. Who was it that said, 'A man may believe many times, without knowing once'? And it is so absurd to consider this a question of right and wrong, anyway. It 's merely a question of what is the most sensible thing to do."

Clare was trembling all over now, and knew that Ardis would despise her for the weakness that she could not conceal.

"Why must I always show when I am hurt?" she thought. "Oh, I must stop this — I must, I must."

Ardis went to her, and took one of the cold little hands in hers.

"Suppose we both forget all about this," she said. "I will agree not to say anything to the girls about your plan, if you will make the same promise. Oh, Clare, I did n't think that you would let anything — even the Glee Club — come between you and me!"

Clare struggled with herself for several minutes before she could speak, and then she said, "I — love you, Ardis!"

"You used to," said Ardis, quietly.

"I do now! Oh, Ardis, don't say that again. I love you always — better than my life. There are people who say that college friendships don't count for much, but those are the people who do not know. Ardis, you know that I love you — that I would do anything in this world for you that I thought was right —" Ardis turned to go.

"Oh, wait!" cried Clare, seizing her hand. She regained her self-control with a sudden effort, and said: "Ardis, the Harland Glee Club is more than a choral society of trained voices. It is an organization of strong, sympathetic, intellectual women. It ought to be a power for good — an influence that would make itself felt outside and far beyond this college world! To give an annual concert for the College Settlements would imply no extra labor, no individual expense. We are here, as you say, to sing. It is our duty to sing, our pleasure to sing. Why not make it our *glory* to sing, and let some of that music go back to the God that gave it?"

"You have heard what I had to say," replied Ardis, "and if there 's anything I detest, it is useless repetition, particularly in a scrap. I don't see why every scrap should not be conducted according to parliamentary law. Let each side make out a careful analysis of all the objectionable things that it has to say to the other, and say them in order. Then some one would be somewhere, when the scrap was over."

Clare threw herself down on the bed, and buried her face in the crackling depths of a pine pillow, that spoke remotely of summer sunlight and the damp fragrance of wood-paths. Her courage departed as she heard Ardis close the door behind her, and she thought, "What shall I do! Oh, what shall I do!"

She could eat no supper that night, and when she started out for rehearsal, she knew that her last vestige of self-confidence was gone. The rain had stopped, but there was a thick fog, that seemed to gather up the silences and bring them so near that they walked beside her. Sometimes she thought that she heard faint whispers not far from her ear; once she felt the touch of mysterious fingers upon her forehead. But she knew that a certain room in Music Hall would be full of light and song and laughter, that it would be warmer than the fog was cold.

"What can I say to make them want to do it?" she thought. "Ah, I wonder what Ardis has said to them already! Perhaps they will not listen to me."

She pushed open the great door, and went down the hall to take off her wraps.

"Oh, Miss Deland," called Gladys Campbell, coming out of the rehearsal room, "May Churchill is

going to cut to-night. What do you think of that?
She says the fog gets into her throat."

" I'm devoutly glad of that," thought Clare.
" Come here and kiss me, Gladys. I don't believe
that I can lead at all, unless you do."

" Miss Hathaway says you want to give a big
concert before Christmas," said Gladys, accepting
the kiss as a matter of course. "*I* don't want to
give a concert, Miss Deland. It's no fun to get
up and let people see what a lot of sticks we are."

She spoke with the playful assurance of a spoiled
child who has not the remotest idea of what it means
to be a Freshman.

" Gladys ! " said Clare, turning upon her suddenly.
" do you know what you are saying? "

Gladys collapsed, and did not speak again for the
rest of the evening.

After all, it was not so hard for Clare to say what
was in her mind, when she had once begun. She
told them what she thought it ought to mean to be
a member of the Harland Glee Club. She said that
it would be very hard, if you were little, to wake
up on Christmas morning and not find anything in
your stocking, and that it would be harder still
if you had no little stocking to hang up. It would
also be hard to have no Christmas dinner, especially
if you had to see other children whose parents gave
them not only dinners and breakfasts, but pink sugar
animals to eat in between-whiles.

She said that if the women's colleges took no
interest in little poor children at Christmas time, who
could be expected to? And then she reminded
them of the Man who had been a little child Him-

self, and who said, "Do this in remembrance of me."

The scriptural quotation may not have had direct reference to giving a charity concert, but it made no difference, so long as, with a single exception, it was a unanimous vote.

"Will you speak to the President about this, Ardis," asked Clare, after rehearsal, " or shall I?"

"I shall have nothing to do with it," was the answer; and accordingly Clare went to the President the next morning.

"I fear that this concert would be more beneficial to the College Settlements than to the members of the Glee Club," he said, when Clare had stated her plans. "Of course such a performance would require extra rehearsals, and there seems, at present, to be more danger from over-work in recreation than in the departments of study."

"The Glee Club is a very important department of study," said Clare, with dignity, " because it teaches people how to keep their tempers and be a useful part of a valuable whole. It is also the best possible form of recreation, because it takes one's mind off from the ordinary routine of work."

"Two very good arguments," said the President, with the suspicion of a twinkle in his eyes.

"And to give a concert is only second nature to people who love to sing. Music was meant to be heard; and if it is n't heard, it reacts on itself, and does ever and ever so much more harm than it would by being sung at a concert. You see, the girls are learning new music all the time, and if it is n't sung pretty soon after it is finished, they get tired of it and lose all their first enthusiasm. And it's easier to sing before an audience than in a stuffy little room, because the Glee Club, like every other musical organization in the world, needs the stimulus of outside encouragement to do its best work."

"I see," said the President, gravely. "But do you think that you could prepare for this concert without the usual number of extra rehearsals?"

"Certainly," replied Clare. "You yourself have often said that if people learn their lessons well every day, there is no necessity to cram for examinations."

The President smiled.

"And if you'll let me give the concert, I'll promise to do it with only two extra rehearsals — short little ones — only to get the programme in order, and show the girls where they are to stand."

"And how about the Banjo Club? You do not seem to have included them in your promises."

"Oh, they can play the same things that they played last year. Nobody will know the difference."

The President appeared to yield, but refused to give his definite permission until the matter had been brought before the "Ladies-in-charge." These same ladies were to hold a meeting the next Saturday afternoon, and he told Clare that she might come for her answer on Monday morning.

Clare wandered restlessly around, outside College Hall, while the meeting was going on, hoping that she might discover something from the faces of the matrons as they went back to their various houses; but this was of no use at all, because every matron knew that it was her duty to appear non-committal.

Mrs. Halifax was the last to come out, and when she saw Clare lurking around the college entrance she walked slowly over to the Storey House steps, then stopped and beckoned mysteriously. Clare ran up to her, and they both looked around to make sure that nobody was in sight.

"It's all right!" whispered Mrs. Halifax, quickly. "Now run along home and get your supper."

Clare thanked her and did as she was told, wondering meanwhile if it was not the people like Mrs. Halifax who made the world kind enough for other and very young people to live in!

Ardis relented at the last and presided over the sale of the tickets, for this would be expected of her by the college at large, and she did not care to invite criticism. But she refused to do anything else, and, as time went on, the continued friction and opposition became so unendurable that Clare thought seriously of resigning her position on the club.

One afternoon, not long before the concert, she was seized with a very bad headache, and as there was to be an important rehearsal that night, she sent for Ardis to take her place.

"Why not postpone the rehearsal?" asked the Assistant Leader, who was much annoyed at finding Clare in bed. "It is very demoralizing for a club to be drilled by two different people with entirely opposite ideas. I would only undo what you have done."

"But you know how we have been in the habit of singing the music. The girls know the songs well enough already; but, unfortunately, we can't be content with 'well enough.' This music must be perfect."

"Then you had better come down and attend to it yourself. I don't think that I could achieve perfection in any line. That must be left to the people who have more confidence in themselves."

"Then, if you absolutely refuse to take the rehearsal to-night, will you please tell the girls that there isn't to be any?"

"No, I won't — for the reason that I want to hold a short business meeting to decide how many tickets are to be given away."

"There are to be no tickets given away!" said Clare, sitting up in bed. "What is the object in having a charity concert if the tickets are to be given away?"

"Charity sometimes begins at home," said Ardis, smiling, "and it has always been the custom for each member to have six or eight tickets to distribute among friends. Of course, you, being the Leader, would have a few more."

"But do you realize that giving away these tickets would make nearly fifty dollars less for our Settlement children? I have counted up, and, Ardis, it must not be done. Why, you know, Dr. Page let us have our programmes printed by the man who does the Analysis slips for him, just because he knew that we wanted to save expense. And Mr. Hughes and the night-watchman both offered to give their services. And then to think of our taking tickets to give away! You know that this is not to be a society event, like the March concert, but all very simple — given in the afternoon, among the holly, and with the dear Christmas Carol at the end. It is different from the other concert, Ardis. Can't you understand?"

"I will bring the matter up before the club to-night, and perhaps, if you are not there, they may have a chance to exercise a little individual judgment for themselves."

Clare said nothing; but when Ardis had gone away, she cried.

"I am the weakest character in the world," she thought. "I am not fit to be at the head of any-thing. But no, it is not the real Clare that cries! It is the other one who is always getting hurt, — the one who is n't strong. Oh, I don't like that other one!"

She struggled into her clothes while the household was at supper, and when the Glee Club girls assembled for rehearsal she was there to lead them. The matter of the tickets was decided in a very few minutes, and Clare's mind was set at rest by the knowledge that none were to be given away. Then she tried to conduct the rehearsal, but looked so ill that the girls rebelled, and Kathleen Carey took her home.

When the afternoon of the concert came, every seat in the chapel had been engaged for over a week, and chairs were placed in the German room, or in the hall outside, for the people who had only tickets of admission. Mr. Hughes, the janitor, took in money at the front door, and the night-watchman, who was a firm friend of the Glee Club, received the tickets at the chapel entrance above. The great hall was beautifully trimmed with holly and Christ-mas greens, and each one of the ushers wore a little sprig of holly in her gown.

Clare was delighted to find that her audience was

composed of the people whom she would have liked most to see there. All the young Faculty, who boarded or took meals at Miss Taylor's had bought tickets, and old Dr. Burton occupied a seat in the front row, next his son. Even the gardener walked in proudly with a ticket that had been secured a week before, and two of the " scrub-ladies," whom Clare sometimes encountered after college hours, appeared in their best clothes. Mr. Henley, the druggist, was sitting near Mrs. Flannagan, of the famous chocolate cakes; and the man who kept the second-hand bookstore was there.

As the concert was for charity, the President had allowed it to be advertised down town, and a number of country people had driven in to hear the Harland Glee Club sing. Near the back row, in one of the transepts, Clare spied her old friend of Sophomore year, — the one whose barn had been theirs on that memorable Decoration Day when they were caught in the rain. She went up to shake hands with him and his wife; and then she asked about the two iron-gray cart-horses who had kindly contributed their nose-bag, and the gentle cow with the tan-colored spots on her sides.

" Be you in the show?" asked the farmer with interest, observing Clare's white gown; and both he and his wife looked highly gratified when she replied that she was.

There was something about that audience that caused a strange choking sensation to rise in Clare's throat, and when she went to gather her little flock around her, she felt that they were nearer than they had ever been before. One of them told her that a lady who could not come had just sent in five dollars for the children of the College Settlements, and Clare said: " Oh, how many pink transparent sugar animals and fat yellow oranges that will buy! Come, my dear ones — my dear ones, we are ready to begin!"

The first number was received with a great deal of enthusiasm, which increased as the programme went on. The Banjo Club played well, and alternated pleasantly with the more serious work of the others.

"They sing wonderfully well," said one of the townswomen who had journeyed long in the music world. "Who has trained them to sing like this?" she asked of an usher with holly in her hair.

" Miss Deland is the Leader now," answered the Sophomore, with that pretty air of pride in a valuable possession which one Harland girl is very likely to manifest in speaking of another. "Our Glee Club has always been trained by one of the students. We wanted Miss Deland to have her name on the programme, even if the others weren't; but she said that it didn't make any difference who the Leader was, — that they all did it together."

" This is truly a Christmas concert!" said the lady, smiling, with the tears in her eyes.

Before the intermission came it had begun to snow, and it snowed softly all through the final numbers, and the "dear Christmas Carol" at the end. Dr. Page had promised to play the carol upon the big organ, and he slipped in unseen while the Glee Club was singing "Fair Harland." Now, he himself had composed the music for " Fair Harland; " and when the Glee Club reached the last verse, there came suddenly from the organ those same beautiful chords ·

that every one loved so well, and organ and Glee Club finished their college song together. Then Dr. Page played the prelude to the Christmas Carol, the Glee Club opened their hymn-books without leaving the platform, and the whole audience joined in singing, " It came upon the midnight clear, That glorious song of old,"—that same glorious song that the snow-flakes may have heard before they floated down through the winter night to drift against the chapel windows.

Every one hurried away when the concert was over, for it was nearly six o'clock, and downstairs there was a confused scramble of college girls talking about the music, Wyckham men stamping through the hall with their coat-collars turned up, and townspeople searching in vain for their wraps.

It is characteristic of all musical performers to disappear as soon as an entertainment is over, and one Glee Club girl seldom sees another between the time when the last note is sung and chapel the next morning. But when Clare pushed open the side door and ran out into the snow, she was touched to find that several of her girls were waiting upon the steps to say good-night.

" Did n't it go off splendidly? " asked Isabel Bovey, taking Clare into her arms.

" And did n't we sing well? " asked Virginia, triumphantly. " We could n't go home without hearing you say that we sang better than you had expected."

" I knew that you would sing well," answered Clare ; " you always do ! "

" Yes, because we have you," said Faith. " We wanted you to know, before we went home, that we did it all for you to-night, Clare. We tried our very best because of you, little dear! "

Clare tried to say something more about the singing, but the words would not come.

" Oh, my dear ones," she cried, " good-night! " and in a minute she was running blindly towards home, with the snow in her face, scarcely looking or caring where she went because of that pain in her heart. She had decided to resign the Glee Club leadership in the morning.

CHAPTER XVIII

THE LEADER OF THE GLEE CLUB

"DID you know that we took in one hundred and seventy dollars?" asked Kathleen, as Clare came into Music Hall the next afternoon. Ardis had called a business meeting of the club, to decide upon the final disposition of the money, but there seemed to be some difficulty in obtaining a quorum.

"Where *is* everybody?" asked the Manager, indignantly, pacing the floor, notebook in hand.

"Here, on the radiator!" answered Kathleen, lifting Clare into that exalted position.

"If she would only have helped me, I could have stood it," Clare was thinking, "but I cannot do it all alone. Oh, Ardis, Ardis, Ardis!"

"Who's there?" called out Kathleen, as the big door slammed again.

"'Thou seest I am one who weeps,'" said Faith, coming in with a blast of icy air. "It's the kind of day when force of character centres in the end of the nose."

Kate Dervish and Virginia Paul dropped in as if by accident, and a number of others appeared from music-rooms where they had been loudly practising until their time was up. When two more had been forcibly extracted from the college reading room, where they were keeping guard over a book, there were enough people to vote, and the meeting came to order. Seventy-five dollars were assigned to the New York Settlement, fifty to Dennison House in Boston, and twenty-five to the Settlement in Philadelphia. The expenses of the concert had been ten dollars, and the club suggested that the remaining ten should be divided up among them, to buy Christmas presents with.

"The Banjo Club voted beforehand," said Clare, "that whatever money was left over should be given to them, and Beatrice Adams said that she hoped we would respect their decision."

There was a hoot of derision at this; but Beatrice Adams, the leader of the Banjo Club, won her point, because she had realized that a sense of humor is the highest common factor between musical organizations in the same college.

"It's all right that they should have the ten dollars, anyhow," said one of the girls, "because Kathleen broke all the strings in two banjos by sitting on them after the concert."

"Well, if the instruments were on top of each other, how could I sit on one without sitting on the other," protested Kathleen, indignantly; "and besides, I did n't sit on either of them."

"Oh, Kathleen!" expostulated Mary Donnelly, softly.

"Well, I doubt if I did; and Whately says 'deliberate and confirmed Doubt, on a question that one has attended to, implies a verdict of *not proven*.'"

"There is not much doubt that you 'attended to' this question," said Clare, laughing; and then she stopped and gave a kind of gasp, wondering if she had the courage to do what she had come to do, and not feeling sure but the planning of it had all been a bad dream.

"Girls, there is something that I wanted to say to you," she began, and then the sweet familiarity of the faces before her made it almost impossible to go on. She stopped and said to herself, " You must n't cry; no, you must n't cry. If you cry, I 'll kill you."

" I 've been thinking," she continued with an effort, "that I 'm not very strong anyway, and that perhaps it might be better — "

" Clare," interrupted Faith Bentley, reading in her face what she was about to say, " wait a minute — you must wait — you don't know — " She had risen from her seat, and the girls looked at her in astonishment.

" This is not exactly parliamentary, Miss Bentley," said Ardis. "Perhaps the Leader would like to finish what she was going to say."

Faith looked at Ardis, and Ardis looked at Faith, and suddenly Ardis went white up to her delicate temples, and turned her face away.

" We will — dismiss the meeting, then," said Clare, looking puzzled. " The matter that I wanted to speak of can wait until next term."

The meeting adjourned more quietly than usual, and Faith took Clare by the hand, saying: " Come into the organ room a minute. I must speak to you and — explain. I saw what you were going to do," she said, as soon as the door was closed, " and I know that you have been driven to it; but, Clare, I tell you that you simply must not resign. You must n't — that 's all! "

"It is harder for me than for any one else," said Clare, "but circumstances that you know nothing of have forced me to it, and I've made up my mind that it's right."

"'Circumstances that I know nothing of,'" repeated Faith, scornfully. " Perhaps you forget that I'm with her on the editorial staff."

" I did n't mention any names."

" No; neither did I. Oh, well, Clare, I may be material and pointless and violent, but I'm not a fool!"

" I never thought that you were until you interrupted me this afternoon. I don't think you quite knew what you did — that's all."

" I suppose you know that if you resign, they will put Ardis in your place. There's no one else."

" Yes, I know they will. She will make a very good Leader."

" Clare, Ardis must not be at the head of this club."

" Don't you think she could do it, in addition to her editorial work? She is strong, you know."

"Oh, yes, her 'Prism' work would n't interfere in the least, not in the least; she would n't allow it to. It would be against whatever principles she thinks she has."

" Faith, what do you mean? I don't believe you know what you do mean."

" Do you consider that you are resigning on your own account or on that of your club?"

" On account of my club. I'm so tired with continual — well, I'm so tired, most of the time, that there is n't enough left of me to lead them."

She determined not to let Faith know that Ardis had left all the work of the management, as well as that of the leadership, to her, and that this strain, in addition to the constant opposition, was more than she could bear.

" You were a great fool to make Ardis Assistant Leader," said Faith.

" I 'm a great fool to care about things as I do. That's the principal direction in which I show my folly. If I cared less, I might be able to do more; but as long as I can't help caring, and I have n't enough strength to both care and lead, the leading must be given up. You can call it lack of self-control if you like; I don't care what you call it."

" Don't you know that you can lead better, when you 're tired to death, than another person could, who had twenty-horse power of muscle? This club does n't need a policeman; it wants a musician."

" Thank you," said Clare; " but I know that I can't do justice to my club when I 'm worried all the time, so I think it is merely decent to turn them over to some one who can. Perhaps you don't think that I care; perhaps you don't know that they are so much of myself that when they are gone, there will be very little of me left — even less than there is now. The college has n't given me so very much, Faith. I have never held any office in my class. I have just been ' little Clare,' you know; that 's what they called me, — ' little Clare ' — and that 's all I meant to them. And then, at the beginning of the last, this most precious gift came to me as my own, — something for me to love and care for, something that was all my own. They are mine — *mine*, do you understand? And I must give them up because I can no longer do well by them — because I love them well enough to give them up. But, oh, the Monday and Thursday nights! I could bear it better if it was n't for that. There will be the Monday and Thursday nights all alone."

While Clare was speaking, Faith had been undergoing an ethical struggle which yielded no supremacy to either side. She had stumbled into one of those complex situations, peculiar to small places, in which every one bears so distinct a relation to everybody else that the slightest misadjustment ends in a spiritual fracas.

"The welfare of our Glee Club is worth more than the feelings of any one girl, no matter who she may be," she thought; and then she decided that it was her duty to tell Clare what she had discovered about Ardis. Not very much, and not who the girl was whose place on the "Prism" had been stolen away; but enough to make Clare turn white, and draw one or two long sobbing breaths, that hurt Faith more than they hurt Clare.

"Can you ever forgive me?" she asked, wiping away a few miserable tears on her brown "pussy" mittens, which sizzled pathetically when tossed back on the radiator.

"It was right to tell me," said Clare, looking somewhat dazed. "It is the Glee Club, you know, only the Glee Club — no girl who could do such a thing — I wish it had been any one but you who told me, and then I could have thought it was a lie. But you said that Miss Carlisle knows — that you found it out by accident from — who was it? Never mind, but you said that Miss Carlisle knows."

" One of the Ninety-four editors told me," said Faith, " and I would n't believe it, because we all loved her, you know, — the President of Ninety-five."

" She was an easy thing to love," said Clare, in a low voice, " very easy, very easy indeed. But one must think only of the Glee Club, — always of them. It was right to tell me; I understand. Only, now that you have told me, can't you go away and leave me alone with my dead? "

When Faith had gone, she thought, " I won't believe it until I 've asked Miss Carlisle."

But the next day, when there was an opportunity to ask Miss Carlisle, she found that she did not dare; and then she knew that it was all over. She said to herself, " Christine must never know ! "

One morning vacation had come, and she was driving down to the station with some of the other girls. The snow was shining with a newly formed crust, and Christmas greens hung in all the windows. " Merry Christmas, Clare," called some one from somewhere. " Merry Christmas ! Merry Christmas ! Good-bye." The words came back to her that night when she was awakened by hearing people singing in the street. They were young men coming out of the Club House next door, and their song was: " Hark ! the herald angels." It was very beautiful, and Clare sat up in bed to listen. " I do wish," she thought, " that some of my girls could sing bass ! "

The song died away into the starlight and stillness, and she lay down again thinking of the college and of the great·deserted ·chapel, with the holly berries dropping down, one by one, into the shadows; and then she thought of the Music Building, empty and dark.

" Oh, Ardis ! " she cried, " it is n't Merry Christmas. It can't be Merry Christmas any more. But it's ' Good-bye ' ! "

Ethel Deland was married on New Year's Day, and in the excitement of being a one and only bridesmaid, Clare found less time to think of her woes. But they returned in full force when she went back to winter term, knowing that she must begin now, and relinquish the ideal that had been the dearest possession of her college life. And such things must always die a lingering death. One is forced to wait by their bedside, night after night, and witness all their pain, until one morning they are gone; and with them is gone something that used to be a part of ourselves, but which we should not know if we met again.

Clare could not believe that the real Ardis was so different from the one she had loved. There were the same dear eyes and hair, the same sweet, merry ways, — the same Ardis in everything but what meant so much to Clare. The girl Ardis had existed in her imagination only, and now the girl Ardis was dead.

" But I promised to stand by her unto death," she thought, " and now the time has come. She has died in a different way from what I meant, — that 's all."

Clare wondered what relation the girl that was left bore to this other one who had gone, and who had torn away so much youngness in the going.

"I wonder if she could lift her hand like that, in just that one dear way that she alone knows, if she were so different from what she used — no, she never was, she never was! And it was not her fault that I idealized her, and made her all kinds of lovelinesses that she was not. She never pretended to be different. It is I who made the mistake. And it was 'unto death' that I promised. That means as long as I myself am alive. It shall be so." And with this determination in her heart the new term began.

One night there was to be a lecture by Charles Dudley Warner in the Gymnasium, and while Clare was at supper, Ardis came up to ask if she would be willing to omit the Glee Club rehearsal that evening.

"The lecture doesn't begin until half-past seven, so I hardly see how it can conflict with rehearsal," said Clare, "but if you 're sure that the girls would rather not have one, why, of course, it does n't make any difference to me."

"Well, I only know what they said," replied Ardis, "and I admit that it is n't exactly constitutional; but we can hold a business meeting to-morrow, and vote on it. Resolved: That rehearsal should be omitted last night, so that we could all have time to dress for the lecture."

"All right," said Clare, laughing, "but you will see that they all understand about it, won't you? It would be dreadful if any of them went over there, and we did n't come."

Ardis promised, and took her departure, thinking: "It is quite evident that Faith has n't told her anything that I would not like her to hear. But I wonder why she did n't resign that day, when she had herself all worked up into the proper state of excitement!"

It was not an ordinary college lecture that night, but an entertainment given by the Hadley House, which had secured Mr. Warner through the offices of Miss Carlisle.

When Clare arrived at the Gymnasium, there was such a crowd about the two entrances that she soon became separated from Ruth and Christine, and did not reach the basement until after they had gone upstairs. While she was in one of the dressing-rooms, taking off her wraps, she overheard May Churchill talking loudly to some one just outside the door.

"We went over there, and waited half an hour," she said, "and not a soul turned up! And we would n't go away, because of our loyalty to that Leader of ours. A nice kind of Leader she is, too, to tell some of us that there was to be no rehearsal, and let the rest find it out for themselves. It 'll be some time before I burden her with my presence again — I can tell you that."

"I am afraid that there has been a misunderstanding," said Clare, coming out of the room. "Ardis told me that all the girls had been, or would be, notified about the omission of the rehearsal, and I did n't know about it myself until supper-time. I understood that none of you wanted to have one to-night, because of the lecture."

"Oh, don't try to lay it off on Ardis," said May, rudely. "You 're the head of the club, and if anything goes wrong, it is you who are to blame. I suppose that it is very easy for you to leave the club

in the lurch, the first time that you want to go anywhere; but you'll find that it isn't so easy to get
them together again, the next time you want them,
that's all."

Clare's eyes blazed suddenly, and she began, " Do
you mean to say — " Then she thought, " No, they
are like my children. I mustn't let myself be angry
with them." But for a minute she would not trust
herself to speak.

" If I were you I wouldn't try to lie out of it,
either," said May. " The few of us that were over
there can fix up an alibi for you in good form."

" Oh, May, don't! " said the Glee Club Sophomore,
in distress. " What will she think of you? "

" I don't care *that* what she thinks of me," said
May, shaking her fist in Clare's face; and then she
turned and walked away.

" Don't mind her," implored the girl, stopping a
minute behind. " She wouldn't have said what she
did, if it hadn't been for being so disappointed in
you ! "

Then the two went upstairs, and Clare was left to
gather up the fragments of the encounter as best
she could. She knew that the situation was one for
which she had not been trained, and with which she
was powerless to deal. What ought you to say to
people who shake their fists in your face and call
you a liar? Refinement is always helpless in the
presence of vulgarity, because vulgarity does not
fight fair; it attacks with slung-shots and sand-
bags, and great jagged pieces of iron, while refinement is meekly preparing to defend itself with
pins.

"I'll read the dictionary!" cried Clare, with a sudden explosion of wrath. "I won't be beaten next time, for lack of names to call her!"

Then she remembered what the Junior had said about proving an alibi, and began to laugh. "May was absolutely ridiculous," she thought. "I suppose that I ought to be proud of having such a bright set of girls on the club!"

People often said that Clare's sense of humor had been her salvation.

"But I never heard of any one speaking to a Leader as she spoke to me. What's the matter with me, anyhow, that I can't inspire a decent amount of respect in the girls? I wish I were taller, and not a fool, and could talk straight when I have anything to say!"

And then the words of the Sophomore came back to her with a reproach more pathetic than she had realized at the time. "She wouldn't have said what she did, if it hadn't been for being so disappointed in you!" Clare buried her face in her hands, and sat down on one of the steps. She heard a faint rumble of applause in the Gymnasium above, and knew that the lecture had begun.

"May was right," she thought. "I *am* the head of the club, and when anything goes wrong, it is I who am to blame. I ought not to have trusted Ardis to tell the girls. I ought not to have left anything to her, when she has failed me so many times. But it is hard not to be influenced by a person that you love — oh, so hard! And the girls have found out now that I am nothing but a failure from beginning to end, and aren't afraid to tell me so; and if I'd had any strength of character at all, I could have slain her with a look."

She went upstairs in time to hear the last half of the lecture, and comforted herself, that night, by thinking, " Well, you're a fool, anyway, and you might as well get used to not expecting to be anything else!"

But she was forced to be something quite different before the month was over, for May Churchill was as good, or as bad, as her word. She not only cut nearly all the rehearsals, but encouraged the younger girls to do the same; and as Ardis refused either to record the absences or collect fines, the Glee Club rapidly verged upon demoralization. Clare stood it as long as she could; and then she informed Ardis that she would like to have a talk with her in some place where they would not be likely to be interrupted. The tower stairs were chosen for the scene of the fracas, and they both jested about it pleasantly, as they toiled up, hand in hand.

" I hope you know what you're going to say," said Ardis, when they had comfortably established themselves, " because, if you don't, you're pretty sure to get rattled."

" Fortunately, I do," said Clare. " I wished to inform you that your conduct with regard to the Glee Club is absolutely outrageous and unendurable, and that I won't stand it any longer."

Ardis looked somewhat surprised, but made no reply, and Clare went on: " As Assistant Leader you are a complete failure; as Manager you are worse than nothing. You cut rehearsals whenever you feel like it, and your influence on the younger girls is hopelessly bad. You are destroying the old traditions of law and order in the club, and spoiling whatever chance we may have of doing any decent work this year. Now I've said what I wanted to, and you can talk all the rest of the afternoon, if you like."

Clare had often wondered how Ardis looked when she was angry, and now she found out.

"I have been neglecting my duties as Manager, have I?" she asked. "Perhaps you may have forgotten that you have taken most of those duties out of my hands. Everything that I did, or tried to do, you opposed, and had voted down by the club. Most of the things that it was my duty to attend to you preferred to manage for yourself. How in the world am I going to tell which part of my work you want me to do? You have left me so little that I'm sure I don't know what it is; and it is very like you to blame me because the girls have been cutting rehearsals. Is it my fault that you are no longer able to interest them? They were enthusiastic over you at first, but every enthusiasm is followed by a reaction, and now you attack me because the reaction has come. If you make the rehearsals a bore, you need n't be surprised if the girls stay away."

"It is n't that at all, and you know it!" said Clare. "May, and some of the others, are mad because they were n't told that there was to be no rehearsal the night of the lecture; and very likely you will say that you were not to blame for that, either. Well, I suppose you were n't, for I ought not to have trusted you in the first place."

"I would n't talk about 'trusting,' if I were you,"

said Ardis, rather bitterly; "wait until you have proved that you can be trusted yourself."

"If you have an imaginary grievance against me, I do wish you'd settle it with me alone," said Clare, desperately, "and not take it out in neglecting my club."

"Since this discussion is likely to resolve into personalities in any case," said Ardis, "I think it would be a good time to explain to you that I understand all about that Junior-usher committee business of last spring. I understood at the time; and yet you consider yourself a friend to be trusted! Isn't it fortunate that the person who is in the wrong always has the satisfaction of thinking that he is in the right!"

"I don't know what you mean about the committee business," said Clare. "I didn't hear anything about it until after the girls had spoken to you. And then, too, you had given me to understand that Christine had just been appointed. If there was any double-dealing in the matter, I don't think that it lay on my side."

"Do you mean to say that you didn't have anything to do with it — that you didn't get up the whole thing? I wish I knew whether to believe — "

"Oh," cried Clare, "you never doubted my word before! But it doesn't make any difference," she added wearily to herself, "I wonder why it doesn't make any difference — any more." And she gripped her own hand tightly, to keep herself from answering the question.

"I wanted to speak to you about a new Assistant Leader," she said. "I find that the work is getting too hard for me, and no doubt you will be quite willing to surrender the position to some one who has more time."

"If you appoint a new Assistant Leader after promising the office to me, I shall resign from the club."

This was a contingency for which Clare was not prepared, and at first she did not know what to say. It would give rise to much unpleasant comment in the college if the Glee Club Manager were forced to resign because she could not get along with the Leader; and Clare did not want her girls to have anything unpleasant to remember, in connection with that year. So far the trouble between Ardis and herself had been of a private nature, and she wished it to remain so.

"If you put it in that way, I can do nothing," she said. "Of course you know that I will do nothing. You have very little mercy in you, after all."

She realized that it was quite useless to continue the discussion, and rose to go. "But I have had the pleasure of saying some things to her," she thought, "and perhaps she'll remember afterwards what they were."

But in thinking it over afterwards, she came to the conclusion that what she had said to Ardis was less likely to be remembered than what Ardis had said to her.

"If they find the rehearsals a bore, it *is* my fault, and I've tried so hard to make the work interesting. I think it's too bad."

She had always made it a point to tell the girls all the funny stories that she heard, and encouraged

314

them to do likewise; and they had seemed to have very good times together. But as Ardis said, the rehearsals must have been growing more stupid, or they would not have stayed away.

"I wish I were a lovable kind of person, like Ruth," she thought, " or dear and funny like Christine, and then perhaps they would n't desert me ! "

She took a piece of paper, and wrote down all the good qualities that she thought a successful Glee Club Leader ought to have, —

1. Ability to transpose and harmonize; sing, place and train voices, play a good accompaniment, carry four different parts in your head at the same time and not go crazy, and write new music when necessary.

2. A sense of humor. (*Very* important.)

3. Inexhaustible patience.

4. Self-control.

5. Steady nerves.

6. The strength of a horse.

7. Good Christian principles.

8. Some personal magnetism.

9. Not be a fool.

(Clare's definition of a fool was " to care too much about everything, and let people see that you do.") Her mouth drooped more and more, as she went through the list, crossing out all the things that she was not. She knew that she was a Christian, as far as having the principles went, but also realized that she very seldom acted up to them. A sense of humor she was certain of, because she often suffered as much from not being able to laugh as from not being able to cry. And most of those musical

315

characteristics she had been born with, so it was not especially to her credit that she possessed them now!

Finally, a plan occurred to her by which the Glee Club could be apprised of its misdemeanors in a way that would be both delicate and effectual. And the next day she wrote "Very important" on the notice for the bulletin board. It was very icy weather, and the Glee Club girls did not walk to rehearsal that night; they slid. But they were all in good humor when they arrived, because it had been entertaining to watch each other fall down on the way.

"Tired, Honey?" asked Kathleen, when Clare came into the room. "Let *me* distribute the music."

Rehearsal went unusually well, and when it was over, the Leader said: "I want you to stay a few minutes, and hear something that I have to say to you. It won't take long."

"We're going to get a blowing up," whispered a Sophomore to May Churchill.

"No, you're not," said Clare. "If you won't come to rehearsals out of respect for your college and honor for your club, it is not likely that anything that I could say would make any difference! But I have noticed the great lack of interest that has prevailed of late, and have come to the conclusion that we all need a rest. I think that if we were not very tired and ill, nothing could blind us to the importance of this Glee Club work, and the loyalty to our college that it implies. I would like to suggest that we take a two weeks' vacation from rehearsal, and then call a business meeting to decide whether we care to continue the work during the remainder of the year."

There was a horror-stricken silence, and then one girl said breathlessly, " I 've invited three men up to the March concert."

" Yes, a number of people have asked friends," said Clare; " but it would be very easy to explain to them that the club has lost interest in the work, and that there will be no concert this year."

" Oh-h!" exclaimed somebody else; and again there was a silence, which gradually became fraught with alarm. Some of the girls thought that Clare's mind had become unhinged through anxiety.

" There were the mid-years," murmured some one from the second-alto row.

" Yes; and if you remember rightly, we had no rehearsals during the week in which the examinations were held."

" If we don't work pretty hard, we can't give the March concert, can we?" ventured one of the girls.

" Oh no," said Clare, unconcernedly. " We have a reputation to keep up now, and of course we would n't want to have it said that we had deteriorated since Christmas."

" I move that we don't have any vacation," said Kate Dervish.

" I 'm sorry," said Clare, " but I think that I shall take a vacation, whether the rest of you do or not. It 's been very tiresome, coming down here, night after night, to find so many absences, and I really feel that I need rest. Of course you are at liberty to continue the rehearsals under the Assistant Leader, if you like. I myself will meet you in this room two weeks from to-night."

There seemed nothing more to be said, and the girls filed out with troubled faces, casting furtive glances at Clare as they went. Some of the more righteous were bursting with triumph, while others suffered distinctly from amusement. Kathleen came up and felt of Clare anxiously, on her way out of the room.

When they were all gone, Clare seated herself on the table, a favorite place of hers, and took up a copy of the " Musical Courier." May Churchill looked in as she was passing the door, and uttered an exclamation of disgust. " The Treasurer forgot to take back the benches," she said to her friend, who was waiting in the hall. " Come in here, Gladys, and take a hand with these."

The two girls carried back the benches to the music rooms from which they had been taken, and then May came in alone, and shut the door.

" I should think you 'd be glad to get rid of us for two weeks," she said. " We 're not worth caring about ! "

" Come here," said Clare, holding out her arms. "You may think I 'm very silly, and I don't doubt that I am; but I really don't see how I 'm going to get along without you for two whole weeks! I 've just been thinking about it. It will seem as if my world had gone out."

" I 've been an ass," said May, cheerfully. " I wanted you to know."

Clare understood that this was meant for an apology, and said, " It was a horrible misunderstanding

318

all around; but we 'll forget that it ever happened,—
and not do it again!"

"You'd better rest up a lot in the next fortnight,"
said May, "and after that I'll promise to make that
little Gladys Campbell behave."

Clare smiled inwardly, but said: "That would help
me ever so much, May. I don't believe we have
the remotest idea how much we influence the people
that are around us. The younger girls all look up
to you, and—it is so easy to want to be like the
people we love!"

May flushed suddenly, and turned away. She was
a magnificent creature, with blue eyes that looked
red in certain lights, and an abundance of personal
magnetism that would always make her a positive
influence for right or wrong.

"It is n't always easy for you to be good, either,
is it?" she asked wistfully, looking at Clare.

"May, I have perfectly horrible times with myself,
and you know it!"

"Yes, you wanted to kill me, fast enough, the
other night. I respected you for it."

"My only comfort is to believe that all force was
put into the world for good. It would n't be sensible
to say, 'Don't meddle with fire, for fear that you
will be burned.' We've got to have fire, and manage
it so that we *won't* be burned. But, oh, it's hard!
May, don't you suppose that I know?"

"But what good does it do, about influence and
all that, if people don't know just how hard—if
they don't think that you try?"

"I have asked myself that same question so many
times," said Clare, "and I can't— Oh, May, I do

believe that people judge us for the direction in which we are struggling, and not for how far we have gone!"

"I'll be your prop in sorrow and disaster," said May, crossing the room with her usual boyish stride. "When in doubt, play May Churchill, and you'll find she takes the trick. Good-night."

She had quite forgotten about Gladys, and nearly fell over her, as she sat waiting on the steps.

"Oh, go home," she said impatiently, "you little fool!"

Gladys departed indignantly, and May strolled down the concrete walk, gazing absently at the oblong light of the matron's window in the Hillard. Then she stopped short, as if in meditation.

"I wonder!" she said.

CHAPTER XIX

IN THE HEART OF MARCH

THE students of Harland College celebrate St. Valentine's Day very much as the children do, except that, after people grow up, there is not so much pulling of door-bells and scampering away to hide around corners. There is a Valentine box in every campus house, and after supper a dance or some other kind of entertainment, followed by the opening of the box and distribution of the valentines. These are funny or pathetic, or both, as the case may be, and there are a great many opportunities of telling people, in a good old-fashioned way, just how much you love them.

The girls of the Taylor household did not have a Valentine box, because most of them had been asked down to the campus that evening; but a number of very nice valentines came in the course of the day. Christine received one from Louisa, the pug-dog, speaking in slighting terms of her vanished cat, and of the superiority of canine acquaintances in comparison with feline. Louisa was stout and unsatisfactory; her skin fell in tawny folds and draperies about her useless neck and waist, and she was too deaf to understand half the names you called her; but she had brains.

ACROSS THE CAMPUS

When the girls first came to Miss Taylor's, Louisa had a way of barking frightfully and ferociously in the upper hall while they were trying to study, and for many weeks they restrained their resentment out of consideration for Miss Taylor. But one day the crisis came. Christine emerged from her room with wild growlings of wrath and an open umbrella, and Louisa was so taken by surprise that she fell backwards down the entire length of the stairs. Christine counted the thumps with satisfaction from behind her door, and knew when the bottom was reached, because she heard Miss Taylor applying restorative measures in the room below.

The next day Louisa appeared in the upper hall, with a plaster over one eye, and barked cheerfully at Christine's door. It was evidently a prearranged plan, for when the door flew open, the dog crouched grinning and enthusiastic at Christine's feet, with every white tooth gleaming cordially in the dusk. Her whole canine form was converted into one trustful and corpulent wag, which so touched Christine that she sat down on the floor and took Louisa into her arms. From that day forth they were firm friends, and Louisa accompanied Christine to the basket-ball game, with a bow of Ninety-seven gold on her tail. People mocked at Christine for allowing her affections to be won through flattery, but she always retained a soft spot in her heart for the deaf old dog; and when she returned to Harland as an alumna, several years later, the only tears of association that she shed, were over the grave of Louisa in the garden, — a part of the pathos and absurdity of those college days that were gone forever.

Clare's valentines were mostly flowers, for her friends knew how much she loved them, and how long she could make them live, by dint of careful nursing and persuasion. Clare possessed capillary powers of enjoyment, that stretched out, like tiny fingers, into infinite space.

That afternoon she asked Christine to come into her room for a little while, saying that there was to be a concert. " But you must n't tell any one," she added, " because they 'd laugh."

When Christine went in, she found Clare sitting before a semicircle of vases and bowls filled with flowers, which she had arranged like instruments in a little orchestra.

" Here are my first violins," she said, pointing to a bunch of white violets, " and the purple violets there on my right are the second violins. Those daffodils over at the back are the horns, and the red carnations are the cellos and double-basses. The maiden-hair fern and smilax are the flute notes — look how delicate and rounded they are. Sidney Lanier makes the notes of his flute rose-colored, but to me they have always been green. Now we will have the ' Ride of the Walkyrs.' Listen, and see if you don't hear the galloping of horses."

Christine was familiar with Wagner, and as she followed the movement of Clare's hand, which " played the invisible instrument in the air," she was sure that she heard the beat of distant hoofs. Nearer and nearer the Walkyrs came, up through the wind and sleet, dashing past with wild cries and sudden flashes of armor, until the unearthly galloping grew fainter and far away. One tiny shadow of a horse in the clouds, and a long wake of scudding gray; then nothing but wind and rain and darkness.

"That was magnificent," she said, as Clare's hand came to a pause. "Your first violins are in excellent tune. Do you know who sent them to you?"

"No, do you?"

"Yes, and I'm sure that the girl would be delighted if she knew what a prominent place you had given them."

"I sent you one too," said Clare. "It was a verse. I sat up last night after I was sleepy, and wrote it; but I sha'n't tell you which one it was."

"I did n't get but one, so it is n't necessary. My others were all grinds — mostly about my departed brindled syllogism. If I were you, I'd put the orchestra in water now. All performers expect something to drink between the acts."

"They 've been in water all the time," said Clare, "so perhaps we ought to have had the Rhinemaidens' chorus instead of the Walkyrs. But was n't it a nice concert, Christine?"

"It was beautiful!" said Christine, warmly. "I wish that Stephen could have heard it."

Clare often felt, nowadays, that the music in her was growing up, and it grew so much faster than she did that it seemed as if she herself must give way at the seams, and be replaced by a new one. But the Glee Club was a continual safety-valve for superfluous energy in this direction, and it was the kind of work that paid. The girls had returned with fresh enthusiasm to their rehearsals, and were singing better than ever before, better than they had ever thought that they could sing, but no better than was expected and demanded by their Leader.

"Whenever we begin to feel that there is *anything* we can't do," she would say, "we have only to remember that we are members of the Harland Glee Club!"

The result was that when the tickets for the March concert were placed on sale, every seat in Assembly Hall was gone in less than an hour. The next day it turned out that there would not be room in College Hall for half the people who wanted to go, and Ardis obtained the permission of the President to give the concert in the Opera House down town.

"We are the stuff," said Kathleen briefly, when the second set of tickets went on sale. "Single file, please," she added in one of her most characteristic second-alto roars, as the long line of applicants, reaching from the hall downstairs, began to push towards the chapel door.

"Do you wish me to risk the life of one who is dear to me by intrusting myself to this rabble?" inquired Christine severely of Clare, whom she encountered in the German room. "Author of all evil, can I get into the library without having my ribs dispersed, or receiving a punch in the head from that soloist of yours?"

"You ought to feel honored to receive a punch from such a source," said Clare. "Come down to the Opera House to-morrow, and hear Kathleen sing 'The Elephant Slinger's Dream.' It's never on the programme, but she generally throws it in at rehearsals."

"The Opera House! I warn you I shall go absolutely mad if you get me onto that stage. I shall act all of Shakespeare and most of Marlowe. And you should just see me do the swan part in 'Lohengrin,' especially that place where the swan falls to pieces. You would think it was a real bird!"

"But I don't think that even the stage is half so dramatic as music," said Clare. "Music has to be dramatic to succeed at all. It's got to have plenty of exciting situations, and plot interest, and murders, and elopements, and — jokes."

"What wag's wit is this?" asked Christine, thoughtfully. "Have you done your Hegel for to-morrow?"

"No, I was just going in to get the book."

"I'll go with you," said Christine, with alacrity. "There isn't but one book, you know."

The next evening Clare wrote this letter to her mother: —

My very Dear, — Early this morning the frost got onto the trees, and the sunrise got into the frost, and I felt as if I should burst because I couldn't tell some one how much I liked it. So I went downstairs and played the "Faschingschwank" as loud as I could, for of course I thought the rising-bell had rung. But it hadn't, and just as I was in the middle of that big, bangy part where Schumann brings in the "Marseillaise," in sailed Miss Taylor in a fuzzy gray wrapper; and out sailed Louisa, with the barks preceding her faster than you could count, and both of them informed me that it was not yet six o'clock. So I gathered up my scattered chords, and retired; but on the way upstairs, I overheard Ruth and Christine upbraiding each other in their room. Each one seemed to think the other responsible for the noise.

IN THE HEART OF MARCH

Yes, I know it was inconsiderate of me, but my clock fell down behind the bookcase last night, and I've lost the handle off my umbrella, so I couldn't poke it out again.

You should have heard our first rehearsal in the Opera House this morning! Oh, it was — now, Clare, don't you be a fool, but it was, just the same. And when the curtain went up, with the calm majesty that only a curtain who does n't stick can assume, and there was the great house full of shadows, with the violin stands tossing up their arms, like skeletons of music long forgotten— there, I *will* be a fool if I want to. And the Kerry Dance! Why, we make our own selves cry, we sing it with so much expression. I only hope that the audience will be as much moved as we are.

And then the girls are so dear; I don't believe that any Glee Club was ever half so dear! They want me not to get tired, you know, and save me in all kinds of little ways; and it is n't the saving that counts so much as the knowing that they care. And they are enthusiastic, and just exactly right, and, oh, I love them, I love them! Yes, I'm studying hard too. It is n't *all* Glee Club, although my letters have been pretty full of it lately.

Another new song came walking into my room last night, and sat down. Of course I was terribly busy, but did n't want to seem inhospitable, so I said, " Just wait until after the concert, and I'll write you out, but I really can't attend to you now." And it said, " I refuse to be put off," and chased me all over the college. And yesterday afternoon it dragged me up and down stairs by the hair, and fired things on top of me until I gave in and wrote it all out. And here I am now, with lessons unlearned, and a feeling of resentment against all my friends. People say, " Don't you enjoy writing music? " Oh, oh, don't I ! What a horribly egotistic old letter ! But you're the only one in the world that I can talk to like this, so you ought not to mind, being all that I have, you know.

Your own little CLARE.

P. S. Does n't it make you wild to think of our Ethel being a Mrs. anybody?

P. S. I upset the ink-bottle down the front of my new skirt, but I don't think that it will hurt it very much, and Christine gave me some more ink.

The day of the concert came at last, and Clare spent the afternoon on her bed, rolled up in a steamer rug, with a " Please don't disturb " sign out, and Christine on guard in the hall. She heard carriages dashing up from the station, and the voices of men and girls, as they went laughing past the house. Somebody came upstairs and said, " Every flower in the town has been sold, and they say that all the carriages have been engaged for to-night."

Christine said, " Hush ! "

At five o'clock the front door slammed, and the maid called up softly : " May I take these flowers up to Miss Deland now? There's five boxes of 'em, and they litter up — "

" Hush ! " said Christine again.

" Oh, I wonder if they're violets," Clare thought, sitting up in bed. " I wish I could go to sleep."

The light in the room grew dimmer, and then went out. Some one came and listened at the door, and Clare said to herself, " Shame on you, not to be asleep ! "

To tell the truth, she was suffering from a violent and unprecedented attack of stage fright. " I feel as if a barn were sitting on me," she thought. "You'd better go away, barn!" For she realized that she must not let the Glee Club know that she was nervous.

"This is what people have talked about before, and I never understood," she thought. "It goes to your knees, and makes them feel as if they were n't there, and it loosens all the muscles of your teeth."

Ruth and Christine dressed her for the concert, all in white with bunches of lilies of the valley at her neck and shoulders; and the housekeeper and maids and even the cook came up to look at her before she started. Everybody in the house was going to the concert, except Miss Taylor and Louisa, who had gone to take tea with a relative in the country.

"You ain't scared, be you, Miss Deland?" inquired one of the maids, observing that she was unusually pale.

"No!" answered Clare, sternly, and then wondered where the voice had come from.

When they reached the Opera House, she slipped on to the stage, to try over the hardest accompaniment once more, and one of the ushers said, "You are not nervous, are you, Miss Deland?"

"No!" answered Clare, with such violence that the usher retreated in alarm.

But when the audience began to arrive, Clare was obliged to give all her attention to the Glee Club girls, who were so enchanted with the spectacle that they persisted in thrusting out their heads, so that they could be seen from the house. They also scraped acquaintance with the men who managed the lights, and found out what you did when you wanted the performers to look purple or green. Clare did not dare look at the audience until after the first few numbers, and then she thought that she had never seen anything so pretty in her life. Twelve hundred people in evening dress, and not more than fifty of them over twenty-three years old! And their enthusiasm was enough to make a Leader feel comfortable down to the tips of her toes, for the representatives from other college Glee Clubs — Harvard, Princeton, and Yale — understood how to give the right kind of applause, and labored manfully, hand and foot.

Her attention was distracted by a slight commotion in the house, caused by Kathleen Carey, who had turned the green lights on the Banjo Club. The effect for a minute was ghastly, and then, before the unhappy performers had recovered from the shock, they appeared twanging luridly in a violent glare of red. Clare managed to get across the stage and pluck Kathleen from her sinful occupation before anything else could happen; but when the Banjo Club came off the stage, Beatrice Adams presented the other Leader with a distinctly unmitigated piece of her mind. She might not have been so severe, if Clare had not laughed; but Clare did laugh, even while she was assuring Beatrice of her mortification that such a catastrophe should have taken place.

"Talk about ruling by love alone," said the Leader of the Banjos, indignantly. "What that Glee Club needs is a right good trouncing!" And they got it before the evening was over.

Clare's stage fright had gradually abated by the time that the intermission came, and she was beginning to feel that the Fates might be propitious during the rest of the programme. But the Fates had evidently decreed that the illumination of the Banjo Club should be avenged.

When she and Ardis started to go down into the house to receive the sympathy and encouragement of their friends, they encountered Ethel Lindsay at the stage door.

"Oh, Clare," she began, "I think it's a perfect shame that the girls aren't doing any better to-night. I never heard them sing so badly — and after you've worked so hard too!"

Clare had always placed implicit faith in Miss Lindsay's musical criticism, and this sudden attack quite took her breath away.

"What — what do you mean?" she asked, rather tremulously.

"Why, they're singing abominably — that's what I mean, and I don't believe it's your fault, either. It's simply because they're not trying. I always told you that you wouldn't be able to do anything with them, unless you were more severe."

Clare looked to Ardis for support in this unhappy emergency, but none came.

"So you, too, consider the concert a failure?" she asked; and when there was no answer, she realized that Ardis had deserted her again. She was too young to appreciate the fact that Miss Lindsay might possibly be wrong, and far too tired to bring any reserve strength to bear upon the matter. So she simply turned around, and went back to the stage, and sank down quite hopelessly in an imitation rustic chair, with hard, imitation ivy leaves that hurt her face when it was pressed against them.

Outside, in the audience, the laughter and congratulations went on. Then somebody asked, " Where's Clare?" and Christine went to find her.

"Why don't you come out?" she demanded, when she caught sight of the dreary little figure in the rustic chair. "Everybody's asking for you, and the other girls are getting all your compliments."

"Where's Clare?" asked Ruth, opening the stage door and shutting it again in the face of a Wyckham Freshman, whose low mutterings died away into wrathful silence.

"Why doesn't somebody bring her out?" inquired Professor Burton, appearing from the other side of the stage.

Clare found it impossible to explain, in the face of such a multitude, and fled into one of the dressing-rooms, where she was presently joined by Christine.

"Now, who's been saying ridiculous things to you?" she asked, taking Clare into her arms; and this unusual demonstration made Clare feel better immediately. She told Christine who had been saying ridiculous things to her, and said that she knew she had disgraced the college. Ethel Lindsay was a reliable musical critic, and very likely Clare's own fondness for the Glee Club had blinded her eyes — or ears — to their real failings.

"Where did that girl sit?" asked Christine, fiercely.

" On me, principally. I haven't recovered yet."

" And you intend to take the judgment of that one person against the enthusiasm of an entire audience? Why, don't you know, you little goose, they're

saying that they never heard a Glee Club sing like this,
—that it's wonderful, marvellous, and things of
that sort. Clare, I should think you'd have more
backbone!"

"That's just the trouble at present. I haven't
any backbone. You see my spiritual strength is
entirely dependent on cod-liver oil, and I've forgotten
to take it lately. I haven't even been able to appreciate my own jokes, and that shows that I'm pretty
far gone."

"You see if she doesn't go home in detachments
to-night," said Christine, between her teeth. "But,
Clare," she added gravely, "I shouldn't like to be
dependent for spiritual strength on something that I
couldn't swallow!"

The ten minutes' intermission was over, and the
girls began to come back to the stage. Clare heard
them gathering in the "green-room," ready for the
second half of the programme, and the color left her
face.

"I'm stage-frightened, Christine," she said, breathlessly. "Really, it takes the stiffening out of you, a
thing like that. You see it was the first criticism of
any kind that I'd heard."

"Professor Burton says that this is the most successful affair of the kind that has ever been given
at the college," said Christine, encouragingly; but
Clare made no reply.

"Come, brace up," said Christine, looking a little
anxious; "you mustn't let yourself give way like
this. Don't you know that you've got to be an
honor to your college to-night; that we're looking
to you as the one who will bring new glory to our

class, who will be brave and true and strong, because of Ninety-five?"

Clare did not answer, and Christine opened the door. " Come in here, Kathleen," she called. " Help me fill these glasses from the spigot; we want to drink to the health of Ninety-five."

"To the finest class alive!" said Kathleen, waving her glass at a perilous angle over Clare's head, " from which may I never transplant my personality."

"Come, Clare," said Christine, with a clink of glasses, " To the finest class alive!"

"That was a good thing to mention," said Clare, setting down the empty tumbler. " Of course we must not be cowards, — we that wear the green!"

She motioned to Kathleen to follow her, but before they reached the Glee Club the sound of vituperation came to their ears.

"I see a voice!" exclaimed Kathleen, dramatically. "'Now will I to the chink to spy, and I can hear my Ethel's face.'"

"Stop!" said Clare, with a frantic clutch. "It can't be that Ethel Lindsay — "

But it was. She had kindly consented to oblige the Manager by giving " a little informal talk to the Glee Club."

"You don't do credit to your training, those of you who were on the club in Ninety-three," she was saying, " and the rest of you do such careless work that you can't even keep together. You take advantage of your Leader — "

"I beg your pardon," interrupted Clare, " but I don't think that any one of them would take advantage of my absence to say things that they would not dare to say if I were here!"

"Is that the way you acknowledge Miss Lindsay's kindness?" asked Ardis, looking exceedingly displeased.

"I don't want to be rude," said Clare; "so perhaps it would be as well to explain to Ethel that what my club does, and the way it sings, lies entirely between the girls and me. We understand each other very well, and do not need any discipline from outside."

"And we've heard from the front of the house and the middle of the house and the back of the house," muttered Kathleen, explosively, "and if you sat anywhere else, you can go chase your grandmother."

"Hush, Kathleen!" said Clare.

"'Contemptible peanut!" continued Kathleen, squaring up to Ethel in a pugilistic fashion. "Only grant me the obvious pleasure of cracking your invidious shell."

"Kathleen, you're a disgrace to the club," said Ardis, angrily.

"'If an ass kicks me, ought I to resent it?'" quoted Kathleen, with a bow.

An impatient round of applause from the house reminded the girls that the intermission had been very long, and Clare said quietly, "Come!"

Before the last half of the programne was over, the audience had gone wild, and people said, "That Leader's head will be turned by all this. I don't believe that any girl could stand it." Poor Clare!

After the concert May Churchill said to Ardis,

"Come over to the Hutcheson some time to-morrow evening. I want to have a talk with you."

Ardis and May had spent one year at the same preparatory school before coming to college, and although they had seen very little of each other since then, Ardis felt that May was still her friend. She had worked very hard to make Ardis Leader of the Glee Club, and had therefore begun the year with a certain amount of antagonism against Clare. Ardis remembered this, as she pushed open the swinging door on the second floor of the new dormitory, "Hutcheson," and walked slowly down the long hall. She found May tilted back in a rocking-chair against her bed, smoking a cigarette, and making some pretence at copying an omitted lecture from the note-book of a friend.

"Have one?" she asked, with a lordly flourish of the arm towards the cigarette-box on her desk.

"No, I thank you," said Ardis, turning away in some disgust.

"You used to," said May, with a broad grin. "What's come over you in the last two years? Reformed?"

Ardis declined to reply.

"Perhaps you don't remember who gave me the first one, then?" continued May.

"If that's all that you wanted to talk about —" began Ardis, impatiently.

"It was not," replied May, rocking her chair forward with a determined thump. "I wanted to tell you that you'd better let Clare Deland alone."

"Why don't you let her alone yourself? You only make a mess of things when you interfere.

336

And besides, what do you expect to get out of it? You can't persuade me that you have developed a disinterested affection for Clare."

" I would n't try to persuade you, if it was n't true, because you have n't the necessary capacity for containing so large a lie. If you try to pour a three-quart lie into a two-gill measure, some of it is pretty sure to slop over on to the floor. It can't all be believed."

" You might believe some of it to-day, and the rest to-morrow," said Ardis, smiling.

" You 're trying to digress," replied May, screwing the lighted end of her cigarette through a piece of paper. " What I want you to do is to have a new Assistant Leader appointed the first thing next term."

" We don't need but one."

" We have n't that! And besides, it 's unconstitutional for the same person to hold two such important offices at a time, especially when that person does not fulfil the duties of either."

" Do you know that I could have you put off the club for speaking to me like that ? " asked Ardis, quietly.

" You might have, before last night; but now they 're so down on you that you would n't stand any show at all. That 's why I deferred my conversation until to-day."

" If it was nothing of any more importance than that, I think that I can dispense with your society," said Ardis, turning to the door.

" Wait a minute," said May, without looking around. " What I wanted to say was, that if you don't see about that Assistant business pretty soon,

I shall tell the whole Glee Club about that little editorial affair of yours."

Ardis took her hand from the door, and noticed that the fingers trembled slightly.

"I must be tired," she thought with a smile.

"You need n't think I don't know about it," continued May. "I know all about everything that concerns you. But I think that, with the exception of Faith Bentley and a few of the Ninety-four editors, I 'm the only girl who does know."

"Well, what is it that you think you know?" asked Ardis with an unexpected quiver in her voice. "I must be very tired," she thought.

"Oh, I know any number of things," said May, amiably. "I have discovered, for one, what kind of a girl Clare Deland really is. She 's just as much of a firebrand as the rest of us, but she has principles, so she keeps trying to put herself out; and that makes her in a violent state of sizzle all the time. It 's the sizzle in her that gets into her playing and makes the shivers go meandering down your spine when you hear her, and causes your toes to snap. And when she talks to you about being good, she really is n't talking to you at all, but to herself; and I wish to God that I 'd had a friend like her at just the time when I ought not to have had a friend like you!"

"Why have n't you stated your exhaustive knowledge of Clare and myself to the world at large? I did not suppose that you had ever refrained from telling anything that you knew."

"I 'll tell you why," said May, throwing down her cigarette. "It 's because I was fool enough to still care for you; that's why. It was because I remembered the old days when we used to be friends, — when I thought you were everything that was perfect, and believed that you would be my friend always — and help me to be good."

Ardis had turned very pale.

"You've burned a suspiciously round hole in that bed-spread," she said quietly.

May's eyes flashed, and she rose to her feet. "Clare told me once that it is natural for us to want to be like the people that we love. Do you understand what that means? Do you know that an older girl can sometimes change the whole life of a younger, by the way that she looks and thinks and feels? Do you know what it means for one person to have absolute faith in another? No, you don't, because you haven't any faith in you! And after you had upset all my philosophy, and laughed me out of my poor little 'Now-I-lay-me' habit of saying my prayers, you threw me over entirely, and left me to shift for myself."

"May," said Ardis, unsteadily, "you must remember — it was different with me — from what it was with other girls. I never had any chance."

"I'm sure I don't know what you mean," said May. "You're not the only person whose mother died when — "

"*Don't* speak to me of my mother!" cried Ardis, quickly; and May stopped, touched by the sudden break of pain in the girl's voice.

"Then if, as you say, you never had any chance, did that make you determine that nobody else should have one?"

"No," exclaimed Ardis, facing her suddenly. "I was young and in the wrong, but I never meant to harm you. I outgrew myself, and outgrew you as a part of that self that I wished to forget. I wanted to forget! I wanted to be different. But there is no mercy in this world for the people who make mistakes. Every one expects you to do the same thing over again, and watches eagerly to see if you won't. And the combination of so many wills is sure to influence yours. 'Give a dog a bad name and hang him,' means to give him the name and then drive him into hanging himself. It would be a great deal simpler to hang him in the beginning. But people don't ever seem to think we are sorry for what we do. Oh, people are merciless! There ought to be a God."

"To swear by, anyhow," said May. "By the way, are you going to see about that Assistant Leader business?"

"No, I'm not."

"Then you don't mind my telling —"

"You can tell what you like and to whom you like. If the story is believed, it will be a relief to be stoned by people for whom I have some respect, instead of by myself and you."

"You have some pluck," said May, approvingly. "Ardis, you're such a horrible combination of good and bad qualities that it's like playing at hide-and-seek to find out what you really are."

"I'm tired," said Ardis, pitifully.

"Heavens and earth! I should think you were. Here, sit down here a minute. No, don't try to talk. Oh, Ardis," she cried, burying her face in her friend's lap, "I did n't think it would hurt you so much. I did n't know — I did n't understand."

Ardis turned her white face towards the window, and did not speak. A warm wind, smelling faintly of spring, stirred the curtain now and then, but for a long while that was the only sound in the room. Then Ardis lifted May's head from her lap, kissed her on the forehead, and went downstairs.

The next day the sound of coming flowers had gone from the wind, and the sky had retreated into itself. A few tiny snow-flakes began to wander aimlessly through the air, as if searching for something to do, and these were followed by others whose mission was more obvious. Two days later the world of Harland was one dazzle of white and blue, and rumors spread through chapel that the lake was again in a condition for skating. By four o'clock as much of the college as had learned its lessons was flying joyously around on the ice, with frequent collisions, and exchange of frost-bitten pleasantries through the bracing air.

Kathleen and her friend, Mary Donnelly, '97, were having a race, thereby causing consternation among the beginners who were staggering in their path. Christine had persuaded Clare to come out, and was rewarded by seeing the color gradually come back to her face.

"Now, don't you feel less vindictive, on the whole?" she asked, as they wound up with a magnificent slide towards the skate-house.

"Yes," said Clare. "I'm sorry that I said everybody I know is a fool."

"But you stood up for Ethel Lindsay, though, and

said that she did n't mean to be unkind. A speech like that would naturally be followed by a relapse."

"But I 'm sure she did n't mean to be unkind. She has always been my friend, and even helped to get me the Leadership. I insist that she did n't mean to be unkind!"

"You neglect your opportunities in the way of rage. I myself was furious with every one in the house, including that beardless supe with the little Derby hat over one ear."

"I feel as if we ought not to mind anything, as long as it went off well," said Clare. "Leaders always realize that but for the kindness of Providence the most awful, unutterable things may happen."

"I don't know what else you 'd call Miss Lindsay! But, Clare, you are wonderfully optimistic for a person who 's always getting sick. I believe that I should swear."

"I think that optimism is the only rational doctrine — that 's why. You have to see the bad side of things anyway, and if you can see the good too, why, that shows that you 're just so much more broadminded."

The snow talked cheerfully under their feet, as they walked up College Lane, and turned in at the campus gate. A golden light crept on ahead of them over the white slopes, and they stopped to look back at the three little sunset pictures framed in by the windows of the factory tower.

"Talk about crying over spilt milk," said Christine, moodily. "We have a perfect right to, when it turns sour on the floor!"

342

"Christine," asked Clare, slowly, "were you ever disappointed in any one that you cared very much about?"

"Once," said Christine, after a pause.

"Do you think that any one who really cared for you would be willing to let other people attack you, even if she herself often did?"

"My standards of friendship are all gone to pieces, so I'm not a good person to consult."

"Do you mean to say that you haven't any friends left whom you can trust?"

Christine solemnly drew off her glove, held up two fingers of one hand, and put the glove on again.

"One of them is Ruth," said Clare, pathetically, "and of course the other must be Ardis; so I don't see where —"

"It isn't Ardis," interrupted Christine.

"Then it must be me."

"It is."

Clare looked thoroughly mystified.

"But about Ardis — it can't be that all your little disagreements with her have led to anything as serious as this."

"Perhaps I'm hard to get along with."

"That's evading the question. I see you don't want to tell me; but sometimes — Christine, I wish you *would* tell me, I'm so —" She broke off suddenly, feeling that she had stumbled upon dangerous ground.

"If Ardis has ever hurt you," she said, "I know that it must have been unintentional, because she loves you dearly. In fact, I believe you're the only person in college that she does love."

"Oh, Clare, you don't know what you're talking about."

"I don't often, I admit; but to-day I do. I know that Ardis loves you."

"And I know that she does not. But please don't ask me how or why I know, because I shall never tell you." She turned her face away, and Clare saw that she was very pale.

"Christine!" she said under her breath; and then all of a sudden the truth flashed upon her.

"What's the matter with you?" asked Christine.

"Oh, nothing — go home. I mean, don't wait for me. I think I'll stay out till supper-time."

"Is it another song?" inquired Christine, sympathetically, for Clare had been "taken that way" before. "I suppose she didn't even hear me," she thought with a smile, as she went on up the icy path.

Clare stayed behind on the Observatory steps, and watched the three tower pictures until their light was only a faint yellow glimmer against the sky. She could still hear the sound of distant laughter from girls coming home through College Lane. A Freshman, accompanied by a Wyckham friend, went by with a merry clash of skates, and both greeted her enthusiastically as they passed. Clare did not know the girl, but a Freshman is never afraid to bow to a Senior when that Freshman is reinforced by a man.

The supper-bell rang in the Hadley, and somebody upstairs threw open her window to close the blinds. Clare had a momentary glimpse of bright curtains and pictures, and a bowl of violets somewhere, before the shutters were slammed to. Then she rose and walked home.

"Sometimes you can't forgive people," she thought; "sometimes you have had to bear too much. And yet I promised to stand by her 'unto death.'"

There are times when we are too tired to engage in any moral struggle, no matter how small; when we can only stand with face towards the sky where the sun has been — and wait for another day!

CHAPTER XX

ELIZABETH DANE was sitting alone in the editors' room of the old Gym, looking at the back door of the Warren House opposite, and trying to get inspiration.

It was Saturday afternoon, and the day was full of the early spring; soft calls, and bird notes, and sunshine drifted in through the open window. Then something else followed.

"Here are the proofs," said Rachel Winter, vaulting in after them. "There they are, right under your foot, and Mr. Ball says he wants the editorial right away."

"I only hope he may get it," said Elizabeth, wearily. "I've already spent two hours reading copy for the Contributors' Club. You didn't happen to see Ardis anywhere around, did you?"

"No; she generally keeps out of sight when there's anything to be done."

"Well, did you remember to tell them that the word they couldn't read in the leader was 'that' instead of 'true'?"

"Yes; I said it wasn't 'true,' and he asked why it was that the editors always put in such a thunderin' lot of things that wa'n't so! Aren't you coming to the rally? It's nearly four o'clock."

346

"No, I'm writing for the cause, and that's more noble than going over to listen. You need n't say anything to Ardis if you see her. Very likely she's planning to help later on. Poor old Rachel, you look tired out! That's the fourth time you've been down to the printer's to-day, is n't it?"

"Only the third," said Rachel, cheerfully. "Good-bye, and come over if you can."

She swung herself out of the window, and Elizabeth was left to concentrate her scattered energies upon a plea for the new Chemistry Building. Everybody realized, in a vague sort of way, that the college was poor, but few people understood how hard it was sometimes for the President to make both ends meet. The class-rooms were becoming more and more crowded every year, in proportion to the rapidly increasing size of the college, and although the professors were often at their wits' end to know where the next recitation could be held, there was no money to remedy the urgent need. But the demand for a new Science Building had now become imperative, as the old one, which was small to begin with, was utilized by Chemistry, Physics, Zoölogy, and their laboratories; Geology, Physiology, Mineralogy, and beginning German; and an inoffensive German or Geology student could scarcely help suffering pathetically from the daily and uncongenial companionship of H_2S or PH_3.

The Councillors of the two upper classes had been going around during the past week, getting subscriptions among the girls, and this afternoon a mass-meeting was held to discuss results. Excitement waxed high when the report read that nine hundred and eighty-seven dollars had actually been raised, or pledged, among the students alone!

"It lacks only thirteen dollars of a thousand," said Councillor Wyman, impressively. "Is there no one here who will help to make up the even sum?"

A Junior called out, "I'll give a dollar," and this encouraged a small Freshman who had been fidgeting impatiently, to say, "I'll give five."

Other offerings were quickly made; and when the thirteenth dollar was pledged, the whole chapel united in triumphant applause.

"We all know," said Ruth Burritt, rising, "that the college is in terrible need of everything, except people to love her and stand by her through thick and thin! [applause] and that the Alumnæ are working very hard to get us a library, so we can't reasonably expect them to help us about this new building. But we can each of us do something if we fully understand that every little counts for much. So let us make our beginning, and pass it on to those who come after us, trusting them to realize, as we do, that when our Alma Mater calls on us for help, she must not call in vain!"

This speech was greeted with tremendous enthusiasm, and then Ardis Hathaway rose, saying, "The Glee and Banjo Clubs would like to contribute two hundred dollars — the proceeds of the Easter Concert — to the fund for the Chemistry Building."

The Leader of the Glee Club, who had just come into the hall, flushed crimson as she heard this, and walked up to one of her first sopranos, who was applauding vigorously in a back row.

"Stop clapping for yourself!" the Sophomore beside her was saying.

"I was n't!" answered the girl, indignantly. "I was clapping for my Leader!"

"When was this business meeting held?" asked Clare, slipping her arm around the girl's sweet neck, for she had heard the reply.

"This morning, before chapel. Why were n't you there? We all wanted to talk it over with you."

"I did n't know anything about it. I was ill yesterday, and this morning there was nothing to do at the college, so I stayed at home."

"The sign was up yesterday," said the soprano, looking troubled, "and we thought of course that you knew about it."

But she understood as well as Clare did that the leader of a Glee Club does not usually learn of its business meetings from a sign on the bulletin board!

"Never mind," said Clare, gently; "the money has gone just where I would have wanted it to."

She could scarcely complain of the Glee Club Manager to this child. But it had hurt all the same, as little things sometimes will; for she felt that it had placed her in a false position, — with the Glee Club, who would think that she was not interested, and with the other girls, who would give her more credit than was her due. "It was just a little unnecessary," she thought, as the mass meeting adjourned; but she knew that it would be of no use to speak to Ardis about it.

"Did you know that Mr. Field is coming up next week?" asked Leonora Kent, slipping her hand through Clare's arm. "Be thankful that you're not on the Dramatics Committee, and walk over to the Storey with me this minute. We had a meeting in Kathleen's room half an hour ago."

Leonora had been elected Chairman of the Dramatics Committee because of her executive ability and her good temper, — two really excellent qualities which are not always found in combination. It would be a crucial moment when the trainer, Mr. Field, came up to pass judgment on the girls who were trying for parts in "Twelfth Night," and Leonora was proportionately concerned. Of course the committee always made its own choice of characters, but this choice did not invariably coincide with that of the trainer, and the students were awaiting his advent with uneasy minds.

The annual Shakespeare play at Harland had resulted from the discovery made by both Faculty and students that the best way to understand Shakespeare is to "go and do it." And the fact that even the minor parts were taken by intelligent and sympathetic people, who had made a careful study of the great master, did much to obviate the difficulties that would naturally lie in the way of unprofessional work. Well-known critics had gone so far as to say that the "Shylock" of Harland surpassed any that they had ever seen, although they did add afterwards that "they could not understand it;" and the famous "Nick Bottom" of Amy Lennox had attracted the attention of Sargent himself, who besought her to give up her High School engagement in the West and go upon the stage. The Dramatics were always so popular that there werc generally half-a-dozen applicants for each part; and as the people who did not apply spent most of their time in coaching those who did, the whole play was thoroughly known by every one in the class before the first performance took place.

As Clare and Leonora approached Kathleen's room, they heard her roaring savagely, "'Oh, for a stone bow, to hit him in the eye!'"

"Ow, go away!" expostulated a milder voice. "Your next cue is 'where I have left Olivia'!"

"'Fire and brimstone!'" broke in Sir Toby, with an audible kick.

"No, no, you came in too soon; you ought to have waited for—"

"'Bolts and shackles!'" shouted Sir Toby again.

"'Oh peace, peace, peace, now, now!'" expostulated the prompter as the door opened, and Kathleen advanced towards her friends, with a feather duster in one uplifted hand, inquiring ferociously,—

"'Shall this fellow live?'"

"'You must amend your drunkenness,'" said Leonora, disarming Sir Toby with a clever turn of the wrist.

"'Out, scab,'" said Kathleen, pointing derisively at Clare; "this is a Dramatics meeting."

"We're not all here yet," said Leonora, establishing herself on the divan. "Now go ahead, Virginia, and give us Maria."

"'A dry jest, sir,'" replied Maria, dropping a demure little courtesy, "but you don't catch me doing my part again until Sir Andrew comes."

"He doesn't belong to the committee, and neither do you, so clear out, Ginny!" said Kathleen, good-naturedly. "We can't have the whole caste spouting around in here."

Clare and Virginia took their departure when the others came in, and the committee set to work.

"To tell the truth, I'm not certain about Sir Andrew yet," said Leonora, consulting her notebook. "What would you think of Miriam Smith?"

"She lithpth," answered Kathleen, briefly.

"Well, how about Peacemaker Adams? She's wild to have a part."

"She also lithpth," said Kathleen again.

"No, she doesn't, — you're thinking of Pomona. But perhaps we can work both those in, as a ' Lord, Priest, Sailor, Officer, Musician — ' "

"No!" howled Kathleen, "not *that!*"

"' And other attendants,' " finished Leonora, severely.

"Minnie Appleyard is the best for Sir Andrew," said Mildred Wyman, decidedly. "She's so fat that she'll be funny if she doesn't act at all."

"No, sir! *I'm* going to be fat!" said Kathleen. "I've got the promise of all the sofa-pillows in the house."

"One of you ought to be thin," objected Lucile Murray.

"But it won't be acting at all if a fat girl plays a fat part. Let the corpulent one say, ' I am thin,' and *act* thin, by my hat! Then it'll be real art."

"Kathleen, be still," said Grace Reade, impatiently. "I think there's no doubt that Edith will get Orsino, don't you?"

"There's no one better," replied the Chairman; "and you, Grace, are pretty well fixed as Sebastian.

Amy Allen and those others can't begin to come up
to you."

"I think it depends entirely on who gets Viola,"
said Grace. "It is certain that I look less unlike
Elsie Dane than like Ardis. I don't see why Ardis
is n't willing to try for Olivia, anyway. She's the
only beauty in the class."

"Because she prefers to be first in everything,"
said Mildred, with a smile. "I think we all understand our friend Epicurus by this time. Now about
Malvolio, — I'm going to try for that, although of
course I shall get left. And Faith is pretty sure of
the Clown. I'm simply wild to see her skipping
around the stage in red curly shoes, and hear her
sing, ' Hold thy peace, thou knave!' "

"Yes, she does it well enough, if she be so dis-
posed," said Kathleen, condescendingly, "and so do
I too. ' She does it with a better grace, but I do it
more natural.' "

" ' Very sweet and contagious, i' faith,' " said
Grace, suppressing her friend with a sofa-pillow,
"but for heaven's sake, keep still till this meeting
is over."

"I wonder if Christine is going to try for anything?" said Lucile.

"She's kept pretty still about it, if she is," said
Mildred. "But then, she's not much given to
prating of her intentions."

" ' A fustian riddle,' " came in a smothered voice
from under the pillow, " ' And O shall end, I
hope!' "

It did end when Mr. Field came up the next
week. An anxious group assembled outside the

Athletics room in the old Gym, where the trials were to take place, and much amusing conversation was heard on the stairs. Some of the competitors were nervous, but most of them were in riotous spirits. Ardis Hathaway, who was trying for Viola, sat by herself on an upper step eagerly studying her rôle, while three Sir Andrews were holding a solemn rehearsal of their part, in unison, interrupted at times by the Clown, who playfully observed, "'How now, my hearties, did you ever see a picture of *we three ?*'"

Another candidate for "Viola" sat in her lonely sanctum downstairs, sorting over the last relay of proof sheets for the "Prism." Her previous trials for the part had met with enthusiastic approval from the committee, but on account of the work which one of the editors had left undone, she would be unable to see Mr. Field that afternoon. The injustice and exasperation of it all came over her in wrathful gusts as she listened to the hilarity outside. Most of the editors were trying for some part in the play, and she was therefore reluctant to call upon them for extra work, although she knew that they would not refuse. But Elizabeth realized the full extent of her responsibilities, and understood that when there was a deficiency on the staff the editor-in-chief must supply it. And the fact that she was working her way through college made the situation still more trying. Tutoring and sewing occupied all the outside time that might otherwise have been given to the study of her part, and now the few spare moments that she had saved for it were urgently demanded by the "Prism."

TRYING FOR DRAMATICS

"I suppose I might as well give it up!" she thought, turning to the great pile of proof sheets that awaited her.

There was a soft tap at the door, and the Class President came in.

"Why aren't you upstairs?" she asked, laying her hand for a minute on Elsie's hot forehead. "You ought to try for your part now, while you're feeling fresh, and not put it off till the last of the afternoon. Ardis has just gone in."

"I'm afraid I can't," said Elsie, with the suspicion of a quiver in her voice. "There is work to be done, — and this is my first duty, you know."

"Yes, but can't it wait a few minutes, only this once? It may make all the difference about your getting the part."

"Yes; but the work ought to be finished to-day, and somehow I don't like to put it off. You see it's our last number, and I've determined that it shall be a good one. Of course it's a disappointment; but I suppose that a person like me ought not to expect to go in for anything that's only pleasure, anyway. I ought to sit down and be thankful for my little attic room, with the smell of the turnips coming up from the kitchen; and not want pretty clothes that fit, and not want to go to the Prom because it will cost a dollar, and not want to try for Dramatics when I really haven't the time, and — Oh, Ruth, it is so hard to crowd the youngness out of one! I try and try, but somehow it will always keep cropping up."

The tears had come to Ruth's eyes, and she answered, "Yes, I know!"

355

"I'm ashamed of having spoken like that," said Elsie, taking up her pen. "I didn't mean to, and I seldom do. But you're so dreadfully sympathetic that you always affect me like a kind of spiritual door-mat, on which to wipe off my troubles."

"Is it only proof-correcting?" asked Ruth, suddenly. "Why, Elsie, if that's all! Mr. Packard taught me how to correct proofs one summer when he was on the 'Lampoon.' It's nothing at all, if you know how. Just let me take that page a minute and I'll show you."

"You do know how," said Elizabeth, approvingly, as Ruth gave evidence of her skill.

"Well, then, you go straight upstairs and let me finish this work. I can do it as well as you, and it's very important for you to see Mr. Field to-day. Oh, Elsie, don't say no. Please, please, don't be unreasonable and everything! I'll be so careful, and I know why it is that you have extra work this afternoon, although I respect you for not telling. But I'm President of my class, and it would be wrong for me to stand by and see unfairness like this without trying to prevent it. That's what being a President means. You know, Elsie, you know, yourself. And then — Oh, Elsie, that night when I was sick, and you sat up and nursed me! Don't you remember? And the next morning there was no breakfast, because we had run out of supplies, and it took all our money to pay for the medicine that the doctor ordered. And I had to lie there and see you go off to work, knowing that you had had nothing to eat!"

"It's true that we've had some experiences together," said Elsie, giving her a warm hug, "but don't cry, Ruth. I'll let you correct the proofs if you want to, and I'll go upstairs and do my best, honestly I will, only — *don't* cry, Ruth; and thank you, dear."

When she joined the group on the stairs, Kathleen was contesting hotly with "a Sea Captain, friend to Viola," who considered that his turn ought to come next.

"'I cannot be so answered!'" said Kathleen, severely. "As for waiting around any longer in this slip-shod, heterogeneous fashion, it's myself that won't stand it. Beshrew me, if it isn't enough to turn a black cat maltese!"

"'Sir Toby, there you lie!'" drawled one of the Marias from a top step. "You know that you wouldn't go away for love or money."

"Mr. Field wants the next Viola," said Leonora Kent, coming to the door. "Is Elsie Dane here?"

Elizabeth quickly responded, and Kathleen and her Sea Captain immediately engaged in a scuffle.

"'The offenth ith not of such a bloody nature,'" remonstrated Pomona Adams mildly, from the window-seat. "Oh, girlth, here comth Mith Arnold, reading. She'th got a Shakethpeare from the Library."

"I borrowed hers, that's why," said Kathleen. "I didn't know she was going to try for anything."

"'Be not afraid of greatness,'" murmured Christine, entering the hall.

"'Fie on him, Jezebel!'" called Kathleen over the banisters. "Take off those yellow stockings."

"Oh, I hope she'll get Malvolio," said one of the girls.

"So do I," agreed Kathleen. "If she doesn't, Philippa Fairbank will, and that high and mighty air of hers is one too much for me. She looks at me as if I were a mouse suspended by the tail. 'Go off,' she says, 'go off!'"

When the final result of the trials was made known, it seemed that the selection of the Dramatics Committee had been, in the main, approved. But Mr. Field had seriously objected to a fat Sir Andrew Aguecheek, saying that he ought by rights to be a slim knight, of meagre proportions. Accordingly Miss Appleyard was relegated to the part of Antonio, the Sea Captain, and Freda Hastings took Sir Andrew.

"I wonder why we hadn't thought of her before," said one of the girls. "That deadly serious air of hers will make it all the funnier."

"She's bow-legged, too," added somebody else. "It couldn't be better."

Nobody but Kathleen had tried for Sir Toby, as the other girls did not dare compete with her. Christine emerged triumphant as Malvolio, although Mr. Field declared that the acting of Philippa Fairbank in this part was nearly as good. The trainer was to come again in two weeks, and meanwhile rehearsals were to be directed by the Professor of Elocution.

The first one was a memorable occasion, for all the minor parts insisted on being present in every scene, and it was with difficulty that they could be ejected to wait until their turn came. The relations between Viola and Olivia were, unfortunately, somewhat strained, as Elsie Dane had come off victorious, and Ardis found it hard to forgive her. At first she refused to take any part at all, but Mr. Field finally persuaded her to accept Olivia, although her behavior at the time was such as to infuriate the loyal members of Ninety-five.

"To think of having to be teased," said Mildred Wyman, indignantly, "when so many girls are simply dying for a part!"

"Well, you see," said Mr. Field, conciliatingly, "she's so confoundedly pretty;" and the girls realized that it would be quite useless to reason with such a man.

Clare Deland was to have the general supervision of the music, although the actual work of training the choruses and wrestling with the orchestra would be done by Faith Bentley, who had more time. The editors went off duty in April; but the demands on the Glee Club leader would become steadily greater now, until Commencement. Clare did not mind this at all, for the training of her class in the Ivy music is the proudest as well as the most loving task that a leader has to perform; and the Glee Club prospects for this term had been much improved by the happy return of Margretta Nolenski. She had appeared with a smiling countenance at the first spring rehearsal, and Clare wondered afterwards why it was that Ardis and May Churchill exchanged significant glances when she came in. She might have wondered still more if she had known just how large a fracas had been averted by the timely presence of this young Polish-American.

But Clare was thinking of something else at present, and, strange to say, it had nothing to do with Glee Club. The competition for the Ivy Poem had now begun, and no one knew who was trying for it, but everybody who sat up late was suspected. Clare had always been fond of writing verses, although she could seldom be persuaded to let any one see them; but a few simple little things in the "Prism" had caused Miss Carlisle to say, "If you were not so much of a musician, you might be an unusually good writer."

Clare remembered that Dr. Page had once remarked, "If you had not so many outside interests, you might be a remarkable musician," and wondered if she ought to annihilate herself. But now her attempt at an Ivy Poem was done, and, to complicate matters, the music had come with it! "It belongs with it," she thought, "and yet the same person never gets both. If the words succeed, the committee won't take the music, and if — what is more likely — the words fail, the music will be of no use, anyway." It was Clare's first experience in setting her own words to music, although she had composed many songs, and she felt much as a mother does who makes the clothes for her own child. But she said nothing about the little musical garments when the words were handed in. At the end of the allotted time, it was announced that Miriam Smith had won the competition, and Clare tried to forget how disappointed she was. "But I'd be an abominable pig if I wasn't glad," she thought, "when Miriam looks so happy."

The Ivy Poem is very often written by some one

who has never written anything before. This girl had never been admitted to a society; she had tried for the Glee Club, and failed; she had tried for Dramatics, and failed. Nobody in her class knew anything about her; but what difference did that make, now that she had written the Ivy Poem! Her father and mother would see it on the Ivy Day program, under the class seal, and hear it sung after the Oration, while the class President was planting the ivy beside the college walls. And they would be delightfully, even ridiculously proud, as only the best fathers and mothers can.

And after all, it was the music that had meant the most to Clare. She went down to Dramatics rehearsal that afternoon to help Faith with the "catch" in the second act, and while the girls waited for a delinquent member of the caste, they asked her to play something. She had tried in vain to forget the one dear melody that had followed her about for the last few weeks, but it was waiting always at her fingers' ends, and this afternoon it played itself before she realized what had happened.

"What is it, Clare?" asked Orsino, from his perch on a step-ladder. "Oh, do play it again! Is it one of yours?"

A tall, pale girl rose from one of the stage boxes, where she had been sitting, unobserved, and said: "I know what it is! It couldn't be but one thing. I know what it is!"

She pulled a rumpled piece of paper out of her pocket and tossed it over to Clare, who saw that it was the first rough draft of the Ivy Poem. And what was stranger still, the music went to the words!

"Don't say anything about it now," she said quickly, for the coincidence seemed almost too surprising to be true. The words of the poem were beautiful and simple, and Clare felt satisfied that they were a hundred times better than her own; but the music —

"I want to see you after rehearsal," said Faith, who was on the Song Committee; "but how in the name of all that's wonderful you managed to finish that music to-day, when you didn't see the words until this morning —"

"I didn't see the words until Miriam showed them to me just now," said Clare, laughing; and Faith looked so mystified that she promised to explain later on.

That evening Clare met Faith and another member of the Ivy Day Committee in Music Hall, and the two Seniors listened to their Ivy Music.

"It's a song that understands," said Faith, looking out past the dusk on the college steps. "It has the haze of the meadows over it."

"And the strength of the mountains too."

"And the scent of the arbutus, — oh, Clare!"

"It has something else," added the other Senior, after a pause. "Do you know, if you weren't such a happy kind of person, with more friends than you can attend to, I should almost think that you'd lost something you cared for. That's what makes us want to cry when we hear it, although it isn't a sad song."

"Wasn't it strange that Miriam should have got it?" asked Faith, hurriedly. "We never supposed that she could write, although she is certainly a passionate lover of the college. The other night I found her with her arms tight around that stone pillar on the side porch, and her cheek against it, and I should have stopped to call her a fool if — well — I hadn't been crying a little myself."

"You inconsistent old dear!" said the Senior, walking rapidly to another window. "But it's a good thing that we've been too busy so far to think much about what it all means."

It is really surprising how little time there is for sentimentalizing in that last spring term at college. Anxiety for the success of Dramatics, appointments on the Commencement Committees; Æsthetics and Philosophy papers long overdue, are all absorbing subjects of interest; and it is only in quieter moments — at vespers, perhaps, or in the warm twilight of the campus evenings — that the college girl remembers "these things are the last!"

"I can't realize that we're actually going abroad when it's all over," said Clare to Christine one afternoon, as they walked down to the Opera House. "And yet it's what I've longed for ever since I can remember, — music study in Germany. And to think that you're really going with us! Oh, Christine! how do you suppose it all happened?"

This was the plan that Mrs. Deland had been cherishing in secret for several years; and it was going to come true!

"Of course we shall travel very simply and live in small pensions, not hotels, but we shall have such fun among ourselves that other things won't make any difference."

"Fun! Well, I should rather think so! I'm so

glad that my mother said I could go! I was afraid at first that she would n't. But having Stephen over there will make her feel more comfortable about us."

"Yes; but if your brother is studying architecture in Paris, I don't see that we shall be very likely to run across him often in Berlin."

"He 'll come and see us, of course, and you and he will probably spend most of your time at the Wagner-Vereins. I like Wagner myself, but not in allopathic doses; so you can't count on my society more than five hours a day."

The friendship between Christine and Clare had grown steadily, from the time when Pippa came singing through the early morning, and taught another girl that all was yet right with this heart-breaking world. They had said nothing about it, but each knew from that day that the little barrier of misunderstanding was gone at last; and sometimes they felt, although they never spoke of it, that a common loss had drawn them together.

The Opera House was cool and dark as they pushed open the stage door, and Christine experienced a wild thrill of exultation as she looked up at the scenery suspended over her head, and the ropes which crossed and recrossed in mysterious tangles. There was something inspiring also in the stiff little imitation hillocks, with false, curly moss stuck on to them, like the false whiskers on the hero. She rejoiced that she was going to be Malvolio, and went through her part with so much spirit that the little audience applauded vigorously when she left the stage. She waited a few minutes to see the midnight carouse of Sir Toby and his friend, aided by the sprightly Maria; and while groping her way through the seats in the orchestra circle, she ran against Philippa Fairbank, who was watching the rehearsal from a dark corner.

"Why, what's the matter?" asked Christine, in alarm; for Philippa, the stately and severe, was unquestionably weeping.

"Oh dear, is it you? I didn't suppose any one would come down here," was the dismal reply.

"I'll go away if you'd rather. But please tell me — no, I'll tell you instead. I have a boat engaged for this hour. Let's go up and take a row."

The Athletic Association had purchased a few boats the year before, and by writing one's name very forcibly on top of any others that happened to be on the slate, one of these crafts could be secured for a short time. The lake was too small to be judged by its quantity, but its quality was all that could be desired. Nobody had been upset, nobody had contracted malaria, and everybody's disposition had been improved by the innovation.

Philippa was much pleased that Christine should have asked her to go, and insisted on carrying the oars down from the cellar of the old Gym, where they were generally concealed. The boat-house was not then built, and the one remaining craft rocked gently at the end of a somewhat uncertain little dock.

"Let me row," said Philippa, as they got in. "If I don't row I shall talk, and I don't want to do that."

"Why not?" asked Christine, taking the oars. "If something is bothering you, you'd better get it out. I won't listen if you don't want me to."

She pushed off, and stood with the dripping oar in one hand, watching the drops scurry off in circular ripples behind the boat.

"I thought when I came here," began Philippa, abruptly, "that I'd be something more than President of the H. A. C. W., but I'm not.

"I wanted," she continued, as Christine did not speak, "to do something of some account here, but I haven't."

"What set you to thinking about that?" asked Christine. "It's the way we all feel."

"Not those of you who succeed. Why, I'm not even in a society."

Christine's face darkened. "That doesn't mean anything, Philippa. At least it means so absurdly little, in comparison with the suffering it causes, that one often becomes impatient at the very existence of such organizations. They aren't what counts after we leave this place. It's our friends that count, and our studies, and the campus, and the mountains, and everything in this world but one little society pin!"

"Did you think that before you got in?" asked Philippa, quietly; and Christine laughed.

"No, I didn't," she admitted.

"Then the best solution of the problem is to meekly accept the law of life, by which some shall be taken, and others left?"

"It would be much better to abolish the universal tendency to exaggerate what is unknown. The best part of being in a society is that it teaches us to gauge them at their proper value. It would be quite impossible to persuade non-members that the society girls do not have a certain amount of contempt for them. And yet being in is the very thing of all others that teaches us to respect the people who are out; for knowing, as we do, the number of girls who get in and don't deserve it, and the greater number who deserve it and don't get in, we can't help understanding that the universe does not begin and end with membership."

"But afterwards, when one is an alumna, — to come back year after year and find the same society wearing the same dear pin, and being proud of it — "

"Don't!" said Christine, "you hurt me. I've been through it all myself so many times. And although I love my society dearly, I think that I shall always remember — "

"What?" asked Philippa, curiously.

"Oh, nothing, — an unpleasant experience that I had in my Sophomore year, that's all. It's over now, but somehow one doesn't forget!"

"You can afford to forget a great deal, now that you are Ivy Orator, and in the Dramatics too."

"Yes, but that isn't real success. The beginning and end of our trouble here is that we are always confusing what we want to be with what we want other people to think us! If only we could make ourselves understand that to do our best is all that can be expected of us, — if only we could grow old enough to realize that it takes all kinds of people to make a world — "

"If only we would be satisfied with doing the work of a toe when we'd rather do that of an ear," interrupted Philippa, grimly.

"Never you mind, a toe has plenty of sentiment! I respect my toes, especially when they're stepped on, and don't complain. But college is a pretty complete little world in itself. Some of us have got to be toes, and do a toe's work. But the toe happens to be a rather important member of society in the long run. Just imagine how our high-lights would limp without them!"

"It's a cruel world — sometimes," said Philippa, slowly.

"All worlds are. And this one is not unlike others. It *is* a world with great passions and struggles, and real victories — or failures. It's a very real world, after all."

"And disappointments are the greatest reality in it."

"Yes, I believe that disappointments are the worst things we have to contend with here, except, of course, ourselves. Our temptations lie mostly in the direction of success. There is no doubt that we all want everything that's going, and will get it if we can."

"Not always!" said Philippa, thinking of the Junior presidential election, the year before.

Christine pulled in her oars, and they drifted into the cool shadow of the banks.

"After all," she said, half to herself, "it's a dreadful responsibility to be young, — to know that the chance is yours, and that the future is only a 'perhaps,' which, if you care enough, can be made into a 'must and will'! I don't mean mere outward

368

distinction, but that 'most of the best' that it is in us to do. And then there's the afterwards, when we can remember that we tried. The remembrance of having tried must be all that one needs in old age, I should think. And to really try, means to try for the one hundredth time, after ninety-nine failures. Just the same old law by which so many leaves must live and die before we see one flower. And yet the leaf cannot be considered a failure, — unless the caterpillars eat it."

"Oh!" exclaimed Philippa; and then she remembered having heard some one say that Christine's sense of humor was greater than her sense of propriety. She wondered if her companion was thinking of the fuzzy, brown-and-black caterpillars with effective shading, or the smooth, objectionable caterpillars, that one does not like to meet.

"Those are some of the things that I shall try to say in my Ivy Oration," continued Christine. "I only hope that I can say them right; I only hope that I can say them truthfully and well. Oh, this old oration is no joke, I can tell you! Sometimes I wonder how it is that people can get inside of an opportunity and not feel the awful solemnity of it all. It's like the silence in a cañon. But it must be broken by your voice; and what is anything that you can say, compared with the meaning of that silence? Well, life's queer."

"'Speech is but broken light upon the depths of the unspoken,'" quoted Philippa, sympathetically.

"True; that's what I thought the other day in Philosophy, when I flunked dead. It helped to console me for having said nothing."

"'Which is the properest day to drink, — Saturday, Sunday, Monday?'" came in a mediæval duet down the woods path: and Sir Toby and the fool appeared, skipping hand in hand.

"'Every day is the properest day, so why should I speak of one day?'" replied the fool in her sweet soprano.

"'I had rather than forty shillings I had so sweet a voice to sing as the fool has,'" said Christine, cordially. "Come aboard, fool, and give us an oar home! You, too, Sir Toby, seem to be in want of exercise."

"'Excellent! why, this is the best fooling when all is done,'" said Kathleen, accepting the invitation. "But, unfortunately, all is *not* done. I haven't looked at my Ethics for to-morrow."

"And you can't cut, now that you're in Dramatics," said Faith.

"If you see me there to-morrow," responded Kathleen, gloomily, "you may know that it's against my deepest inclinations."

"Like the old woman who departed this life," said Christine; "and when a sympathetic neighbor asked the afflicted widower if she was willing to go, 'Willin' to go!' he repeated in surprise, 'she was 'bleeged ter!'"

When the girls reached the dock, a little group of Sophomores were waiting for the boat, and one of them shyly observed, "Here's to Ninety-five!" as its crew disembarked. Christine left her friends at the campus gate and walked home through College Lane. There was still an hour before supper, and she determined to spend it in wrestling with the Ivy Oration, which was not yet finished.

"My oration must not live to be ashamed of me," she thought, going to her desk. "I wonder if it knows that I'm young, and is trembling all the time at what must follow? I respect you," she said, taking up the loose pages that lay before her, "and therefore I'm afraid of you. It's just the same way with the people whom we fear. We're really not afraid of them at all, but of ourselves, for fear that we shall say or do some idiotic thing that will forfeit their esteem forever. I wish I could flavor you with genuine inspiration, my dear, but at present everything desirable seems to be second hand. Life is really a vast intellectual pawn-shop, with all its ideas neatly ticketed on their shelves."

But she knew perfectly well that she did not believe this about the ideas, and trusted that her own were not really pawned, but only cross, because of the heat.

She seized her irresponsible fountain pen and set to work; and just then Ruth came in with the Ethics references for to-morrow. Ruth generally looked up references for them both.

"Do you think," she inquired, "that everything — every person and every emotion — was put into the world for good? That evil is only perverted good, and not a positive quality at all?"

"I don't know," said Christine, stopping to tie a piece of blotting-paper around her pen. "How about a poor photographer? Do you think that there was intended to be any good in him?"

"No," replied Ruth emphatically, remembering the bad Senior pictures; "I shall give that as an example in class."

"Well, do you think — " she began again.

"No," said Christine, severely; "don't you see that I'm writing?"

"Christine," ventured her room-mate timidly, after a protracted silence, "what made you put the can-opener in my work-basket?"

"Yes. Perhaps. You'll probably find it in Sidgewick," was the irrelevant answer.

"Oh, I pity any one who has to room with a girl that writes," thought Ruth, as the supper-bell rang; and decided to spend the evening with a friend.

But even then the oration did not get on very fast, for Christine kept thinking of Philippa Fairbank. She was conscious of having thought about her a great deal that afternoon, and wondered why it was that she could not forget their conversation in the boat.

"After all, it's nearly over," she thought, "and that girl feels that she hasn't had anything worth having. And here I am, trying to write an oration on the compensations in failure!"

She closed her notebook impatiently, threw it on the floor, and went out into the warm spring dusk. Leonora Kent lived at the farther end of College Lane, but Christine preferred to go through the hole in the fence, and take a long cut across the campus grass.

"It's different from other grass," she thought, as she felt it soft and cool beneath her russet ties. "I wonder why!"

The apple-blossoms were all white this year, which gave the back campus a peculiarly ethereal and spirit-like appearance; the hammocks were found half full of drifted petals every morning. But to-night they were occupied by their rightful owners, curled up in groups of two and three, exchanging jests or whispered confidences.

"Is that you, Christine?" asked some one as she passed; but Christine hurried on without answering.

She found Leonora working by the dim light of a kerosene lamp. "They forgot to fill it to-day," she apologized, "and it smells horribly. I'll blow it out."

And somehow Christine found it easier to say what she had come to say in the dark.

"I think, Nora," she began, "that I shall have to give up Malvolio, after all. The Ivy Oration takes more time than I thought it would, and — Philippa Fairbank really does the part a great deal better."

"Oh, Christine!" said Leonora; and if it had not been dark, her classmate would have seen how disappointed she was.

"I'm sorry," said Christine; "but you see — "

"Yes, I see through you, if that's what you mean. And probably you think I don't know just how exactly like you this arrangement is! But do you really feel that you owe her so much as that?"

"Perhaps I shall write a better oration," faltered Christine; for the sacrifice had cost her a struggle, and she knew it.

"Of course it is for you to decide, but — it isn't as if she was a friend, or anything like that. Do you think that she'll appreciate — "

"She must never know," said Christine, vehemently. "Promise me that you'll never tell. I trusted you, Leonora."

"I don't betray trusts," was the answer.

"And about her not being a friend. We are classmates, you know! It means a great deal now. It will mean more and more as the years go by."

Leonora felt her way to Christine's face and kissed her tenderly, although she knew perfectly well that Christine was not that kind of a girl. But Christine did nothing more ferocious in return than to slip one arm around Leonora's neck and say meekly, "Please give me another one. Do you know that I really think I've grown to like being kissed? Isn't that humiliating! I never thought that I should sink so low."

"I'm glad you belong to Ninety-five," observed Leonora simply, as they said good-night.

It was past nine when Christine reached home, and as the tired class President was already in bed, she decided to follow her example. But the sleep, when it came, did not rest her. She dreamed that a large white bird with a soft breast carried her swiftly up through the starlight, beyond the place where the dark begins. They reached the outer atmosphere of the world, flew upward, through "white vacancies of dawn," and began to enter the light of another sun. The breast of the bird was warm with this new gold, and sunbeams quivered on its wings. Its name was *Ana*.

"It is a new morning and a new world," she said. "There must be new thoughts here, too." And as they went higher, they reached a fair white forest, where the thoughts clung in whispers to the branches and dropped softly down upon that other world.

And she stopped to fill her arms with the branches, and hear what those thoughts were saying.

"I must take them home," she said, turning to the wings that had carried her. But the bird, ˮΑʋα, was no longer there; and she heard the last electric car grinding past the house on its way back to Laurenceburg. Four bars of white light crossed the foot of her bed, leaped quickly to the screen, and were gone. She heard the car stop a few blocks farther up the street, and then squeak away into silence.

"What *is* the matter?" asked the long-suffering Ruth, turning over with a sigh; for Christine had lighted a candle, and was sitting at her desk.

"Nothing, only I've got to write. I'm sorry. But don't speak to me; I can't help it."

Ruth looked at her in amusement, and wondered if all prospective authoresses had such an undeniable weakness for pretty nightgowns. The changing flame of the wick brought out unaccustomed lights in Christine's hair, which tossed, curly and restless, down to her waist.

"Do you know, you are lovely to-night," murmured Ruth, drowsily. "It really is a pity that —"

"Go to sleep!" replied Christine, sternly; and Ruth obediently turned her face to the wall.

Christine sat there, still thinking of the bird ˮΑʋα that had carried her beyond the light of the stars, and finished the Ivy Oration.

CHAPTER XXI

THE COMING OF THE ROSES

"Yes, that old fellow was a character," said Professor Burton. "He flunked the whole Physics class one day on the question, 'What did Galileo most need?' and of course we answered everything, from 'sandwiches' to 'a telescope;' but none of those went, and at last he said, 'An assistant.' So we remembered, and coached the next division waiting outside, for he always asked the same questions of both classes. And when he demanded to know what Galileo most needed, the whole room answered in unison, 'An assistant!'

"'Gentlemen,' said the old chap, with a gratified smile, 'if you will believe it, I put this same question to every gentleman in the first division, and not one of them could answer it!'"

Professor Burton and several of the Seniors were standing by a window of the Physics room in Lincoln Hall, for the "Symposium" was giving a tea. These entertainments of the "Symposium" were considered by many to be not only unique, but dangerous in character, — partly because they did not occur oftener than once in three years. Lemonade and coffee were served in chemical beakers and test-tubes, and something generally blew up before

376

the afternoon was over; but this added an atmosphere of expectancy and plot interest to the tea, which most affairs of the kind do not achieve. Everywhere could be heard the whirring of water and the soft tinkle of glass. A little zinc battery reacted unassumingly in its retreat of H_2SO_4, and a row of Helmholtz resonators stood like children in a class-room, waiting to answer when called upon. The group around the camera-obscura was usually the most lively, for the instrument was aimed at the street, and strange figures appeared on the ground glass. Now and then a horse trotted past, with quick little wiggles of its inverted legs, or a man walked by on his head, — the sound of his footsteps seeming quite out of proportion to the size of his feet.

"Are n't you coming to our Faculty Reception to-night, Professor Burton?" asked one of the girls. "We 'd like to hear some more stories of your aged friend."

"I 'm coming to the reception because I want to meet your illustrious class. But I sha'n't bring any more stories, because you know it 'll be your duty to entertain me, and I never like to interfere — "

Somebody claimed his attention just then; and as he turned away, Mildred said, "After all, I believe that he is the nicest person on the Faculty."

"Except Miss Carlisle," objected some one who was not a "Scientific."

"Well, what I like about him," said Ruth, "is his consideration for old Dr. Burton, in not allowing himself to be called 'Doctor,' although he is really a Ph.D. It's a little thing, but awfully dear, I think."

"Old" Dr. Burton was a retired minister, and his son had once said, "I want you to be the only Dr. Burton." It was, as Ruth said, a little thing, but very characteristic of the man.

"He isn't dependent upon his teaching at all, — did you know that?" asked a Sophomore in a Chemistry apron, who had come to oversee some experiment. "His mother came from the town where we live, and my mother used to see him when he was a child."

"Really?" asked Mildred, forgetting for a moment the Sophomore's tender age. "Do you remember how he looked in kilts?"

"No," answered the Sophomore, joining in the laugh that followed; "but my mother used to know Mrs. Burton, and thought she was one of the dearest people that ever lived. She was very young, you know, when she died."

"We didn't know," said Ruth, gently.

"And Dr. Burton never got over it, they say. He was a good deal older than she, but they loved each other — very much."

"Then you must at least have seen the Professor, — after you were born," said Mildred, respectfully.

"No, not until I came here. They moved away from Springdale when 'little Ken,' as they called him, was only four years old."

"Christine," said Ruth, when she went home, "you really ought to have come to the tea this afternoon. We heard some interesting facts about your friend Professor Burton."

THE COMING OF THE ROSES

"He isn't my friend any more than he is every-body's," replied Christine, coldly. "What were they?"

Ruth told her; but instead of expressing a suit-able amount of sympathy, she only said: "Well, you don't seem to have discovered anything more extra-ordinary than that he was a boy once, like other men. What strikes me as far more unusual is that he is a boy still. But, Ruth, don't talk any more now, for I want to finish this Hegel before supper."

They both went to the Faculty Reception at the Hutcheson that evening, and Christine managed to secure a delightful though brief conversation with Miss Carlisle. Then she sought out Madame Rigault, having always cherished a secret admira-tion for that lady's dramatic temperament and wit. But Professor Burton was talking to half-a-dozen Seniors at the other side of the room, and did not appear to see her.

"He's an insufferable bore not to come and speak to me, when he knows that he's the only man here worth talking to," she thought. But this was not true, for most of the Harland Faculty are worth talk-ing to, especially when they listen to what you say.

Christine went out on the piazza, where eight stout Japanese lanterns sputtered overhead, and the tables were occupied by discarded ice-cream saucers. The twilight would soon be replaced by a cheerful moon, and she followed the path out to the back campus, where everything smelled delightfully fresh and cool. The hole in the fence showed black against the gray, but she did not turn towards it immediately. She thought of the Senior flower-

379

bed, and walked slowly back to the Observatory steps.

A gentleman in evening dress was coming up the slope in the opposite direction; but Christine did not see him until he was nearly upon her, and then she could not help looking a trifle annoyed.

"By Jove!" said Professor Burton, smiling, "did you run away too? So did I."

"I was there for a very long time," said Christine, in self-defence, "but it's too hot to stay indoors to-night. And besides, I wanted to think."

"And the presence of the Faculty interfered? Well, I've noticed that difficulty myself, sometimes, in class."

"If I had ever been one of your students," said Christine, resentfully, "I'd go home."

"Please stay and talk to me, instead. I want to know what you would like to think about, if the presence of the Faculty did n't interfere."

"You were thinking very hard yourself a minute ago," said Christine, "and I had n't really begun, so suppose that you make the first move."

"Figuratively, you mean? It's much too warm, as you say, to go indoors. But if you insist upon knowing, I was thinking about an article that I've just been reading on stomachs. There's a man in Switzerland who says that he could take one out, and the patient would be happy and good, and live up to his ideals just the same."

"I don't think that I should like to submit my ideals to such a test," said Christine, gravely.

"Nor I, either. It would mean too much dis-tinction. I should be afraid that people would love me for that alone, and not for what I really was. Now it's your turn."

"Well, I was thinking about something very different from stomachs, and yet often influenced by them, — genius."

"It's too big a subject to think about, all in one evening, — that is, unless you're old enough to have discovered that genius is chiefly good hard work."

"It's something besides that, as you know perfectly well."

"Yes; genius might be defined as the ninth wave, if it did not frequently turn out to be the seventeenth or the one hundred and forty-third. I'm inclined to think that there's no law or reason in it. An angel stands at some mysterious gate through which new souls must pass, and every millionth soul, for instance, he seizes by the ear, and says, 'Here, you go and be a genius!' And the soul may be born in the body of a Scotch peasant or a king, in a German foundling or an American farm-hand; but whoever he is, he has to go and be a genius, and he has to stand it, and so have his friends."

"Do you think," asked Christine, uncertainly, "that if one isn't a genius in a certain line, it's wasting time to keep on working in that line, — only because you love it, you know?"

"People seldom 'love' to do things that they don't do tolerably well," said the Professor. "With the exception of music, — which is generally perpetrated by the fools who have rushed in, — the survival of the fittest still prevails. Nowadays, if a man does a thing badly, we kill him. He has to care a great deal for his art, to keep on building until he's out of conventional range. Then he can sit there and dangle his legs, and nobody can hit him. But I certainly think that we can often judge of a person's aptitude for his art or science by the devotion that he has for it. If his devotion is genuine, it must have been aroused by a genuine taste."

"That's rather encouraging; but, after all, aren't there more exceptions than there are accordances with this rule?"

"If I were a rule, I should certainly spend most of my time knocking my exceptions in the head. They're so much more valuable when there aren't too many of them. But for a young person, the way lies open and clear. You don't need to be an exception when you've got enough grit to be a rule. What you want to do is to go ahead in the line that you're pretty certain you were meant to take. Being a genius is merely a speculation in futures, for people won't believe that you're a genius until you've proved that you aren't a precocity. But work is certain and real."

"And geniuses must work hardest of all."

"A genius has the heaviest load of responsibility that any one can bear. It isn't a credit to him if he surpasses other people. It would be a disgrace if he didn't. But in any case a man's got to work like — well, he's got to work, and no one has a right to stake out his capacity for him until he's proved himself a fool."

"Then the only thing to do is to work as hard as ever you can, no matter how trifling you are, and wait until afterwards to find out what it all means."

"Exactly," said the Professor.

"And the more bay windows you can build into your house, the more rooms you'll have that get the sunshine."

"The really great man," said the Professor, as if thinking aloud, "is not great because he is different from other people. He is great because he is like so many different kinds of people. And this prismatic quality of his makes him hard for ordinary mortals to understand. Therefore they fear him, — whereas he is invariably meant to be loved."

The gentleness in his voice made Christine wonder if they were not both thinking of the same Great Man, — of the one who had not where to lay his head. But she could not speak of this to him now, although she realized afterwards that they had known each other very well for a few minutes that night.

"Tell me about your writing," said the professor, suddenly.

"Well, there's nothing to tell, — except that I wish the world was not so impatient of young people who try to do things! It says 'Wait until you're older;' but how in heaven's name are we ever to get anything done if we don't begin?"

"Perhaps you would sympathize with the man who found the world such a trying place that he wanted to get off and walk."

"No, I'd rather stay on and travel. I'm going to Europe this summer with Mrs. Deland and Clare."

"To be gone long?"

"Probably a year."

"And you really think that your work calls you so far away from home?"

Something in his voice made Christine turn to look at him, and then she realized that she had never really looked at him before. She knew indefinitely that he was tall and rather serious, with a fine wide forehead, that gave dignity, not eccentricity, to his face. But now she noticed that his eyes, which might have been any color, happened to be gray, with pupils that dilated quickly when he spoke.

"I love my work better than anything," she said.

"That is a pity," he remarked, after a pause; "because if you cared for your work only less than a few other things, you might succeed."

"What do you mean?" asked Christine, curiously.

The college clock struck nine, and the Professor sprang to his feet, saying, "Good heavens! I had an appointment with Comstock in my den at eight-thirty this evening! But don't waste any sympathy upon him, Miss Arnold, for he knows how to amuse himself in my domains, and there'll be a whole pandemonium of microbes in the air if I don't go down and tie him up."

"You'd better hurry," said Christine, laughing.

"Thanks, and — Miss Arnold, I've enjoyed this Faculty Reception extremely."

When Christine went home, she found Clare alone in her room, looking out at the campus. Clare did not speak when the door opened, so she went and curled up beside her on the bed. Then "What kind of a time did you have?" came simultaneously from them both.

"Well, I met the new Lit professor," said Clare, "and he's handsome, but rather shy. I went around under the stairs to get a drink of water, and he was there, sitting on the cracker-box."

"I wonder that Ardis didn't tackle him. She prides herself on reassuring bashful men."

"Oh, she was out on the piazza, talking to Dr. Comstock."

"What business had that desirable M.D. at a Faculty reception?"

"He'd come to look for some one, they said, — Professor Thorne, I think. But he must have forgotten about it, for I met him and Ardis walking down College Lane together as I came home."

Christine began to laugh, and explained the joke to Clare, adding, "I feel sorry for Dr. Comstock if he really cares for Ardis, and I'm afraid that he does."

"Don't you think," asked Clare, hesitatingly, "that it's better not to have men around — I mean in that way, of course — until we're out of college? Of course I don't know many men, but I've always noticed — in the cases of girls who do — that they interfere dreadfully with the work."

"Yes," said Christine, "I think that, as a rule, the best college girl doesn't go in for that sort of thing, any more than the best college man does. The men are interested in their teams and societies and college magazines, and girls are only incidental until later; and that's the way it should be with us."

"We should do college thoroughly while we're in it," said Clare, "and then — "

"Do the other thing thoroughly when we get out, if we want to," finished Christine.

"I suppose that you have n't any theories about 'the other thing,' as you call it, yet, have you?" asked Clare, bashfully.

"Yes, I have, — but only one. I believe that a woman, in order to be worthy of the man she loves, should first have been worthy of herself. *He* may not be worthy. I 've known of some that were n't. But what I mean is, that she must be worthy of her love for him! A life that has been what Drummond would call 'a tragedy of aimlessness' is not the right kind to bring to a clear-sighted man, who knows what life means. It 's not what 's going to help a man towards his manliness! But I think that we must have caught the spring fever, to be talking so much about 'the other thing.' We never did before."

"Perhaps it 's because we 're older," said Clare.

"In that case we ought to know better. But the abstract man can't hurt anybody, especially if he does n't turn up; so let 's not be too hard on him."

This spring had been full of new experiences for Christine. Strange, awakening impulses had walked by her side; but when she turned to question them, they were gone. "Perhaps, as Clare said," she thought afterwards, "it 's because we 're older!"

The mornings grew warmer now, and the forsythia bush in front of the Storey tossed out its yellow

spray like a fountain of sunbeams over the turf.
The hymn at chapel was often, —

> "Summer suns are glowing
> Over land and sea," —

a song that will always suggest sitting by an open
window in recitation and planning to go down
town, directly afterwards, for ice-cream soda.

> "Life is dark without thee,
> Death with thee is bright."

It seems so much more like a love-song than a
hymn, in that last spring term at Harland! The
days vibrate with a sweet intensity that alternates
with a most inexcusable sleepiness; and it is hard
to stay awake at Analysis, no matter how beautiful
the music may be. Even the irrelevant strains of a
brass band under the window supply but a temporary
distraction. And then all of a sudden it is the farewell meeting of Phi Delta Kappa. The plans of
the entertainment are concealed from the Seniors,
and it is a great surprise to them all, when, after
the Society paper and the little play, they are invited to come over to the Storey House for refreshments. Mrs. Halifax meets them at the door and
takes them into the sitting-room, where a great
open fire snaps a cheerful welcome and dances in
miniature over the keys of the old-fashioned piano.
It is a rainy night, and the girls pile their gossamers
in a shimmering heap on the hall table, while three
extra umbrella stands extend their hospitable arms
to the blaze.

"This piano is always kept open for you, little

girl," said Mrs. Halifax, pinching Clare's cheek. "I hope you remember." And Clare slipped her hand into the matron's, saying, "How like you it was to think of all this for us!"

"Don't forget that I have some of the best Phi Kaps in my own house," said Mrs. Halifax, glancing at Kathleen, who was bringing in the ices. "Bless my heart," with a sudden filling of the eyes, "how I shall miss the little torment!"

After the refreshments had vanished, they turned down the lights and sat around the fire, singing, talking, and laughing until late. The tune of "Where, oh, where," was saved until the last — not because of the "Jolly Juniors," or even because of the "verdant Freshmen" — but because of the "dear old Seniors," who would soon be far out "in the wide, wide world."

> "They 've gone out from their Alma Mater,
> They 've gone out from their Alma Mater,
> Safe now, in the wide, wide world."

"I move that we adjourn," sniffed Kathleen from behind a sofa, and everybody seconded the motion.

The next day was the last Sunday before Baccalaureate, — a time when the Seniors think very hard indeed. It is not a day that is openly set aside for sentiment, and nobody expects you to be sad yet; but how can you help remembering at vespers, when you listen to that organ — and the President knows exactly how you feel! He talks to every one in the hall at first, and it is only at the end that he puts in those few words for you alone, that will go with you as long as you live.

THE COMING OF THE ROSES

He speaks of Who it is that has been with you through it all, and made the disappointments easier to bear; for he understands that even a little world may have its sky and its sea. And he speaks of the Christ who is here, of the Christ in the bravery that has overcome all obstacles and is strong, and of the Christ in the hearts of those who love one another. Then there is the prayer, and some of the Seniors cannot look up until long after the Amen.

This afternoon Dr. Page improvised softly for a few minutes, and then led the chords into the prelude of "Oh, rest in the Lord," from "Elijah," and Ardis Hathaway sang it. It was the first time that she had ever sung alone at vespers, although she had often been asked to do so, and her friends were both pleased and touched that she should be willing to sing for them to-day. But others thought: "Perhaps she knows that every one in the class is down on her and wants to leave a good impression before she goes away." And then even these forgot everything else in the sound of her voice: "Oh, rest in the Lord, wait patiently for him."

Christine Arnold clasped her hands tightly together and trembled. It was more like a flower than ever, — that voice, with new sweetness and bloom of tone. "Oh, rest in the Lord!"

And when the song was finished, her classmates could only think, and be glad that she belonged to them.

"There never *was* such a voice," said Christine to Clare that night. "There never will be again. I wonder why it is that the voice is hers!"

389

She had struggled in vain to make herself believe that she cared no more about Ardis; but a disappointment cannot be real if one is able to get over loving the person who caused it! And Commencement has a softening influence upon most of us. When we are not too tired and warm and cross, we forgive all past injuries, and wish to be forgiven in return.

Christine had often been guilty of wanting to be Malvolio again, and could not help wishing that Philippa Fairbank might incidentally break her leg before the night of the first performance. But Philippa continued to flourish, and shame overwhelmed the desires of Christine.

"Ruth," she said one day, "I deserve to be kicked. Kindly kick me."

"Indeed I won't," was the resentful reply. "You've been a perfect dear — since the oration was finished!"

"Then," said Christine, sadly, "I shall be reluctantly compelled to kick myself," which she proceeded to do, three times in succession. But the next day she was wanting to be Malvolio again as hard as ever.

The first dress-rehearsal took place on Wednesday night, and bulging figures in waterproofs scuttled down to the Opera House through back ways. Each new arrival was greeted with insulting shouts of laughter, for wigs did not always fit, and mustaches often brought on such a violent fit of sneezing that they had to be removed. The supes and curtain-lifters were, as Kathleen stated, "at their best," and quite extinguished the eloquence of Sir Toby at one time by whispering loudly, "Turn up them foots!"

The alumnæ, who had now begun to flock back in great numbers, made divers excuses to get into the House, running errands, and bringing messages from real or imaginary friends. One of them, a Ninety-four girl, who had always been known as the "Friend of the Class," waylaid a Senior outside Henley's and said, "Let's take some ice-cream to the kids." That was the only drawback in her case, her disrespectful way of alluding to them. But no one minded a little thing like that when it came to having dinners in her room, and remembering them forever afterwards as occasions of lobster and rejoicing.

"We let in Miss P——, don't we?" asked Orsino, at the stage door, observing that the alumna carried a bundle of thirty spoons.

"Hurrah for the 'Friend to the Class'!" shouted Kathleen, who had smelled the strawberries from way across the stage.

The rehearsal went better for this cooling interlude, although Sir Toby did lose out two of his sofa-pillows in one of the most active scenes, and when taunted with his lack of obesity, replied: "Well, it's myself that wouldn't wish to have the appearance of Araminta Appleyárd in the character of Antonio the Sea Captain. She looks something like the earth might if it forgot to put on the equator!"

"Well, you have stout tendencies too, so don't crow, Kathleen," said Maria, stooping to tie the shoestrings of a very portly priest, who was unable, for obvious reasons, to do it for himself.

"What tendencies, if you please, my fair gull-catcher?"

"Your arms, Sir Toby."

"Never heard arms called tendencies before," said Sir Toby, strutting up and down the stage. "'*There dwelt a man in Babylon, lady, la-dy.*'"

"Poor Leonora will be glad when this is over!" said the priest. "The other night she came to my room to borrow some camphor for a toothache, and when I asked her where the tooth was, she replied, 'In the front row of the balcony, three seats from the aisle, opposite the stage.' It turned out to be an eye-tooth, as one might know; but I've felt uneasy about her ever since."

The next dress-rehearsal was thrown open to the Freshmen, who were always too numerous to be accommodated later on; and on Friday night came the first real performance. Most of the students and alumnæ patronized this, and the last performance, on Saturday, was given for the Faculty and guests.

Sir Toby and the lovely Viola carried off the highest honors, although all the parts were well taken and vigorously applauded. Florence Homer and her ushers were kept busy taking flowers up to the performers, while the fathers and mothers clapped, laughed, and became tearful by turns.

"Who'd ha' thought it!" said a dear old farmer, regarding his stout and priestly daughter with pride. "An' when she come here she was sech a peaked-lookin' gel. Wall, their vittles must agree with 'em, that's sartin."

The Taylor household had reserved seats for its

relatives together, and the three graduating mothers exchanged lively confidences between acts. But nobody sees much of the relatives before Ivy Day, as on Saturday night every one is thinking about the play. And when at last dear Faith had skipped off in her red curly shoes, singing, "With hey ho, the wind and the rain," the audience clapped harder than ever, and the orchestra played its best, for the play was at an end. But the Seniors did not hear all the congratulations that were showered upon them, because they were thinking that this was the end of something else too.

Baccalaureate Sunday came in clear and sweet, like a fine old tune; but the day was up long before the Seniors were. They spent a part of the morning chatting with the alumnæ on the back campus, and when three o'clock came, they were hurrying down to the church in their fresh white dresses, all ready to start from the Sunday-school rooms. The long procession walked slowly around to the vestry doors, between two rows of alumnæ who were waiting to see them pass, and then they heard the music of the organ, and forgot everything but each other. It is the sound of the organ that makes one turn pale sometimes while walking down the sloping aisles, although there is really no excuse for it. And the bunches of white daisies that partition off the Senior seats are exceedingly suggestive of a wedding, — until you remember that there are one hundred and forty-eight others of you, and realize that your time has not yet come!

The service opens with a stirring hymn, and you notice how pretty the choir girls look, up there among the palms, with their fresh flowers and new Leghorn hats. You recollect afterwards that some of them were delightfully sympathetic, while others only looked at you curiously, to see if you would cry. The ushers hover noiselessly about the vestry doors; the congregation keeps up a perpetual waving and rustling of fans, for the day is hot; and the alumnæ in the gallery look down at the Seniors with tears in their eyes, because they are no longer alumnæ, out "in the wide, wide world," but Seniors, who have come back to live it over again with you! And at the end of the service, the girls walk home with such relatives as they have been able to find. A car comes out of a golden haze far down the street, and the alumnæ, who are not dressed up, scramble into it for a long cooling ride before supper.

And in the evening comes the most beautiful service of all. The college chapel is thrown open to guests, and Dr. Page improvises softly on the organ until the dusk has crept up against the windows, and the Seniors are glad that no one can see the look on their faces now. And at last the organ breaks into "Praise God, from whom all blessings flow," and the whole audience rises to sing it.

Clare and Ruth had gone early to save places for their friends, and when they were all seated, Clare went off again "for a minute," as she said; but half an hour passed, and she did not return. Mrs. Deland watched the crowd around the door, and glanced anxiously at the fast-filling chapel.

"Where is the child?" asked Mrs. Arnold of

Christine; and her daughter looked troubled, but only said, "I don't know."

It soon became impossible for any one who was in to get out, or for the people who were waiting outside to get in, so Christine could not go to look for her; and presently the music began.

Clare had gone downstairs to get a wrap of her sister's, which had been left in the reading-room, and just as she was coming out, a Marston House Sophomore thrust a note into her hand

"She's had a telegram," said the girl. "Her father is ill, and she must go home to-morrow morning."

She opened the note and read: —

I need you. Can you come to me? — ARDIS.

"Perhaps," she thought on her way down to the Marston, "I could not have asked more than this, even though she had so nearly forgotten me, — that she should send for me when she is in trouble!"

She found Ardis packing her trunk, assisted by two Freshmen, whose aid chiefly consisted in admiring her various belongings, and sitting upon those that needed to be put in next. They fidgeted uneasily when Clare came in, and finally said that they would go.

"Thank you so much for helping me," said poor Ardis, looking both worried and tired.

"Oh, Miss Deland," exclaimed one of them, stopping on her way out, "just look at this! And on the floor, too, Miss Hathaway! Really, you're pretty careless, if you are a Senior."

She had found a little miniature in a worn velvet

case, and having examined it, held it up for Clare to see. It was the picture of a young and very beautiful girl holding a little golden-haired child in her arms.

"Give that to me!" said Ardis, snatching it from her hand. "Pardon me for my rudeness, but it can't possibly interest you."

"I'm very sorry," said the Freshman, in a subdued voice. "I only looked at it because it was beautiful, but I didn't mean to annoy you."

"It is an old picture," said Ardis, feeling somewhat ashamed, "and both of the people in it are dead, so — I don't keep it around very much."

"I'm sorry," said the Freshman again, as she and her companion went out.

"Is he very sick, Ardis?" asked Clare, sitting down on the floor beside the trunk.

"No — that is — the telegram didn't say he was sick. It was from the housekeeper, and she only said, ' Come home immediately.' "

"Then perhaps it isn't anything very bad. Let me put in these other things. You are tired out."

"No, indeed, I didn't ask you to come down and help me pack, for you know perfectly well that you haven't the remotest idea how to do it! And I'm rather particular about my gowns. What I did want was sympathy, — not the bewailing, conventional sympathy that other people give, but the kind that takes you by the hand and is silent. That's why I sent for you."

"It was very good in you," said Clare, softly. "I'm glad you did. I don't know how I could have borne it if — you hadn't."

THE COMING OF THE ROSES

"I want to say good-bye to this place," said
Ardis, turning down the gas, "and you must come
with me. It won't take long, for none of the things
that I want to take leave of will care. Caring is
what consumes the time and energy of the world.
Doing claims but a small share."

"Where shall we go first?" asked Clare, as they
started out; it was all that she could say.

"Down College Lane. You can hear the frogs
better there. I wonder how long it will be before
all these old shanties are swept away, and the campus reaches down to the lake. Now up by the
green-house, — don't step on those plants, Clare.
Why, what's the matter with your eyes? How
young and uncertain our botanical gardening looks!
And let's stop for a minute on the Observatory
steps. I shall always remember that we can see the
lake from here. And then the hammock, up between the spruce-trees, where — Let's stay here a
minute longer for ' Auld Lang Syne.' " They visited
each favorite spot on the campus, and stole into the
great, empty Gymnasium, where the wind sighed in
the shadows, and rustled the fading wreaths left
over from the Junior-Senior reception. And then
they went into the little old organ-room in the
Music Building, where Clare asked, "Won't you
sing?" And Ardis answered, "Not to-night."

But she wiped off the familiar keys very tenderly
with her handkerchief, and closed the instrument as
gently, Clare thought, as if she were laying a rose
in the hand of a child that is asleep for the last
time. And then they went out, and sat on the
College steps with their arms around each other.

397

Dr. Page was playing "Elsa's Entrance to the Cathedral," and the faint cry of the "Swan's Song," drifted out through the open window. After this came a suggestion of Mendelssohn, and the grave march of Schumann chords; for the player wandered along in a musical twilight of his own, stopping to look closely in the faces of those whom he met. Long lanes he traversed, with the scent of cinnamon roses through the dusk, and crowded city streets, with the quick pulsing of hurried feet. Then the breath of the arbutus crept into it all, and Dr. Page was playing the "Ivy Song."

"Oh, I had forgotten!" Clare said, as Ardis took her hand; but she remembered now that Dr. Page always played the "Ivy Song" at the end of Baccalaureate Sunday.

"Clare," cried Ardis, suddenly, "I must tell you — "

But her voice was drowned by the scraping of chairs in the chapel above, as the audience rose to sing. Then the notes of the fine old hymn filled the evening all around, and Clare and Ardis sang too, because they could not help it: "Praise Father, Son, and Holy Ghost."

"Clare," said Ardis again, "come away, some-where — anywhere. There is something that I must tell you. Come over to the Art Gallery steps. No one will disturb us there."

And when they had seated themselves in the shadow of the great elm, she said: "Clare, my father isn't ill, and I told the housekeeper to send that telegram. I want to go home, because — I haven't any one to walk with Ivy Day or Commencement." Clare started to speak; but Ardis said: "Wait, let me tell you. I was going to walk with Christine to-morrow, you know. We settled that Freshman year, and now she doesn't want to walk with me, and all the other girls that I asked were engaged. I put it off too long, perhaps; but I thought of course — I thought," with a sudden choke in her voice, "that some one would be willing to walk with me."

The bitter fruits of her selfishness had come home to her at last, and she had been hoping, child-like, that they might be different!

"Ardis, I can't believe this, I can't! Oh, it is dreadful!" said Clare. "And you never told me? Why didn't you ask me to walk with you Commencement? I would at least have been better than nobody. And I kept that day open until two weeks ago, in case that you should want me at the last. I had been hoping and hoping that you would want me."

The fact that Ardis had not asked her for one of the three Commencement "walks" was a source of genuine grief to Clare, but she dared not take the initiative for fear that Ardis would refuse; and in this surmise she was quite correct, for Ardis had been intending, until the last, to ask only the most prominent girls to walk with her. And when she had finally decided upon those who were to be favored, the favored ones were already engaged. She then descended to those who were only less favored, but they, too, preferred to walk with some one else. It was humiliating in the extreme, and there was something a little sadder than humiliation in it.

"What makes you think that Christine does n't want to walk with you?" asked Clare, evolving a sudden plan; for she and Christine had arranged the year before to walk together on Ivy Day; and now she understood why Christine had asked her. "But she might have asked me for one day, anyway," she thought, stopping for a minute to bind consolation on her own wounds.

"I 'm sure that she still wants to walk with you," she continued, adding to herself that this was quite true. "And if she is expecting to, it would be dreadful in you to go away. I 'm going to find out this very night, and let you know. It will be easy enough to find out, — and if it 's all right, of course you would n't *think* of going home."

"I could stay over Ivy Day, I suppose," said Ardis, drearily, "and go home Tuesday morning."

"Ardis, you must n't go, you sha'n't go! What do you mean by telling me that you 're going? How dare you go?" Clare stopped to take breath, and regarded Ardis defiantly. "Are you going to be a *coward?*" she asked.

"What would you advise me to do about it?"

"Why, walk three, of course. Everybody knows that there 's an odd number in the class, and if you walk with Grace and me, nobody will know which the odd one is. They 'll think it 's me, if we put you between us, because I 've never been an important person."

Ardis had the grace to blush, although it was dark, and said, "I would never accept it from you."

"Accept it? Nonsense! Which do you think I 'd rather do? Have a few people whom I don't care for think something of no importance about me? or go through Commencement knowing that you'd run away because you hadn't the courage to remain?"

"You forget that our weaknesses may lie in different directions, Clare. You, for instance, don't care at all what people think of you."

"Yes, I do," said Clare. "If people don't like me, I want to knock them down."

"As conducive to affection? Clare, you have called me a coward twice to-night. Did you ever know me to be afraid of physical danger?"

"No. I remember the time when Maude's room caught on fire and you put it out; and the girls told me about that time, this year, when there was a sneak thief in the house, and you went downstairs alone with a candle and scared him away."

"And yet I dislike adverse opinion so much that if I had really expected to meet the thief, I should have put on my best clothes!"

"Ardis, you are driving me absolutely wild! Do say that you will stay to Commencement, and I'll do anything in this world that I can to make it easier."

"If you really cared for me, you wouldn't ask me to do a thing that would drive *me* absolutely wild."

"Perhaps I'd better go home," said Clare, rising. "If you think now, at the end, that I don't care for you, it's all of no use."

"Come back, you foolish, pathetic little child!" said Ardis, drawing Clare down into her arms. "I'm not worth crying over, dear. I don't ever cry over myself any more, just for that reason,

There 's nothing like reason, you know. And I will stay and ' walk three ' at Commencement, if, as you think, Christine will want me for Ivy Day. It won't really hurt me to walk three, because when one has fairly started falling in people's esteem, the velocity increases as one approaches the bottom."

"I 'll go and find Christine," said Clare.

"She won't be at home yet. They were going to sing, or do something, over at the Hillard. And besides, I want to talk to you to-night. I want to tell you — and yet how can I? You 're such a little thing."

"Ardis," asked Clare, suddenly, "why did you say that the baby in the picture was dead?"

"Has n't it been said that ' no child dies so completely as the child who lives to grow up '?"

"I did n't know that your hair was light when you were little," said Clare, as if she had not heard her. "It 's so very dark now. And your mother — Ardis, you look exactly like her."

"No, I look like my father. I 'm sure that I do. And about the hair — I only know of its color through this picture, for everybody who would have remembered about it is dead."

"Your father — " Clare began; but Ardis said: "He 's a man; and besides, he did n't see much of me when I was little. Of course some men would; but the circumstances were painful, and — Oh, Clare, I never had a chance!"

"Can't you tell me about it?" asked Clare, taking her hand.

"Yes, I will tell you, because perhaps it will make you sorrier for me and help you to understand. Clare, my mother did n't die when I was a baby, — not till long afterwards. But I never saw her when I was a child, because — she had run away."

"Ardis!"

"She left me before I could walk, and went on the stage as an opera-singer. And — there were other things. She had a wonderful voice, and had always been an ambitious girl. And she was beautiful! I don't know any more about her, because my father never would hear her mentioned. We had no near relatives, and my nurse told me that she was dead. I had thought that she was dead until I was nearly fifteen years old. Then she really did die, and I overheard something about it. There was nobody to help me, nobody to explain. I have n't been the same person since."

"My dearest, my dearest!"

"You people who have had mothers to stand between you and your imagination, — to shield you from yourself and the dreadfulness of the world, and keep you from finding out all kinds of things too soon, — why should n't you have high ideals, and beautiful conceptions of what you see around you? What can you know of absolute loneliness? My father used to spend night after night at his desk in the library, thinking, thinking, with his head in his hands, and when I was little, I used to come downstairs for him to kiss me."

"And he did," cried Clare. "He did — because he must!"

"Sometimes he did and sometimes he did n't. One night there was a picture that I had not seen before on his desk. It was one of my mother, I suppose; for when I spoke he started, and looked at the picture, but never looked at me."

Clare had seen Mr. Hathaway two years ago, when Ardis ˙spent a vacation in New York, and remembered him as a tall, dark man, with eyes that were sometimes cynical and more often sad.

"He isn't interested in my Commencement," went on Ardis, hurriedly, "and I told him not to come, because I felt almost sure that he didn't want to. It hurts him to see me sometimes. I suppose because — But you are such a little thing! And that's one reason why I want to go home. I don't like to stay and be a poor alley-cat with no relatives to care; the only one in the class with no one to send me flowers, and be — be proud, you know, and look at me the way your mother looks at you."

She was crying now, although she had said that she was so unworthy of compassion!

"Ardis," said Clare, "you can have half of my mother, and half of Ethel, and half of Ned, too — if you want him," she finished doubtfully, knowing that Ardis had many swains of her own. But she could not have suggested anything better, for Ardis laughed through her tears, and said, —

"I knew that you would do me good, although I didn't expect that you would upset all my plans. But forget what I 've told you to-night, or rather, remember just enough to keep you sorry for me as long as you live. Some day you may hear of a wrong that I did one of your friends here at college — she was my friend too."

And poor Ardis stopped to struggle pitifully with

another rush of tears, as she unconsciously echoed Christine's words of the year before: "She was my friend!"

"You needn't tell me about that," said Clare, kissing her arm through the thin sleeve, "because I know. I've known a long time. And what right would a person like me have to judge you? I'm simply abominable myself, most of the time. And it is true, as you say, that everybody's temptations lie in different directions. We are absolutely unfit to judge each other unless we have been tried in the same direction and have stood our ground. Then we don't care to judge, because we are too busy being thankful. But what I wanted to say was that I love you, love you, love you! Do you understand?"

"I believe," said Ardis, turning rather pale, "that you have been caring a little — right along. I wish I'd known."

And as Clare rose to go home, she was filled with a sweet and pardonable rejoicing that Ardis did know at last!

She found Christine alone in her room, for the Ivy Orator had been sent to bed early, and Ruth was taking care of the relatives. But Christine was thinking too hard to sleep.

"Is it true," she asked, when Clare came in, "that Ardis has had a telegram calling her home? A Marston House girl told us where you were, and said that was the reason."

"She's going home," said Clare, "because she hasn't any one to walk with to-morrow or at Commencement."

" What ! "

" She told me that she had promised to walk with you Ivy Day, and then that — there had been trouble. You must write her a note saying that you are expecting to walk with her to-morrow, and I 'll take it down to the Marston to-night."

" But I 'm *not* expecting to walk with her. There is every reason in the world why I should n't; and besides, I want to walk with you."

" Would you let her go home because she has nobody for to-morrow ? "

" It is n't my fault if she has n't engaged some one to walk with. And if I walk with her, what will become of you? And in any case I know that she does n't want to walk with me. You don't understand the circumstances, Clare."

" Perhaps I understand them better than you think, and I want to tell you something. If you refuse to go with her to-morrow, you will be doing one person a wrong that all the success and self-sacrifice of your college course cannot make up for. You will walk with her to-morrow; you must ! "

" Would you mind telling me why? "

" Because she loves you — is n't that reason enough? And because you love her."

" You forget," said Christine, " that Ardis and I are no longer friends. We found out after a while that we were entirely uncongenial, and have seen very little of each other since."

" I have always thought," said Clare, " that the people who love us place a large amount of responsibility in our hands. We control a certain share of their happiness and self-respect, just as they control a certain share of ours. And the fact that Ardis still loves you makes it impossible for you to throw her over in this way. Before that editorial affair, when you found out what she really was —"

"Who told you?" asked Christine, turning upon her.

"Never mind; it's enough that I know. But before that happened, she understood that you did not know her at all, and that your respect for her came through not knowing. But now all that is changed; you do know, and if you make her understand that you still care for her, she will think that there is something left in her to respect. Then she will begin anew, and live up to your opinion."

"She does not care for my opinion," interrupted Christine.

"If you set a mark for a person's height one day, and he falls below it, when you come again he will have grown the distance between. It's the law of life, and because this girl loves you, a part of her life has been placed in your hands. It is for you to say whether she shall steal away with her head down, or take new courage and try again!"

"But walking with her on Ivy Day! That's such a trifling thing. I can't see that the question of self-respect is deeply involved in it, except, of course, that seeking her out at the end will give her the impression that I've ceased to disapprove of what she did. It wasn't the wrong to me that I minded, but the horrible wrong to herself — the lack of loyalty and uprightness and moral stability — and everything. I don't mean to say that I'm one particle better than she. I know I'm not; but I happen to detest her particular kind of failing. And I don't doubt that she detests mine with equal cordiality. So what is the use of forcing us into one another's society?"

"Do you really think that you would be countenancing what she did by walking with her fifteen minutes to-morrow morning? Does the doctor who provides the medicine vindicate the presence of disease? Do you think that the person who lends a helping hand connects himself by necessity with the trouble that caused the downfall?"

"No; but I can't explain it to you, because we're arguing from different points of view. If she still cared for me —"

"Oh, Christine! if you could have heard her voice to-night when she spoke of you and said, ' She was my friend!'"

"Don't!" cried Christine, thrusting out her hands as if to ward off something that would hurt her if it came.

"Has it ever occurred to you that you could never, if you lived a thousand years, despise her as much as she despises herself? And are you sure that you know how many temptations she has struggled and struggled with, every day of her life, before she made this one mistake? Wrongdoing is seven-eighths under water, like an iceberg; and for every time that a person yields, there must have been at least seven times that he wrestled for life with the dreadful thing, and threw it down and overcame it. I haven't had an easy time myself, and I know."

"Possibly I do, too. But you persist in misunderstanding me, Clare. I'm not whited sepulchre

THE COMING OF THE ROSES

enough to keep Ardis at a distance only for what she has done. But what she did has convinced me that she has ceased to care for me, and, such being the case, I don't see why I should thrust myself upon her."

"Suppose it should turn out, after all, that she did care for you," said Clare, quietly. "It would be rather a bad thing to look back upon, wouldn't it, — to remember that you'd thrown her over?"

"Yes." The color had gone from her face now.

"It would be even worse to remember that than to think that you had descended to the level of Christ, and taken her by the hand! You see even if she didn't want your love, she would need it all the more. No woman ever gets enough love in this world, and no person can have too much. To forget everything that has happened, and help her to begin again, — that's what Christ meant when he said, 'Love one another.'"

"What shall I say in the note?" asked Christine quietly, going to her desk.

"Write it just as if you were both in the long ago, when it wasn't necessary to explain."

Christine thought a minute, and then wrote: —

DEAR ARDIS, — Please don't forget that you promised to walk with me to-morrow. CHRISTINE.

"Will this do?" she asked, handing it to Clare.

"It isn't for me, so I won't read it; but you know whether it will do or not, and so will Ardis."

She studied Christine's face curiously for a minute, and then kissed her on the forehead, as if satisfied with what she saw.

409

"Wait," called Christine, as she went to the door; "if I walk with Ardis to-morrow, what is to become of you?"

"Oh, I shall be all right," was the cheerful answer. "I'll look out for myself, I promise you."

She was not gone long, and when she came back, Christine was still sitting at her desk; but the room was dark.

"I've brought you something," said Clare, feeling her way to the window. "It was thinking aloud, or else I shouldn't have found it. They were late this year, weren't they? But perhaps it was because they didn't want us to go. You are the Ivy Orator, so I thought you ought to have it."

She slipped a cool, long-stemmed flower into Christine's hand, and went softly out of the room. Christine lifted it suddenly to her face, and when she laid it down again her eyes were wet.

It was the first of the Senior roses!

CHAPTER XXII

"THE GLORIOUS CLASS OF NINETY-FIVE!"

Ivy Day opened with a soft mist over the trees and through the grass, but the people who understood South Harland knew that this would burn away before long. Clare had a Glee Club rehearsal at eight o'clock, and they practised with the Banjo Club for the grand *pièce de résistance* of the evening. When they came out to chapel, the awning was already flapping over the seats arranged in front of the side entrance, and the Junior ushers were flying about like distracted kittens. Chapel was longer than usual, and the Seniors barely had time to get into their white dresses and down to the Hillard House before ten o'clock came. And it is quite certain that no Senior would have made her appearance at all, if it had not been for the obliging underclass friends, who put in the final stick-pins, tied the ribbons that went behind, and took the Ivy Day roses out of the washbowl, where they lay muffled in a wet towel.

"How do you feel, Christine?" asked some one, as she escaped from the kodaks which pursued her across the lawn, and joined her classmates on the Hillard steps.

"I am thinking of Ninety-five," she said. And when the long procession had wound slowly down past the Warren, and up the Storey House walk to the college steps, it was the thought of Ninety-five that was with her still, and helped her to be unafraid.

The Leader of the Glee Club did not walk in the procession, to-day, behind the Class President and the Ivy Orator, as other leaders had done, but was "late in dressing," she said, and joined her class from the reading room when it reached the steps. The tuning-fork which she carried in her belt gave the pitch for "Fair Harland," and after this came the "President's Welcome," which Ruth delivered in her sweetest and most straightforward way. And then a distinguished-looking man near the front, with white hair and flashing gray eyes, placed his hand on his wife's, as she said nervously: "Oh, *do* you suppose the awning will come down over our heads? It would frighten her to death if it did."

And Christine, who would have "fought and bled and died" for Ninety-five, delivered her oration as a daughter of that white-haired man should have done, saying what she had to say bravely, "truthfully, and well." And through it all she saw her father's face; and after it was over, the sound of his voice as he said, "Well done, Christine!" meant more to her than all the congratulations of Faculty and students combined. They were strangely alike, these two, — she with her rigid purity of honor, and he with the remembrance of one senatorial term lost because he had adhered, in spite of opposition, to that firm uprightness of principle which often goes astray in political campaigns.

"Papa, I want you to meet Clare," she said; and

when the Leader of the Glee Club looked up timidly at this six feet two of senatorial dignity, she saw something in his face that was so like Stephen and Christine that she forgot to be afraid of him at all.

"Why did n't you walk in the procession?" he asked quizzically. "My younger son told me to be sure and look at you, but you gave me no opportunity until the music began."

"Oh, Clare, what did you promise me?" asked Christine, sorrowfully. "You said that you'd look out for yourself, and I was so excited over the oration that I did n't stop to ask how you'd do it."

"Never mind, let's not talk about it," said Clare, who was visibly embarrassed; and in an undertone she added, "Did you see how happy Ardis looked?"

But she could not help remembering the moment of weakness that had come to her while she stood waiting, a solitary figure in the reading room, and saw her class, the class of Ninety-five, come over the campus without her! "But I suppose it was silly," she had thought, wiping away a few furtive tears, "to hope when I came here that somebody would love *me* best — best of all, as those two have loved each other from the first."

Some one called her away just then, and Christine told her father what Clare had done.

"H'm! — must have good blood in her," he said briefly. "Who's her father?"

"Her father was Captain Stanley Deland, of the First Maine Cavalry, during the war; but he died before Clare was born."

"Seems to me I remember the name. They were all regular devils for courage, — the First Maine;

so the girl has a right to a backbone of her own. There must be a lot of good, hot, fighting blood distributed around amongst these girls. They ought to have inherited considerable grit from the glory of the old flag."

"They have," said Christine, proudly; "for there are more ways than one here of showing courage!"

"Are you acquainted with Dr. Kendrick Burton of the Biological Department?" asked the Senator, unexpectedly. "Professor Walcott, of the Smithsonian, wished to be remembered to him if we met, so perhaps you would be kind enough to introduce me, my dear."

It was obvious that the Senator had his eye fixed upon the venerable Geology Professor, who sat sunning himself upon the steps, and Christine found no little difficulty in steering his course away from this impressive personage to a corner of the Science Building, where an enthusiastic and unassuming young man was engaged in oiling his bicycle.

Parents and other attachments were being towed around in every direction by the white-gowned graduates, who seemed to be alarmingly unconscious of the heat, and routed them out of all the corners in which they sought refuge.

The Symposium, which always had its reunion after the Ivy Exercises, now struck up a song of praise to CO_2, set to the euphonious tune of "Monkey, Monkey," and rendered in at least seven different keys. There was a general rush to the windows of Lincoln Hall, partly to discover what the disturbance was about, and mostly to work upon the feelings of friends inside, who were eating sandwiches and knew how to throw straight. Mr. and Mrs. Hastings and Mr. and Mrs. Wyman were being escorted triumphantly up the steps by their respective daughters, who were members of the Symposium, and Kathleen Carey was explaining to her father that nobody of any importance ever belonged to the Scientific Societies.

"But how if you'd happened to belong to them yourself?" asked Mr. Carey, with a repetition of the same humorous twinkle that Kathleen's friends knew so well; and Kathleen responded, with her usual ambiguity, "It's a very narrow-minded man that can't spell a word but one way!"

Mr. Carey was the kind of man who always carries a pound of Huyler's in each pocket, and is generally good for a long day's outing in a drag, with plenty of lunch and three tin horns. But the most popular of the fathers was Dr. Burritt, whose tales of college sprees long past and of college love still present delighted the hearts of the girls. His stories ranged from the man who dropped a hot fifty-cent piece out to the leader of an early-morning band, to the little girl whose brother was shot in the war, and whom he found and comforted and afterwards married, as any one who looked at Mrs. Burritt might know. And then there were stories of when Ruth was a child, which pleased her friends immensely, because Ruth was so very dignified now; and displeased Ruth herself so seriously that she would go out and take a walk with Mr. Packard, who was never very far off. And after the Glee Club Concert in the evening, the girls took Dr. Burritt into the Hillard House parlor, and made him tell all the stories over again.

415

But the evening was not all spent in story-telling, for when the time came for the Glee Club to assemble once more, and wander about the campus for one last sing under the shadowy elms, every one who was not too tired walked around after them, and listened and applauded by turns. And the people who were there never forgot the sound of the "Kerry Dance," as it floated back through the scent of roses and over the softness of lawns; and the notes of Hawley's "Margarethe" were still singing in Christine's head, as she turned back from the separating Glee Club members to find their leader, who needed her now. Clare was trying very hard not to care too much, but she drew a quick breath when Christine took her hand.

"Isn't it queer," she said, "how love goes down? The more trouble anything like this makes you, the more you love it, and can't get along without it at all. But I told them all about it at rehearsal this morning, — how much they'd been to me; and I spoke to them about the Christmas concert, and they said that they'd always give it. That was what made me feel that it was none of it wasted, — the caring, you know, the caring so much too hard! We have been very *near*, — this Glee Club. We have known —" and she went on thinking to herself of how, though the wide world lay between them, they would be "her girls" still; and of how, as long as she lived, her heart would gain courage, and her soul strength, when she thought of them!

"Christine," said a man's voice behind them, "father's looking for you on the Storey House steps, and perhaps you'd better go to him. The Mater was tired, and I've just taken her home. I'll look after Miss Deland for a while, if she doesn't object."

It was Christine's brother Henry, who had been making a name for himself in the far West, but who adored his sister, as the right kind of brothers should do, and had come on to her graduation. He was five or six years older than Christine, grave, and almost too quiet for his age, — "in dead earnest," as people said, and wasting very little time upon conventionalities. He was not artistic, like Stephen, or original, like Christine, but he gave the impression of having great strength in reserve; and he was absolutely simple, too, as the strongest men are very likely to be. He told Clare about some of the fellows at Harvard whom he had "loved" and had not seen for years, and of how the friendships here at Harland made him want to be with them again. And he said that there was a lot of splendid material for everything in the West, if one had time to "study it out." He liked to be very near to all kinds of men, and had spent several weeks as a common laborer in one of the mining towns. And he understood how Clare felt about the Glee Club: it was worth while to "harden your hands," and all that sort of thing, to turn out a good piece of work like that. "And whenever you get near to the primitive, it hurts, anyway," he said.

And there was something about the bigness of him that took Clare out of herself and out of the college world, and showed her that in the hollow of her hand she held the heart and pith of what she had been striving for. "Enough that He heard it once. We shall hear it by and by."

And long after Henry had gone back to his mining-camp, where the primitive thrives and grows, he remembered a slender, brown-eyed girl with lilies-of-the-valley in her hair, and worked harder than ever.

But while he and Clare were wandering happily around over splashes of lemonade in the grass, and under dancing rows of Japanese lanterns overhead, Christine was searching in vain for her father on the Storey House steps. He had received word from his wife that she was feeling very unwell, and had hurried off without giving another thought to Christine. She looked for him in every possible place on the campus, and then walked up to Mrs. Brett's, the boarding-house on Elm Street, where she had engaged rooms for her family. Mrs. Brett herself came to the door and said, "Well, I was just going down to Miss Taylor's after you, Miss Arnold, for your mother's been ill, and I thought you ought to know. The doctor's upstairs now. But there, dear, don't look so white. It was only a fainting spell, and she's out of it already."

Christine flew up the stairs and into her mother's room, where she found Mrs. Arnold lying on the sofa, with her husband and Dr. Comstock beside her. "Don't tell Christine," she was saying as the door opened; but Christine heard it, and was terrified.

"Oh, mamma, what is it?" she asked, kneeling down beside her. "Somebody tell me what has happened! Papa, what is the matter? Dr. Comstock, *tell* me!"

"GLORIOUS CLASS OF NINETY-FIVE!"

The doctor glanced uneasily from Christine to Mrs. Arnold and said: "There is no cause for alarm, I think; but your mother's general condition is not quite as it should be. The heart action is not particularly good just at present."

"Oh, doctor! how can you?" said Mrs. Arnold, weakly. "To-morrow is her Commencement Day."

"Papa, has she had these attacks before?" asked Christine, in a low voice. But Senator Arnold was looking at his wife and did not seem to hear her.

"Papa, has she had these attacks before, and you *dared* not to tell me?"

"Perhaps it would be better for me to see you a minute outside, Miss Arnold," said the doctor. "You're plucky, I know, and will be willing to leave your mother alone for a while, if you know that it is best. The least excitement," he added, as Christine followed him into the hall, "would not be good for her now."

"I ought never to have come to college," she said brokenly; "I ought never — "

"Nonsense," interrupted the doctor, cheerfully; "the mischief is not of such long standing as that. In fact, it's only just begun. Mrs. Arnold has been overdoing, systematically, for some time, and this has weakened her general condition enough to bring on a slight attack of heart failure. But with proper care and rest it will all pass away; and now that you're through college, there is practically nothing to fear. The care that only a daughter can give will fix her up in no time. Dear me," added the young doctor, gazing pensively out into the darkness, "I wish *I* had a daughter."

419

Christine lay awake for a long time that night, and had not the slightest doubt about the sacrifice that she was going to make. There was only one thing to do, of course, and she would do it. But when morning came, and her mother looked and seemed as well as ever, she wondered if it would be necessary, after all.

"I am simply a horrible, inexcusable black-leg," she thought, "and such a thing as a conscience is an anachronism in my nature. Why it's there I don't know, for it's made me feel like a Seidlitz powder ever since I was born."

And then she thought of what it would have been to go to Europe with Mrs. Deland and Clare, — both of them so simple and Bohemian in their tastes, so enthusiastic over everything, and appreciative of the humorous side of life. She had been to England once with her father and mother, when she was ten years old, and beautiful memories that had never forsaken her made her think of how much more beautiful it would be to go now, when she was old enough to understand. For not to go again after one has been once is almost worse than never going at all, as in the latter case one does not know what has been missed.

"But I've already decided what I am going to do," she thought, "so what's the use of trying to gnaw my own rope?"

She told Senator Arnold her decision, and felt strangely comforted when he replied quickly, "That is better than the Ivy Oration, my dear!"

Of course it was necessary to tell Mrs. Deland and Clare, and send a sad little telegram to the

White Star Line; but somehow the disappointment did not seem so hard to bear when she looked at her mother's face.

"I can't bear to think of the child's making that sacrifice for me," said Mrs. Arnold, holding a small moist handkerchief in one hand. "She says it's because she wants to stay at home and study Washington society, but I know better."

"She's done no more than what's decent," said the Senator, briefly; "but as it happens, she isn't likely to lose by it. If Congress adjourns early next year, we'll all go over, and join Stephen in Paris."

"Oh, can't I tell her?" asked Mrs. Arnold, delighted.

"No," replied the Senator, with his quiet humor; "the Lord does not generally reward his chosen quite so soon. I don't like the idea of a girl making the first part of a sacrifice and expecting her parents to provide the other half later on. Let her feel the full extent of it first, and then — well, we'll see."

The Commencement exercises are not so picturesque as those of Ivy Day and Baccalaureate, but they are much more important, because they involve trustees and a diploma. To speak accurately, no student receives her own, — that must be hunted up afterwards, and exchanged for the one she holds, — but by the time that the exercises are over, she thankfully feels that any one's diploma will do. The guests go early, and are forcibly made to demonstrate the theory that two bodies must and shall occupy the same space at the same time. The alumnæ file gravely in, headed by the Junior ushers with their ribboned wands; and last of all, come the Seniors, led like a chain of white flowers by the Juniors in front; and having taken the front places, which are saved for them, they rise in a body when the President appears, remaining standing until he reaches his seat on the platform.

The rest of the service blends in a memory of music, of prayer, and of helpful suggestions by the Commencement Orator, who is one of the well-known and gifted people often introduced by the Faculty as a stimulus to the girls. But the Seniors have the privilege of deciding who he shall be, and this year he was a man who had a daughter in the graduating class; so that his own little girl, in a white dress, and with a bunch of pink roses across her lap, was looking up at him timidly and eagerly, to hear what he would say. And immediately all the young faces before him, and all the young souls that he must help, resolved into one, and he spoke to the Seniors as he would have spoken to her alone, if it had been for the last and only time. And then the choir sang Marchetti's beautiful "Ave Maria;" the diplomas were distributed, and the service ended with the hymn, "Hark, hark, my soul," which will always be associated in the minds of those who remember, with "the love that lies beyond the word 'Farewell.'"

The President's speech, after the exercises, relieved the tension of the atmosphere, and pointed out to opulent members of the audience that there are noble and disinterested ways of expressing one's feelings. He gave a few pathetic statistics relating to the financial condition of the college, and finally said that the class of Ninety-five had voted to give up its class supper, in order that the money might be added to the sum for the new Chemistry Building.

The applause was long and enthusiastic, for even the under-class girls did not know of this decision; and Ruth Burritt, who evolved the idea, was poked from in front, and prodded from behind, by Seniors wishing to express their admiration. And then the President went on to say that, "in view of the sacrifice made by the Seniors, a gentleman, who shall be nameless, has given the sum of five thousand dollars to this glorious class of Ninety-five, to be used and appropriated by them in any manner that they may think fit; and we ourselves wish to say — "

But the applause by this time had become so frantic that he was obliged to stop, and the Seniors, whose feelings could no longer be suppressed, sprang to their feet and sang "Fair Harland," singing it in tune, too, which was doing very well under the circumstances. And the effect was so spontaneous that no one in the audience dreamed of what had taken place in the Philosophy room just before the Seniors started for the chapel, when a younger member of the Faculty had rushed in, saying: "After the exercises, the President is going to make an announcement, and when he has made it, you get up and *sing.*" So this was why Dr. Page gave the pitch on the organ at just the right time, and everything ended as happily and beautifully as it did. And after it was over, the Seniors and alumnæ lost no time in going to collation at the Wyndham, where the "hungry man was fed."

"'Go frowning forth, but come thou smiling back,'" said Kathleen to a stuffed egg as it rolled under the table. "Oh, girls, how do you reckon that egg feels, when it thinks about what it might have done if it had grown up a rooster?"

"It was better that it should be boiled young," said Grace, solemnly; "an egg is so innocent."

"Yes, it's innocent; but I'd rather have a good lusty beefsteak that has suffered and understands," said Professor Burton, gazing mournfully at his cup of coffee and one thin sandwich.

"I'll get you some salad," laughed one of the ushers, going to the nearest table.

"Yes, do," he murmured gratefully. "Remember that it's my fourth graduation."

But as Christine came in at that minute, the new instalment of refreshments was transferred to a cool place by a window, which the Professor picked out for her. And then the long-suffering Junior went back after more.

"I'm glad that you're not going abroad this year," said Professor Burton, calmly.

"*I'm* not," said Christine, wishing that he would not talk about it.

"Because," he continued, "I generally go to Washington once or twice every winter to attend Scientific meetings, and I have a married cousin there too, who is always pining for my society, Mrs. Reed-Slocum, — do you know her?"

"Know her? Why, of course I do, or rather my mother does. I've never been into society there at all."

"Are you going to be introduced next winter?"

424

"Yes; won't it be horrible?"

"No, it'll do you good. But how about my coming to see you if I get to Washington? I could take you to some very interesting lectures at the Smithsonian."

"Would you deliver them?" asked Christine, unkindly.

"Well, no. But perhaps it would be better to patronize a first-rate dance. My cousin has asked me to several, at different times, but I always wrote and told her that I wasn't out."

"What new theories are you people discussing so seriously?" asked the Junior, coming to bring them some cool lemonade.

"Evolution, from the monkey's point of view," answered the Professor. "We were wondering if he thinks it's an improvement."

"Of course I sha'n't be able to do any work, that's the main objection," said Christine. "Political society is delightful, but complicated. If you'd ever tried to seat people at a Washington dinner, you'd know that it is often a matter of life and death. Sorting over nobility — and we often have that to do, too — couldn't be worse."

"So you really like a quiet life so much the best? Don't you think that you'd get tired of it in the long run?"

"No; I like to travel quietly, or stay at home quietly and work, seeing a great deal of the few people that I care for. It doesn't seem much to ask, does it? But I suppose asking for what we can't have is demanding the most of all."

"A great many people would like nothing better than to change places with you."

"Yes, it was all a mistake some way, — my loving to write most of the time, instead of to entertain and be decently hilarious, like other girls. But I mean to be as good as I can this next year — for a change, and see how it feels."

"And I may come to witness the transformation?"

"Didn't papa ask you to call?"

"Yes; but I wanted you to ask me too, because, you see, we were at college together."

Christine laughed. "Well, you know that I shall be glad to see you, for I strongly suspect that with me it'll be a case of being good and being happy, but I won't have a good time."

"Let me tell you something," said Professor Burton, seriously. "You are going to have the best time that you ever had in your life." And it turned out afterwards that she did, although not for reasons that they either of them then suspected.

When collation was over, Ninety-five had its last class meeting, and voted to give the five thousand dollars to the Chemistry Building. It also determined to work as hard as it could to get more money; and stopped on its way out to annihilate a new-made Sophomore, who was proclaiming her advancement in triumphant tones.

"You're no Sophomore until *we* get out of this college, do you understand?" inquired Kathleen, ferociously. And the girl speedily melted from view.

"Didn't you pass, either?" asked a tearful and disappointed applicant of Grace Reade, whom she met on the stairs. Grace put her hand to her face, and discovered to her surprise that she had been crying.

"I did n't know —" she began, and, taking the girl's hand, she said, "Go home and try again, and don't give up trying until you get here, for there 's nothing like it in this world, — nothing!"

And then she fled away down the hall.

CHAPTER XXIII

THE CROSSING ENDED

ARDIS HATHAWAY had left collation early and gone to Miss Carlisle's room to get a last relay of Bain papers and daily themes which had not been returned. She had intended to say "good-bye" very quickly, and get away as soon as possible afterwards, but this was not at all what happened. Miss Carlisle, who was working at her desk, looked up when she came in, looked at her again, and then, seating herself in a rocking-chair, drew the girl down into her arms.

"My dear," she said, stroking her hair, "don't you know that somebody says even God is willing to give one-and-twenty another chance?"

"But I was twenty-two in November," said Ardis, trying to smile, and then she began to cry instead.

Miss Carlisle rocked her gently for several minutes without speaking, and Ardis thought, —

"Perhaps my own mother would have held me like this if she had been — different. How strange it is that Miss Carlisle and I should be together at all — she a mother without a child, and I a child without a mother?"

"I wish I had a daughter of my own," said the professor, suddenly, as if she had been reading her thoughts.

428

"Suppose — that you did have," said Ardis, falteringly, "and that, for any reason — she had lost her — self-respect. Could you say anything to her that would make her feel as if she still wanted to live?"

"I should say to her: ' Self-respect is the recognition of God in ourselves, and is something that can never be quite lost. It may seem to be gone, at times, but it will return again in our great need, and show us that we are still a part of that God who understands.' Ardis, there have been times in my life when if I had not had God I should have had nothing!"

"I believe in the God that made the world," said Ardis. "But is n't the world, after all, a questionable blessing?"

"That depends entirely upon ourselves. God made the world of flowers and hills, but we must shape the individual worlds in which we live and build the blue of our own sky. Ardis, we make a mistake if we compare ourselves with the people around us, instead of with what God meant us to be! Our capacities for usefulness cannot all be judged by the same standard; some of us — like you, for instance — have better material to start with. I think that, if you chose, there is very little that you could not do."

"But I 've been trying to do things all through my college course — and you see the result."

"No — pardon me — you have n't been trying to do things, but to make people think that you have; and you must admit that there is a difference."

Ardis flushed. "I 've been on the wrong track, I know," she said.

"And there are several by-ways to this wrong road of yours that have made the climbing still more difficult. Why, for instance, do you always try to conceal your motives, and even your most irreproachable feelings, from the world? Of course I'm not speaking of personal affairs at all, but of good, honest, general opinions."

"I don't like to have every one walk in and inspect my ideas as if they were so many mummies in a show-case."

"Your comparison is very apt, because any idea is likely to become mummified if never exposed to the air; and yours are much too original for such seclusion. Besides, don't you know that the soul that no one can see into is the soul that cannot see out of itself, and that when you build a barrier to keep others out, you are also shutting yourself in?"

"I believe in a certain amount of diplomacy," said Ardis.

"Diplomacy? Nonsense! What does a girl of your age want of diplomacy? An ordinary amount of tact is all that she needs. And it isn't necessary to scheme and withhold and misrepresent, with the impulsive outspoken girls who have been your companions. The man who seemed to know most things told us to be true to ourselves, and then we could not be false to any one. And truth is our only means of defence in a world where some people will always be untrue. If we have it, we are safe; if we cast it aside, it may lead, as you know, to serious difficulties."

"Oh! Miss Carlisle," said Ardis, "you don't

know what it has been to me to lose Christine! And I didn't realize how much I cared until it was too late. We walked together Ivy Day, and she was as dear and lovable as ever; but I know that it can never be — the old days; they will not come again. And that wonderful oration! I had no share in it, — had no right to be proud of it, as I would have been if she were my friend."

She was clear-sighted enough not to hold Miss Carlisle responsible for this loss, although it was through Miss Carlisle that Christine knew what had happened. But Ardis felt, in some mysterious way, that Miss Carlisle had been merely the agent of that great force called Retribution, which we all evade at times and must meet at last. And Ardis knew to-day, as she felt those warm arms around her, that the same person may be equally the instrument of a greater force, called Love, which is the greatest of all.

"You say that I do not know what it has been to you to lose Christine," said the professor, gently. "I do know. I have seen."

Ardis did not know how long they had sat there in silence when a knock came, and Miss Carlisle said: "It's a Sophomore who has an appointment with me about a paper, and I'm afraid I must see her. But there is something more that I want to tell you before you go. Christine does love you — she always will; and you can make her respect you if you choose. An opportunity will come if you look for it; but, Ardis, remember always that it is better to fall in *any* one's estimation rather than in your own! Now kiss me, my dear, and write to me

sometimes, if you feel like it; for you know that —
I am very often a lonely person too."

"I didn't tell you what I am going to do next
year," said Ardis, hurriedly. "I 've decided to
work in a college settlement, — not from charitable
motives at all, but because I want to forget, if I
can, that such a person as Ardis Hathaway ever
existed. I shall have classes of girls and children
in music, and I am to sing to them when they want
me to, and help get up little concerts. I couldn't
sing to well-dressed people, who would look at me
and think things; but these little children are different — they come up and take hold of your hand."

"Let me congratulate you most heartily on your
decision," said Miss Carlisle. "There is a tremendous field for work there, and your voice was
put into the world to make people better and purer
than they are. I think it is the materialization of
the mark of God that was on you when you came."

Ardis put her arms around Miss Carlisle's neck
for a minute, saying, "I shall never forget — " But
the Sophomore knocked again, and the sentence was
not finished. There is this about college, after
all, that we never do forget, no matter how old and
tired and disappointed we may be; there is never
a time when we cannot feel the campus grass beneath our feet, and hear, when we listen, the rustling
of the ivies against the college walls.

Ardis walked slowly over to the Music Building,
where a lone violin was playing the "Kerry Dance."
One could almost see the light *portamento* as the
instrument laughed out, "Oh-h, the ring of the
piper's tune," and hear, all too soon, the drip of

rain through the leaves, in a deserted glen from which the merry hearts had fled. She went in search of it, and stopped for a minute outside the organ room to listen. The Glee Club had sung it like that, and one would have known that the violinist was the same person who had trained them.

"I thought at first that you were in Number 7," said Ardis, pushing open the door, "but I suppose you did n't feel quite up to the grand orchestral combination to-day."

Clare had always been fond of trying over four-part songs by herself, singing the soprano, making the violin sing second, and pounding out the two altos with both feet on the pedal piano, which was placed in an adjacent room for organ practice.

"I've just been down to see you," said Clare, stopping, with her bow slightly raised. "Where in the world have you been?"

"Play the 'Kerry Dance' again," said Ardis, going to the window.

Clare played it through once more, and then laid her violin in the case, saying, "If we're going to Phi Delta Kap reunion, we ought to be starting now."

"You're too tired," said Ardis. "Come down to the Marston instead, and take a nap."

"But if you're going away to-morrow morning, this'll be your last chance to see the girls."

"I'd rather see you," said Ardis, simply; and that settled it.

"How bare the room looks!" said Clare, as they opened Ardis's door. "It does n't seem like you any more. I wonder if perhaps the room thinks that it's asleep, and that when it wakes up again we'll all be back here, just as we were before?"

"Clare, what's heaven like?" asked Ardis, in her own unexpected way.

"Tell *me* what it's like," said Clare. "You have known sometimes when you were singing; I've seen it in your face."

"What's your idea of it, I mean?"

"I have always thought that it will be a place where I can have an organ, and a baby, and a grand piano, and a rosebush in my front garden."

"No; what one quality that is different from the world would be necessary to make a heaven?"

"I think it's a place where people don't misunderstand!"

One of the Senior roses stood in a glass on the table, and Clare went over to lay her cheek against it.

"After all," she said, "the whole of our questionings are answered by this! If there had not been meant to be love in the world, God would not have put this here where I can reach it with my hand."

"Lie down and go to sleep, you little thing," said Ardis. "I'm going to sing to you awhile."

"Oh! really? And will you sing the 'Kerry Dance'? The violin can never understand it as you do."

Ardis sat down beside her on the bed, and stroked her hand, and sang, right merrily at first, of Eileen and her lover in the glens of County Kerry, and of the piper's tune. Clare watched the motion of the soft fingers over hers, and noticed the curious pearl ring that Ardis had worn ever since she came to college. Sometimes we learn to associate some little article like this with a certain person, and it is hard, afterwards, to see a thing that resembles it on any one else. It was an old ring made of a black and a white pearl set crosswise, and Clare had once said, "It is like two sides of the same person."

"No," Ardis answered, "it is like you and me!"

Ardis sang on, and suddenly Clare realized that some one had spoken to her.

"I believe I've been asleep," she said innocently, "but I think I heard you just the same. What was it that you said a minute ago?"

"I only wanted you to kiss me," said Ardis; and when Clare had kissed her, she sang again.

> "Loving voices of old companions,
> C-o-ming out of the past, once more;
> And the sound of the dear old music,
> S-o-ft — and — sweet, as in d-a-ys of yore."

The afternoon sunshine deepened and brightened across the floor, and then withdrew softly out of the window without waking the solitary occupant of the room. From outside, on the campus, came the sound of laughter and the tinkle of cups; but through it all little Clare slept, and did not stir until the supper-bell rang through the long halls. Then she hurried downstairs to the dining-room, where some of the alumnæ and all of the Marston House Seniors were gathering to fortify themselves for the night's festivity.

"Where is Miss Hathaway?" she asked of the girl who rang the bell.

"Miss Hathaway?" repeated the maid, in surprise.

"Why, she left on the four-o'clock train, with all her baggage and everything. Did n't you know about it, miss?"

Clare went on through the hall without seeing it, and hurried home. She had a glimpse of white gowns at the supper-table, and met Christine coming downstairs.

"You'd better hurry and get dressed," she said. "We must patronize the pleasant home table of Miss Taylor before starting, as it's quite impossible to be funny on an empty stomach."

"Ardis is gone," said Clare.

"What did you say?"

"Ardis is gone;" and she went on up to her room.

It was not until she began to dress that she became conscious of an unaccustomed pressure on a finger of her right hand. She had not noticed it before, and could scarcely believe that she saw what caused it now. It was Ardis's little pearl ring.

The supperless supper took place in the big Gymnasium, and "P. F." was the only condiment served. As the toasts and class histories had been arranged to come between courses, the intervals had to be supplied by general conversation, and, as Christine had said, "it is hard to be funny on an empty stomach."

Some of the girls were inclined to take a funereal view of the future, while others jested continually to hide their real feelings.

"Well, you can laugh," said one of them, "but you would n't if you were going to take charge of a grammar-school next fall, and teach — brats."

436

"I've got to be a home comfort," said another, "and that's more work than anything."

"Salome and Freda are going to study for an A.M.," said Rachel Winter, "and Leonora for an M.D. Hurrah for Dr. Kent of Ninety-five!'"

"What are you going to do?" asked some one.

"Well, I think that I must be content to shine by reflected glory. My Cornell brother has received a half offer of a professorship in the University of Chicago, and —"

"Why don't you take the other half?" asked Kathleen.

"Because I'm needed at home. But incidentally, I'm going to practise scales until I can play them."

"Every one knows that Kathleen is going to study with Sargent next year," said Mildred. "We'll come and engage the whole gallery on first nights, Kaddy."

"I am!" said Kathleen. "I am going in search of the sublime situation."

"Take care that you don't turn it into the ridiculous," said Grace.

"What is life?" asked Kathleen, striking an attitude.

"An obstacle race, Ardis says," replied Mildred.

"No, — it is an Irish stew, in which some of us is more carrots than others!"

"Ruth maintains a discreet silence about her future," said Elsie Dane, mischievously. "I wonder what she's going to do?"

"We all know that to marry the right man is the best thing that can happen to any woman," said Faith Bentley, impetuously; "so what's the use in being silly about it?"

"Bravo, Fay!" said Edith Standish. "I really believe that your affairs will bear looking into."

"If I'd been engaged, I wouldn't have dared say it," was the answer.

"What are you going to do next year, Philippa?" asked Christine.

"College Settlement."

"And you?" turning to Amethyst Allen.

Amethyst blushed, and replied that <u>she didn't know</u>; but the girls found out afterwards that he was a young travelling salesman, with a good salary.

"Clare hasn't said a word," said Ruth. "I suppose she is thinking of music and Berlin."

But Clare was thinking of a conversation that she had overheard a few minutes ago outside the Gymnasium. While passing a group of Juniors, one of them had said: "Girls, what do you suppose? May Churchill has given up smoking."

"Is it the end of the world?" asked another.

"More probably of the cigarettes. I can't think what's come over her."

This was all that Clare heard, but it was enough to make her happy; for the untamed fire of her own nature had found much in sympathy with May, and of the younger Glee Club girls she had learned to love her little black sheep the most of all.

"Silence!" cried the toastmistress, pounding on the floor. "The Sophomore history is about to begin." And Clare wondered if, by any chance, she had been thinking aloud.

Junior history followed all too soon; and then came the last one, which Grace Reade had written half an hour before starting for the Gymnasium.

438

This was not an example of exceptional negligence on her part, for it is the fashion to write them at that time.

"I don't believe," she said, in closing, "in the class of alumnæ who think that they have a right to criticise everything that goes on at the college after they are gone. We are all familiar with this kind; they come back in dismal hordes and throng the corridors with long faces, saying, 'Oh! it's all changed — it's all changed; it isn't our college any more.'

"Well, — it's in the nature of things that it shouldn't be! Change and growth are synonymous, and our dear college is no less our own because she is rapidly growing from a child to a woman. It is for us to help let down her tucks, and encourage her in good wholesome expansion, instead of insisting that she shall still conform to our obsolete regulations. And we must always remember that it is by us, and not by the undergraduate, that the college will be judged. We alumnæ are the end towards which this glorious means has been tending; the undergraduate is the beginning, but we — *we* are the result. Let us remember that we *are* a result, and that, as a result of this college, our responsibility is almost too great for words. We can ask no more than to be worthy of our President's trust in us, when he said, 'I desire that Harland College should be judged by its alumnæ!'"

The stanch little historian was enthusiastically cheered, and the rest of the evening was spent in song and hilarity. Every one, from the head of the Faculty to Mrs. Flannagan, received a parting three times three, which could not be suppressed even when the janitor came in to turn out the lights. For were they not members of the class of Ninety-five, and did they not know that it was the last time that they could all be together? So they went on cheering in the dark, aided by the Junior ushers outside, who had been holding forth at intervals during the whole evening. But when they ran into each other by accident, their faces were wet.

"One more cheer for Ninety-five," said Ruth Burritt, climbing on a chair. But they were all too hoarse to cheer any more, and holding each other's hands, they passed out into the moonlight, where their Junior friends were waiting to wish them good-bye and "God-speed."

Ruth and Christine and Clare walked home over the shadows of many leaves on the sidewalk, and under the rustlings of other leaves overhead. The moon was riding high over the clouds, for it was nearly twelve o'clock, and the town was asleep. The girls did not speak until they reached the house, for every rush of wind through the trees, every tremble in the grass, reminded them of the time when the woodbine would turn red again on the college walls, and they would not be there to see it!

"I'm glad that it's not good-bye for us yet," whispered Clare, as they said good-night.

"For those who have known and loved each other at college," said Ruth, simply, "it can never be good-bye!"

The laughter died away on the campus, and soon the night was still. The last alumnæ had sung their class songs under open windows and gone home. The weary night-watchman was asleep in the Latin room. And outside, there was nothing but the moonlight; moonlight on the campus, where the grass would soon grow tall and thick, because no longer pressed by eager restless feet; moonlight, on a new little ivy, that must grow — God helping it — Upward, against those college walls; moonlight on the dear river, "deepening to the sea." And beyond the river, the watchers over Harland — watching still.

www.ingramcontent.com/pod-product-compliance
Lightning Source LLC
Chambersburg PA
CBHW031827270326
41932CB00008B/582